W. Lucas Collins

The Public Schools

Winchester--Westminster--Shrewsbury--Harrow--Rugby

W. Lucas Collins

The Public Schools
Winchester--Westminster--Shrewsbury--Harrow--Rugby

ISBN/EAN: 9783337112165

Printed in Europe, USA, Canada, Australia, Japan

Cover: Foto ©ninafisch / pixelio.de

More available books at **www.hansebooks.com**

THE PUBLIC SCHOOLS

WINCHESTER—WESTMINSTER—SHREWSBURY
—HARROW—RUGBY

NOTES OF THEIR HISTORY AND TRADITIONS

BY THE
AUTHOR OF 'ETONIANA'

WILLIAM BLACKWOOD AND SONS
EDINBURGH AND LONDON
MDCCCLXVII

PREFACE.

These notices of the past and present of our Public Schools appeared, like 'Etoniana,' in 'Blackwood's Magazine.' They seemed sufficiently popular to justify their republication in a somewhat enlarged and corrected shape. They are still confessedly incomplete; but they may help to preserve some record of earlier phases of Public-School life, the very traditions of which are growing fainter year by year.

Printed authorities have been freely used. Those which were found most useful, especially such as are of modern date, are named before each School.

The valuable and cordial help which I have received not only from friends, but from many who were previously strangers, is one of the most pleasant recollections of what has been, to the writer at least, a very interesting investigation. The reader will be indebted for any interest he may find in these pages as much to my correspondents as myself.

Some few, to whom I am under special obligation, I may be allowed here to name.

For WINCHESTER; the Rev. ROBERT ALLEN, B.D.

For WESTMINSTER; JAMES MURE, Esq., and the Rev. THOMAS WILLIAM WEARE.

For SHREWSBURY; the Rev. BENJAMIN HALL KENNEDY, D.D., and the Rev. JAMES HILDYARD, B.D.

For HARROW; the Rev. J. READE MUNN, and the Rev. EDWARD HENRY BRADBY.

For RUGBY; the Rev. ALFRED BUTLER CLOUGH, B.D., MATTHEW HOLBECHE BLOXAM, Esq., the Rev. THOMAS LAWRENCE BLOXAM, and the Rev. CHARLES THOMAS ARNOLD.

Many of these names will at least show that information has been sought from the best sources; but for all statements of fact or opinion I desire to be held alone responsible.

W. L. C.

September 1867.

CONTENTS.

WINCHESTER COLLEGE AND COMMONERS.

CHAP.		PAGE
I.	EARLY HISTORY,	3
II.	ROYAL PATRONS,	11
III.	INTERNAL ECONOMY,	20
IV.	FROM ELIZABETH TO THE REVOLUTION,	31
V.	RECENT HISTORY,	39
VI.	PRESENT STATE OF THE COLLEGE,	50
VII.	ELECTION—GAMES,	61
	APPENDIX—REBELLION OF 1793,	70

WESTMINSTER SCHOOL.

I.	THE FOUNDATION,	81
II.	BUSBY,	97
III.	HEAD-MASTERS KNIPE—FREIND—NICOLL,	117
IV.	MODERN HEAD-MASTERS,	129
V.	THE PLAY,	142
VI.	FAGGING,	161
VII.	SCHOOL CUSTOMS AND GAMES,	170
VIII.	SCHOOL BUILDINGS AND SYSTEM,	176

SHREWSBURY SCHOOL.

I. FOUNDATION AND EARLY HISTORY,	193
II. THE SCHOOL UNDER LAURANCE AND MEIGHEN,	205
III. THOMAS CHALONER,	217
IV. DECLINE OF THE SCHOOL,	230
V. THE DAYS OF BUTLER,	237
VI. MISCELLANEOUS,	245

HARROW SCHOOL.

I. FOUNDATION AND STATUTES,	257
II. THE SCHOOL BUILDINGS,	264
III. EARLY HEAD-MASTERS,	269
IV. THE SCHOOL UNDER DR SUMNER,	275
V. DRS HEATH, DRURY, AND BUTLER,	285
VI. MODERN CONSTITUTION,	291
VII. THE GAMES,	304
VIII. MISCELLANEOUS,	315

RUGBY SCHOOL.

I. LAURENCE SHERIFF,	327
II. EARLY HEAD-MASTERS,	335
III. DR JAMES,	353
IV. DR INGLES,	364
V. DR WOOLL,	376
VI. THE SCHOOL UNDER DR ARNOLD,	383
VII. PRESENT CONSTITUTION,	392
VIII. THE GAMES,	400

INDEX,	405

WINCHESTER COLLEGE AND COMMONERS

A

The chief printed authorities are—

Milner's History of Winchester.
Woodward's General History of Hampshire.
Mackenzie Walcott's William of Wykeham and his Colleges.

WINCHESTER COLLEGE AND COMMONERS.

CHAPTER I.

EARLY HISTORY.

The constant ebb and flow of our national life has worked such change in most of our old towns, that the modern English pilgrim who visits Winchester, and spares an hour for the Cathedral and the College, has need to look at his guide-book to remember that he stands in what was, for something like four centuries, the capital of England; where Egbert, and the Conqueror, and the Red King, and Henry the Scholar, held their courts, and which, even so late as the reign of Henry III., disputed precedency with the citizens of London. In the old minster there the most famous of the West Saxon kings were buried; nay, though disturbed by the Danes, their very bones are at this day reputed to lie (somewhat confused indeed, and of doubtful authenticity) in those wooden arks of quaint workmanship—comparatively modern, yet ancient enough to be often taken for the original receptacles—which rest in the choir of the present Cathedral. But any local antiquarian zealous for the honour of his city would have far more than this to tell. Did not the great Arthur himself—"*flos regum*"—build him a castle here in days when the Saxon was not yet in the land? Was not this Camelot? Does not the wondrous Round Table itself, a great fact (only that nothing is so deceptive as facts), hang to this day over the heads of her Majesty's judges, like Damocles's sword, in the Nisi Prius Court there? Again, was it not here that Guy of Warwick slew Colbrand the Dane, that "Goliath of the pagans," and, like a second David, laid the huge head and casque at the feet of Athelstane in the Danemarke? The giant's very axe might have been seen and touched, as a relic of the combat, but that it was stolen, with other treasures, during the Great Rebellion. But if we listen to the store of legends which are written in Winchester chronicles, we shall never get to the College at all, within the compass of these pages; and it is to the College that our special pilgrimage is to be made.

Leave the city streets, then, and pass across the Cathedral Close—stopping for one instant, if you please, to look in through the open door of the noble vista of the nave, and make a short turn to your left into the lane which is called College Street, and which, excepting an undue proportion of pastry-cooks' and fruiterers' shops, has little to betoken the approach to so ancient and illustrious a seat of learning. We pass a long and somewhat blank wall, and stand before the gateway tower of St Mary's College. If your mind is preoccupied with the architectural fame of its great founder, and his princely munificence, you may possibly be disappointed at first sight. Built on the very outskirts of the city, in the warlike days of the Plantagenets, the exterior of the college was designed with at least as much regard to security as ornament. The windows, few and narrow, and closely barred—two or three quaint little oriels which appear in old prints have long been blocked up—give a somewhat blind and prison-like look to the street front, which is not altogether inviting. You have to remember what the good old times of Richard II. were, and what sort of visitors were apt occasionally to knock at your gates and look in at your windows in those days, before you can fully appreciate the suitableness of the design to the circumstances.

"In those days," says the chronicler Froissart, "there reigned in England a priest called William of Wykeham; this William of Wykeham was so much in favour with the King of England that everything was done by him, and nothing was done without him." He did "reign," indeed, for some years, in a very real sense; and might almost have been pardoned if he had written of Edward Longshanks as Wolsey is said to have done of *his* royal patron—"*Ego et rex meus.*" He did something of the kind, which wellnigh got him into trouble, early in his life; for, having been appointed royal surveyor and architect, and in that capacity having rebuilt Windsor Castle for his majesty, he had the vanity to set up in some conspicuous part of his new works the legend, 𝕿𝖍𝖎𝖘 𝖒𝖆𝖉𝖊 𝖂𝖞𝖐𝖊𝖍𝖆𝖒—an assumption which his enemies at court rebuked as being little short of treason. His friends made an excuse for him which it is to be hoped he was much too honest to make for himself, but which enthusiastic Wykehamists, in biographies and otherwise, profess to believe to this day—that he intended to express that the building was the making of *him*; a prophetical foresight of future royal favours scarcely less presumptuous. However, Wykeham—or William Long, for if he had any real patronymic, it was that—weathered that storm, and others more perilous afterwards; became twice Lord Chancellor, and Bishop of Winchester. He was perhaps the greatest pluralist in an age of pluralities, holding something like seventeen canonries in different dioceses, Welsh and English, besides a deanery and an archdeaconry; to which accumulation of good things if any stout church-reformer made objection, it might be answered that he applied the proceeds to better purpose than any ordinary seventeen canons, dean, and archdeacon put together. He did many munificent acts besides, as his diocese and cathedral bear witness; but more especially he founded and endowed, of his own sole charges, the two great colleges of St Mary of Winchester in Oxford (commonly known as New College), and St Mary College in Winchester; this latter as a nursery for the former.

Long before this, Winchester had been known as "a school of kings." There Egbert had placed his son Ethelwulf under the teaching of Bishop Helmstan, and there the great Alfred had sat at the feet of St Swithun. The Saxon Athelwold, whose praise was in all the churches, a true saint and scholar, was in all likelihood educated there; and his biographer, Archbishop Alfric, has an evident pride, near nine hundred years ago, in writing himself down "*Wintonensis alumnus*."* There

* Chron. de Abingdon, ii. 255.

had been a "High School" there from time which had become almost immemorial even in Wykeham's days; and even that, tradition would have said, was a mere modern institution—a temple of Apollo had preceded the monks' cloister. But later and more personal memories influenced Wykeham's choice. In that High School he had himself been educated by a rich friend's liberality; he saw it now falling into decay; he saw young scholars, poor but deserving, much in need of the same help which he had found; and his first idea seems to have been to re-establish and endow his old school for this purpose. He was not a man to do things by halves; and in 1373 he appears to have reopened it at once with seventy scholars, for whose charges he undertook to provide. They were lodged on St Giles's Hill, just outside the city; and there, under Richard de Herton and other masters, the infant community remained for twenty years. Meanwhile, Wykeham was gradually carrying out the rest of his plan; purchasing "Otterbourne Mead" and other lands in Winchester, for the site of his college there, and gradually establishing in Oxford the mother institution —the "New College" of St Mary—which was to receive his Winchester scholars in due course for the completion of their education. Not until that noble foundation, with its warden and seventy fellows, chaplains, and choristers, was launched into full life within those stately walls which are still the pride of Oxford, did he begin to build at Winchester.

Wykeham drew up for each of his new colleges a carefully digested body of statutes. Long as they are, they are worth reading through by any one who still cherishes the idle notion that the monkish teaching and discipline of the fourteenth century were necessarily narrow and superstitious. Wykeham's ordinances, at any rate, are full of sound and liberal wisdom. The nearer our modern public schools can conform themselves to the spirit of old Winchester—for the letter has, of course, in many details become obsolete—the more likely will they be to fulfil their high profession of being seats of sound learning and religious education. He willed that his boys should grow up as Christians, as scholars, and as gentlemen; and he held these qualifications to be intimately connected. He would have them intelligent students of Holy Scripture, that they might be able to teach others; agreeing in this with a man of a very different age, and in many respects very dissimilar spirit— the reformer Melanchthon—that Scripture is little likely to be understood theologically by those who have never been at the pains to understand it grammatically. Therefore he enjoins upon his scholars, above all things, the study of GRAMMAR—" the foundation-stone, the gateway, the source of all other liberal arts and sciences," as he emphatically calls it. They were to be careful to maintain amongst themselves kindness, concord, and brotherly love; " to esteem no man's person," and to hold all distinctions of birth or wealth amongst themselves to be merged in the grand fraternity of letters. To all within the walls of St Mary's College the admission itself was to be a patent of peerage; reverence was to be paid solely to the masters and the "prefects" of their own body. But outside the gates they were to give to the rank and station of such as they met the honour that was its due. So far was the founder from encouraging the notion that the scholar was like to be the unpolished, absorbed, unsocial being which he has been sometimes represented, that he specially recommends to the Winchester boys the observance of the "*curialis modus*"—that graceful and courtly bearing which they had opportunity of studying in the nobles who formed the King's personal retinue. He had taken as his own motto, "Manners makyth man."

The foundation, as the Bishop devised it, was for a warden and ten fellows, three chaplains and three clerks in orders, a head-master (*informator*), an under-master (*hostiarius*), seventy scholars, "poor and in need of help," and sixteen choristers. All still remains unchanged, excepting that the late University Commission reduced the number of fellows (prospectively) to six: the funds which accrue from this suppression being appropriated to the gradual increase of the scholars to one hundred. It has been always held that there was a religious symbolism in the numbers, though Wykeham himself gives no hint of it. The warden and fellows represent the eleven apostles, Judas's place being vacant; the six chaplains and clerks are the six orthodox deacons—Nicolas, by tradition, being a heretic; the masters and scholars are the body of disciples who were sent forth two by two— the Vulgate text giving the number at seventy-two; while in the sixteen choristers are set forth the prophets of the old dispensation, four "greater" and twelve "less."*

The founder was seventy-four years old when he saw the great design of his life completed. On the 28th of March 1393—seven years after the opening of New Col-

---

* Perhaps it is with some notion of carrying out this scriptural symbolism that the college-boys (who have a very curious and copious argot of their own) have from time immemorial called the under porters by the name of one of the minor prophets. The present official is known as Obadiah.

lege in Oxford—the warden and scholars of "St Mary College of Winchester" left their temporary location on St Giles's Hill, and took possession of the new buildings. The good Bishop himself, with his cross borne before him, his warden, John Morris, his "informator," John Milton, and the scholars under their charge, entered in solemn procession, with chant and litany, at nine o'clock in the forenoon. No fellows appear to have been appointed until the following year, and then only five out of the ten proposed.

CHAPTER II.

ROYAL PATRONS.

KING RICHARD granted a liberal charter of privileges to the new foundation, which was confirmed by all his successors, except Queen Mary. The frequent sojourn of the Court at Winchester could not fail to bring a certain amount of royal favour and patronage. Henry VI. was a frequent visitor at St Mary's College, attending the chapel services, and making liberal offerings; and there he found his model for his own foundation at Eton. Whether Etonians will readily confess it or not, now that the daughter has outgrown the mother, it is undeniably true that the Royal College was but a colony from Winchester. The first head-master was William of Waynflete, who migrated from the elder college (where he had taught for thirteen years), with five fellows and thirty-five scholars, in 1443. The bond of connection between the two societies continued to be close and intimate for many generations, although the migration of head-masters took a reverse direction; three at least—Clement Smyth, William Horeman, and Thomas Erlysman—in the course of the following half century, resigning their office at Eton for the more honourable and lucrative position of "informator" at Winchester. Mutual visits and hospitalities between their wardens and provosts kept up the kindly feeling of a common origin; and in 1445 there was drawn up and signed between them an instrument styled an "Amicable Concord," in which, after reciting the identity of object and common interest of both colleges, they undertake to support and protect each other in all lawful causes, ecclesiastical and civil, against all other persons or interests whatever. The use of a common grammar for some years contributed to maintain a feeling of fellowship among the scholars.

King Henry is not recorded to have dined in hall at Winchester, although several of his Court were entertained there on one occasion, when the society laid in "a pipe of red wine," which cost them eight pounds. It does not appear that his successor, Edward IV., ever paid them a visit in person; but in January 1471 he sent one of his men to the college with a lion, and his brother, the unfortunate Duke of Clarence, sent two bears there in the following year,—visitors whom perhaps the boys were quite as glad to see.[*]

When Prince Arthur was born at Winchester, Henry VII. visited the college in state, and was entertained in the warden's lodging. Henry VIII. paid the society two visits, the first time accompanied by the Emperor Charles V. But the Wykehamists regard him as anything but a patron or a benefactor. Not content with forcing upon them the exchange of some of their best manors and advowsons, he did his best to suppress them altogether by the terms of his new statute for the dissolution of

[*] Walcott's Wykeham and his Colleges, p. 154, &c. Warton's Proleg., i. 91.

colleges. John White, then warden (afterwards Bishop of Lincoln), has the credit of having prevented the application of this statute to his own college; and three years afterwards it was repealed by Edward's Statute of Exceptions. King Edward's commissioners insisted, however, on certain reforms; that in future the Scriptures should be read in hall in English, instead of Latin; that each scholar should possess a New Testament; that they should omit from that time forth the singing or saying of *Stella Cœli* or *Salve Regina*, "or any such like untrue or superstitious anthem;" and, amongst other regulations, that there should be "no excessive correction;" which latter proviso, at any rate, was likely to make the new injunctions popular with the college-boys.*

But the Reformation was a time of trouble and disturbance at Winchester as elsewhere. The old and new opinions had their active partisans within the walls of the college. About 1537 (Strype dates it earlier, but he must be wrong), when Dr White was head-master, before his elevation to the wardenship, he had for his *hostiarius* or usher one William Ford. White was a stanch Catholic, as he afterwards proved: his subordinate was amongst the most violent of the Reformers.

"There were many golden images then in that church" (the college chapel), "the door whereof was directly against the usher's chamber. One day Mr Ford tied a long cord to the images, linking them all in one cord, and being in his chamber after midnight, he plucked the cord's end, and at one pull all the golden gods came down. It wakened all men with the rush; they were amazed at the terrible noise, and also dismayed at the

* Wilkins's Concilia, iv. 9.

grievous sight. The cord, being plucked hard and cut with a twitch, lay at the church door. At last they fell to searching; but Mr Ford, most suspected, was found in his bed.

"Mr Ford afterwards had a dog's life among them; Mr White, the schoolmaster, the fellows of the house, and the scholars, crying out and railing at him, by supportation of their master. Violent men lay in wait for him many times; and one night, going into the town, he must needs come home to the college by the town walls, the gates of Trinity College being shut. This was espied; he was watched, and when he came to a blind dark corner by King's Gate, then they laid on him with staves. He clapped his gown-collar, furred with fox-fur, round his head and neck. They laid on him some strokes; but, by God's providence, the most part, in that great darkness, did light upon the ground. So they ran away, and left Mr Ford for dead. But he tumbled and rolled himself to the gates (for they made him past going), and then cried for help; and people came in, who took him up and bare him to his lodging."*

It is impossible to sympathise so entirely with the unfortunate usher as Strype would have us; and one is not altogether surprised to learn that his fanaticism turned afterwards into melancholy, and that he "was tempted of Satan to kill himself upon small occasion." The future career of White equally shows the extreme to which both carried their opinions and feelings. Deprived of his wardenship by the Protector Somerset, White was restored, and subsequently made bishop of Winchester, by Queen Mary. He was selected to preach at her funeral in West-

* Strype's Eccl. Mem., I. Pt. iii. 174.

minster Abbey, on which occasion, says a quaint old anecdotist, Bishop White " made a very *black* sermon," taking for his text Ecclesiastes iv. 2, *Laudavi mortuos,* &c.—" I have praised the dead which are already dead, more than the living which are yet alive." If there was any difficulty in the application, the preacher took care that his hearers should understand it ; for, after speaking of Queen Mary as one who was so much given to prayer that " her knees were hard with kneeling," he proceeded to discourse of her sister and successor as " a lady of great worth also, whom they were now bound to obey, 'for,' saith he [quoting the Latin Vulgate], 'a living dog is better than a dead lion,' and I hope she shall reign well and prosperously over us ; though I must still say with my text, *Laudavi mortuos,* &c., for certain it is, ' *Maria optimam partem elegit.*' " Queen Elizabeth thought this was something more than fidelity to the departed, and deprived him of his bishopric ; " some would have made that a more heinous matter."* He died in retirement, and, though buried in his own cathedral, there is no memorial of him there.

Two fellow-scholars in the same reign, but under a preceding master (Tuchiner), were John Harpsfeld and John Philpot ; they were school-friends, went off to New College in the same year, and graduated together. The first became Bonner's chaplain, and unhappily imbibed much of his persecuting spirit ; he was one of the seven disputants on the Popish side at the Winchester Conference in 1549. The second sealed his fidelity to his Protestant convictions at the stake in Smithfield. Their school-controversies had been of a different kind ; Harpsfeld once

* Sir J. Harington, Nug. Ant., i. 68.

laid a wager with his friend that he would compose in one night two hundred Latin verses with not more than three faults; and, on reference to the master, was adjudged to have won it. One wonders whether the bishop's chaplain had forgotten those early days; whether it was that he lacked the heart, or the influence, to save his old schoolfellow in that day of fearful trial.

To return, however, to the times of the earlier Reformers. The young King Edward, during his short reign, paid Winchester a visit, on which occasion the scholars of the college presented him with no less than forty-two copies of Latin verse. Thomas Hyde, the headmaster at the time, was "a person of great gravity and severity, and a lover of virtuous men," says John Pitts, himself an eminent Wykehamist; "very stiff and perverse," Strype calls him; testimonies which are not quite so contradictory as they seem, when the bias of the witnesses is taken into account. On the accession of Elizabeth, not being inclined to adopt the Reformed faith, he retired to Douai. The feelings of Wykeham's society, as of all collegiate bodies founded under the old discipline, were naturally hostile to the Church reformers, and there was little inclination on the part of the latter to deal tenderly with what many of them looked upon as nests of monkery. The very name of the "College of St Mary" was odious to their ears. In the year following King Edward's visit, Queen Mary was married in the cathedral to Philip of Spain, and the bride and bridegroom attended service in the college chapel; but only twenty-five of the scholars were able to produce congratulatory verses on this occasion; although the restored Warden White, it may be supposed, was not backward in encouraging these loyal effusions—adding, indeed, a copy of elegiacs of his own, more loyal than scholarlike.

Queen Elizabeth paid a visit to the college in 1570. Her scholarly tastes were well known, and the Wykehamists, of course, improved the occasion. George Coryatt and William Rainolds, fellows of New College, met her at the gates with an oration; and she had to listen to no less than forty complimentary effusions, in Latin and Greek verse, by the scholars. A copy of them may be seen amongst Anthony Wood's manuscripts at Oxford; all are in the prevalent vein of flattery, and few have any merit besides brevity. But, if the traditionary story be true (which Etonians also claim), there was one young scholar whose wit and readiness deserved a purse of gold better than Master Coryatt's oration. Her Majesty pleasantly asked him whether he had ever made acquaintance with that celebrated rod whose fame had reached even her royal ears. Both the question and the questioner would have embarrassed most schoolboys; but he replied by an admirable quotation from Virgil—a familiar line, which the Queen was like enough to have understood—

"Infandum, Regina, jubes renovare dolorem." *

It is very ungrateful of the Wykehamists not to have preserved his name. It was possibly the same youthful genius, or at least a very worthy successor, who depicted upon the wall of "sixth chamber"—where, not long ago, it was said to be still traceable—a representation of that

---

* Virg. Æn. ii. 3 :—

"Great Queen, what you command me to relate
Renews the sad remembrance of our fate."—DRYDEN.

same renowned implement of discipline, with the grimly facetious motto underneath—"*Animum pictura pascit inani.*" The Winton rod, in fact, deserves a more special notice than might be thought appropriate in the case of the ordinary birch, whose modest worth (though undeniable) is usually held to be best veiled in obscurity, especially since Mr Tupper's proverbs have superseded Solomon's. This is not a birch at all; it is four slender apple-twigs set into a wooden handle; immemorial custom rules that the twigs should be provided by two juniors, who hold the responsible office of rod-maker, under the orders of the prefect of hall. It is by no means a severe-looking implement; but possibly it must be felt to be fully appreciated. It need hardly be said that it is applied in the ordinary fashion: six cuts forming what is technically called a "bibling"—on which occasion the Bible-clerk* introduces the victim; and four being the sum of a less terrible operation called a "scrubbing." The invention of this very peculiar instrument is ascribed to Dr John Baker, who was thirty-three years warden (1454-87), but of whose acts and deeds little more is on record than the Latin distich in which this contribution to college discipline is immortalised—

> "Si laus est, inventa quidem Custode Bakero
> Ex quadripartito vimine flagra ferunt."

It is very probable that on the occasion of this visit her Majesty was also entertained, as she was by other collegiate bodies, with a masque or stage-play, acted by the scholars. They were certainly in the habit of giving such performances occasionally at this date, as appears from

* The ten senior prefects hold this office in weekly rotation.

the college accounts, and went to considerable trouble and expense in arranging the stage and other appliances —even to the length of removing the "organs" out of the chapel to furnish the orchestra.* The theatrical taste appears to have revived from time to time ; for, in 1742, Dr Burton had the tragedy of 'Cato' acted, in which Whitehead, the future poet-laureate, performed *Marcia* with great applause; and Tom Wharton, under his brother's mastership, wrote prologues for the pieces performed by the boys in the "old Winchester playhouse over the butchers' shambles."

* Walcott, 204, &c.

CHAPTER III.

INTERNAL ECONOMY.

If we wish to know something of the internal economy and general working of the college at the time of Queen Elizabeth's visit, it so happens that there exists a record of it, drawn up by the very best authority, and which enters pretty fully into detail. The head-master at that time was one Christopher Johnson—a man of elegant scholarship, of varied accomplishments, and probably of somewhat eccentric character. He describes himself, in verse which is admirably Horatian, with a sort of pathetic honesty, in an imaginary appeal to one of his scholars not to misrepresent him, in case he should be asked "at home" what sort of a man the master was—

> "Corpore pertenui me dices invalidoque;
> Dormire in lucem, ne lædar frigore; Musis
> Gaudere, assiduum tamen esse negabis; amare,
> Et varias servare vices; quod pertinet ad te,
> Irasci celerem, si quid peccaveris; inde
> Placari facilem, multis ignoscere multa:
> Quanto perditior quis est, tanto acrius illi
> Insistere; hæc de me, quæ sunt verissima, dices." *

* From an MS. copy-book, kept by a boy named Badger, a scholar of Johnson's. The themes and verses which it contains are said to be "*dictata* Christ. Johnson;" some of them at least (as that above quoted) must be his composition.—[Ayscough MSS. 712, Brit. Mus.]

He was a student of medicine as well as a Master of Arts, and occasionally practised in the town of Winchester. After a rule of eleven years as head-master, he took his M.D. degree, and retired to London, where he followed his profession with success for twenty-six years afterwards. Although a very successful teacher in the judgment of his contemporaries, he speaks more than once of the cares of his office as being distasteful to him; and in a series of Latin distiches which he wrote upon his predecessors, he thus expresses his astonishment that one of them, Thomas Alwyne, having once resigned, should, after an interval of twelve years, have allowed himself to have been involved in such a "Charybdis" of troubles again:—

> "Ergo resorberis tam dira, Alwine, Charybdi,
> Nec poteras fracto liber abire jugo!"*

But Latin verse appears to have been his delight; and he wrote not only the set of epigrams just mentioned, but a metrical life of the founder, and a long poem in hexameters (probably composed while a schoolboy), describing the arrangement of the several chambers, the

---

* Others of these distiches (in which each of the wardens and head-masters is commemorated) are very cleverly turned, as for instance—

On Clement Smith, Head-master, 1464-66.
> "Si Clemens fueras, debebas longior esse;
> Turpe per æstates non docuisse duas."

Subsequent masters, it would seem, were not remarkable for clemency; witness Johnson's tribute to the memory of Edward More (1508-17)—

> "Qui legit hic Morum, qui non et sensit eundem,
> Gaudeat, et secum molliter esse putet."

And of his own master, William Evered, he writes—

> "Qui fueras, Evered, meo sensi ipse periclo."

hours of work and recreation, and the peculiar customs of the college as they then existed.*

The scholars at this time were expected to rise at the sound of "first peal" at five o'clock, and were recommended to say privately a short Latin selection from the Psalms as soon as they were dressed. They then swept out their chambers and made their beds (consisting in those days of nothing better than bundles of straw† with a coverlet), and "second peal" at half-past five summoned them to chapel. But these early hours appear to have been as distasteful to some of the young Wykehamists of that day as they are to modern schoolboys; for in a copy of verses, either of Johnson's composition or correction, Melpomene is represented as going round the scholars' beds in the morning, and finding some of them snoring at unlawful hours, to that indefatigable virgin's extreme disgust. At six they went into school, and came out at nine to a breakfast of bread and beer, for which they must by that time have had a pretty vigorous appetite. At eleven they went into school again, and at twelve came dinner. Under the superintendence of the *præfectus ollæ* (prefect of tub), portions of beef, called *dispars*,‡ were served out to the boys in messes of four, with a sufficiency of bread, and beer in large black jacks; the Bible-clerk meanwhile reading aloud a chapter from the Old Testament. The choristers waited at table. An antiphonal grace and psalm were sung, after which the choristers and college servants took

---

* Printed by Bp. Wordsworth in his 'Memorials of Winchester.'
† Hence in college, to this day, clean sheets are spoken of as *clean straw*.
‡ *i. e.*, portions (*dispertio*).

their dinner. Between the two doors inside the hall stood, as it stands now, the *olla* or tub—a strong chest bound with iron hoops—into which all the fragments of the meal were put, and afterwards distributed amongst the poor. Until the last few years the " prefect of tub " (whose duty it was to examine the quality of the meat sent in by the college butcher, and after dinner to see to the proper collection and distribution of the remains) retained his title, though the office had become almost nominal. School opened again at two o'clock; at half-past three came an interval called " bever-time," when the boys had again bread and beer allowed them. At five the school was dismissed, and the whole resident society—warden, fellows, masters, and scholars—went in procession round the cloisters and the whole interior circuit of the college, which was called going *circum*. Thus they passed into the hall, where a supper of mutton was served—one *dispar* to every three boys. Even-song in chapel was at eight, after which, in those primitive days, the young Wykehamists thought it full time to go to bed.

The schoolroom was still " seventh chamber "—*Magna illa domus*, as the founder's directions call it—though, as some of the commoners must have been taught together with the scholars, it is difficult to understand how so many could have found room there without great confusion. Johnson remarks, indeed, that they had no fire in this room, for that the warm sunbeams and the warm *breaths** were quite sufficient; and certainly, if anything like a hundred boys were there collected, that sort of

---

* " Nec schola nostra focum complectitur, attamen omnes
  Phœbeis radiis, halituque calescimus oris."—CHR. JOHNSON.

natural heating apparatus must have been very powerful. But the younger commoners probably seldom came into school, being taught chiefly in the chamber of the warden or fellow under whose charge they were placed; and in summer-time the whole of the scholars usually adjourned for lessons into the adjacent cloisters: a delightful arrangement, from which the latter portion of the "long half" is still called "cloister-time." The tiers of stone seats, which may still be noticed in the deep recesses of the windows, were the places in which the prefects sat when the boys were arranged in their respective *books*—the term still used at Winchester for what in other schools would be called "forms" or "classes." There were then, as now, four books only, though the highest was and is numbered as the "sixth." Then followed the fifth, fourth, and second-fourth. The work of the sixth book comprised Homer, Hesiod, Virgil, Cicero, Martial, and Robinson's Rhetoric. There were twelve college prefects "in full power," of whom one was of "hall," one of "cloisters," one of "school" (called also *ostiarius*,* whose duties seem to have been, in fact, those of a porter, to open the door for the masters), two of "chapel," and one of "tub:" there were also six of lower authority. Tuesdays and Thursdays were partial holidays, on which the boys went out to "hills" twice; once in the morning, returning at nine to breakfast, and again in the afternoon, coming off at three. There they played at quoits, football, and something which seems to have borne a resemblance to cricket—

"Sæpe repercusso pila te juvat icta bacillo."

* This office has been lately revived.

Of some other amusements of the scholars in those days we get one or two incidental notices from Master Badger's copy-book above quoted, from which it appears that they robbed the city orchards occasionally, and that the public bull-baits were a great attraction. Friday was the day of doom, when all arrears of flogging incurred during the week were punctually cleared off.

The upper rooms in the buildings were occupied by the fellows, three in each. The warden had his private lodging "above the inner northern gate," with some rooms east and west of it; the present election-chamber was probably his hall; and from this there is a continuous communication by doors and passages throughout the whole upper storey, which would enable him at any time to visit and overlook the members of his collegiate body. The head-master and his subordinate were lodged together, and the three chaplains had a room in common near the kitchen. Of the chambers below, the scholars occupied six and the choristers one; and it was considerately enjoined, that no occupant of the rooms above was to throw anything down upon their heads, to the detriment of themselves or their goods and chattels. In each of the scholars' rooms were to be three of the eighteen prefects, as enjoined by the founder's statutes; boys "more advanced than the rest in years, discretion, and learning," who were to exercise a supervision over their fellows; so ancient is the system, which, adopted by Eton from Winchester, has long become a recognised feature in all our public schools—the intrusting more or less of the discipline to an aristocracy of the scholars themselves, whether under the name of prefects, monitors, or prepostors. One part of their duty was to instruct the juniors; and this early employment of the monitorial system must have been a very necessary part of the constitution of the school, if, as seems likely, the head-master had at first only one regular assistant. It is still continued in the college under a modified form; each of the junior boys has still his tutor amongst the prefects, the ten seniors having six or seven pupils each allotted to them, whom they are expected to assist in school difficulties generally, and especially in preparation for "standing-up" time, as the junior examinations at the end of the summer half are called. In earlier times it would appear that this kind of deputy-teaching was extended to the younger commoners as well, and led to some degree of abuse and neglect. In 1655, during the head-mastership of Dr Burte, a little boy of six years old was placed at Winchester as a "commoner in college," with other young boys, under the care of one of the fellows named May. These appear to have had no kind of teaching except from the college prefects in turn, who attended at certain hours, and made a periodical report to the master as to how their little pupils conducted themselves, and what progress they were making in their studies. At eight years old this boy was admitted into college. Probably many boys were thus sent as commoners at a very early age, with a view to their subsequent election on the foundation; for, in 1660, one Thomas Middleton petitions King Charles, on his restoration, to grant his royal letters to the Winchester electors in favour of his son's admittance "as a child in Winchester College, where he has now spent three years as fellow-commoner." Of these fellow-commoners, or "commoners," as they are now termed, who have so increased as to form a supplementary body of scholars doubling in number the college-boys themselves, it will be necessary to give some account.

Provision had been made in the original statutes for the reception and instruction of independent students to the number of ten, sons of noblemen or of " special friends" of the college, who, though not claiming the other advantages of the foundation, might yet wish to avail themselves of its sound teaching; with a proviso that these should not be in any way burdensome to the revenues. They paid, probably from the very earliest times, something by way of gratuities to the masters; for one of the "injunctions" of Edward VI., for the regulation of the college, specially provides that the schoolmaster and usher shall " have their accustomed stipend of commensalts (*commensales*), and the warden and fellows to have no part thereof."* Some of these earlier " commoners" were lodged within the walls, and some in a separate establishment, the old College of St Elizabeth of Hungary, standing in St Stephen's Mead. This building, after serving for some years as a kind of hostel to Wykeham's college, was surrendered by the last of its provosts in 1544, and pulled down. The present boundary-wall at the bottom of "Meads" was built partly out of the materials; and corbel-heads and carved stones have been worked in here and there, standing out from the rest of the stone-work in a fashion somewhat puzzling to a curious stranger.

On the suppression of St Elizabeth's College, all the commoners were lodged, some with the warden, some in other parts of the college, probably under the im-

* Wilkins's Concilia, iv. 9.

mediate charge of one of the fellows, and some in houses in the city. Those who lodged with the warden were usually of higher rank; and during some years, in the rolls which have been preserved, there is a distinction between ordinary *commensales* or commoners, and *generosi commensales*, such as was recognised at Eton in earlier times, and is still admitted between commoners and gentleman-commoners at Oxford. In the roll of 1688 the warden's boarders appear as " Nob: Com :" Lord Guilford, Hon. Nathanael Fiennes, Lord Ashley, Sir Thos. Putt, and Sir Thos. Wroth. But this distinction soon disappears, though some of the commoners still continue to be lodged within the walls. The last entry of a "*commensalis in collegio*" occurs in the roll for 1747, during Dr Burton's head-mastership. In his time the college rose rapidly as a place of education for many of the young nobility, and the accommodations were found insufficient. He built what is now remembered by Wykehamists of the past generation as "Old Commoners;" a very much more picturesque-looking building, though probably not so convenient as the present, containing hall, dormitories, tutors' rooms, and prefects' studies. The number of commoners gradually increased, though with some fluctuations, until in 1820 they reached 135. "Old Commoners" was pulled down in 1839–41 to make way for the present building, which was the result of a general Wykehamist subscription; and of which, architecturally and æsthetically, the less that is said the better, as also of certain other modern improvements which successive wardens have made in the college buildings themselves.

The commoners are, in point of fact, little more than

the private boarders of the head-master, attending the regular lessons of the school in company with the boys on the foundation, and amalgamated with them so far as school classification and school work are concerned. At other times they are necessarily a good deal separated, partly by locality, and partly also by a distinct *esprit de corps*. From the time that they began to rival the college-boys in numbers, a certain amount of jealousy has always existed between the two bodies, though both are proud of their common designation as Wykehamists. There is, perhaps, some little assumption of superiority in rank on the part of the commoners, who look upon "College" as in some sort an eleemosynary foundation. The college-boys still wear the gown of black cloth, with a full sleeve looped up at the elbow, and a sort of cassock waistcoat; but the square academic cap, so much affected by provincial "colleges," has been discontinued. The gown, in older times, was worn by the commoners as well—at all events by those who were lodged within the college walls; and the *nobiles* amongst Dr Burton's old pupils appear to have consulted their own fancy as to the colour; some of them, as represented in the series of half-length portraits which he left as a legacy to his successors, appearing in blue and others in red silk gowns. At present the commoners wear no gown at all. They have also somewhat more liberty with respect to bounds, have their own separate ground for football, and in some other respects are not closely associated with the college out of school hours. These things necessarily prevent, in some degree, that thorough amalgamation into one body which is so desirable in members of the same school; but the line of distinction is gradually wearing out, and it is the wish of the present authorities to obliterate it as far as possible. The old wall which used to divide the college "meads" from "commoners' field" has recently been pulled down, which has the practical effect of giving the commoners a right of entrance into what the college-boys are still apt to consider their own peculiar domain. The recent changes, which have made election into college entirely a matter of competitive examination, and have admitted the commoners to compete at the election to the New College scholarships, will do very much to dissipate any foolish notions of the foundationers' position being the inferior one.

CHAPTER IV.

FROM ELIZABETH TO THE REVOLUTION.

The election of boys into college, however it might have been managed in Wykeham's own days, had from time immemorial, until the late reforms, been a mere matter of patronage on the part of the electors. These were, according to the statutes, the warden and two of the fellows of New College, Oxford, and the warden, sub-warden, and head-master of St Mary's, Winchester. They were charged to elect, in the first place, those of the founder's kindred who should be eligible; and, after all such claims should have been satisfied, they were to fill the vacancies with such as were "poor and in need of help, of good character and condition, towardly in learning, of honest conversation, and competently instructed in reading, plain-song, and in *Donatus*"—the Public School Grammar of Wykeham's day.

Much stress has been laid in past days upon the diversion of Wykeham's provision for "poor" scholars to the benefit of the rich. But the best and fairest reading of any man's intentions is what can be gathered from his own practice; and the next best, perhaps, is that in which they were understood and carried out by his immediate successors. Henry Chichele (the Archbishop) was one of Wykeham's earliest "poor" scholars on St Giles's Hill; and he was the son of a Lord Mayor of London, certainly not *poor* in the common acceptation of the word. William of Waynflete, again, was nominated into the college during the founder's life; and he came of a good family, whatever his pecuniary resources might be. Archbishop Warham—"a gentleman of an ancient house in Hampshire"—was a scholar some fifty years after. Indeed it is plain that the kind of education which Wykeham contemplated was unsuitable for any boys except those intended for liberal callings, and to such it seems always to have been very properly confined.

The preference assigned to "founder's kin" in the election soon brought into the field, as may be supposed, young Wykehams and Williamses from all quarters, with others who proved more or less satisfactorily their connection with the founder's family; and gradually the custom obtained of electing two only of these favoured candidates at the head of the roll for admission, and filling up the remaining vacancies by a process of successive nomination by each of the six electors, the warden of New College having the first turn, until the number of vacancies was supplied. In Warton's time, the candidates were merely required "to repeat a few lines from some author suited to their age and capacity;" and the examination under the system which has just passed away continued to the last of much the same character. The successive royal patrons of Winchester were not above asking occasionally, on behalf of some of their dependants, for a "child's" place in college, or a fellowship at Oxford. The Stuart kings, as may be seen from the state papers of those reigns, were very much given to this kind of patronage. James I., on the strength of his somewhat pedantic reputation, interferes so far as to recommend Richard Fitzherbert as schoolmaster; but one is glad to find that he was never appointed. There was, indeed, no vacancy at the time, nor for some years afterwards; possibly the King expected the college to make one. Charles II., in one of these royal letters of request, has the coolness to plead the loftiest motives, recommending one Master Matthew Preston solely as "being wishful to supply that happy nursery with deserving youths." Secretary Windebank got a son elected there by royal favour; and one of the boy's letters home has the honour of accidental preservation amongst the state papers. It is a very stiff and formal little production, becoming a young Secretary of State. He is sorry that "he cannot write a letter worthy of his father's perusal," but "sends him hearty wishes for his welfare," with six lines of Latin verse. The verse is indifferent; but there are less creditable documents amongst the Secretary's correspondence. Queen Elizabeth herself once endeavours to get a Mr Cotton elected fellow, with an immediate view to the wardenship, then vacant; but the house successfully stood out against so very palpable a job.

In the year 1579, under the mastership of Thomas Bilson (Bishop of Worcester), there was something like an insurrection on the part of the boys. They must have had, or thought they had, grave causes of complaint, for they carried their petition before the Queen, and two of the fellows had to journey to court to answer it. Some of them ran away, and it cost Mr Booles and Mr Budd some hard riding (and 10s. 10d. horse-hire) to catch them and bring them back.* How the matter was settled does not appear; but it might have had something to do with Bilson's resignation in that year or the following.

The return of Drake from sailing round the world in his good ship Dragon, in 1580, set all the poets in England versifying to celebrate the happy event. The most successful of these effusions were hung at the mast-head when the Queen went down to sup with him on board his vessel at Deptford. It is said that the Latin verses sent in by the Winchester scholars were generally acknowledged to be the best; but as they are certainly not to be compared with any of Johnson's, they may be content to remain in the limbo of prize-poems generally.†

A school-bill of 1620, for a son of Archbishop Hutton, gives some notion of the Winchester of the Stuarts' days. Master Hutton cost his father "for his dyet at Mr Phillips'" (the fellow with whom he lodged as a commoner), £1, 10s., from August 16th to September 31st, when he seems to have been elected into college. His "scobb, to hold his books," cost 3s. 6d. The boys went once to the royal hunt in the New Forest in a waggon (hired for 4s.), under charge of one Willes and two other college servants; they took their dinner and wine with them into the Forest, and had *coenbum* (mulled wine of some sort) with their supper when they came home. This picnic party cost Master Hutton 6d. extra. But his studies were not neglected: there is a wholesome item in the bill of 4d. "*for birche.*" ‡

* Walcott.
† Milner, i. 375. Camden, Annal. Eliz. (Hearne), ii. 359.
‡ Walcott, 166, 207, &c.

The civil wars came, and the city of Winchester was held alternately for the King and the Commons. Sir William Waller, unable to reduce the castle, vented his rage upon the cathedral, where his troopers hewed down carved work and images with pious ferocity. The college would have suffered equally, but that it chanced to have a friend amongst the rebel authorities. Nathanael Fiennes, fellow of New College and colonel of horse, was a sour Independent, but a good Wykehamist. He occupied his old school quarters with his men, putting in a sort of friendly execution, and thus saved it from wreck and pillage.* The college authorities did not grudge the £29, 5s. 6d. which (as appears from their accounts †) they distributed amongst the guard, though it was a large sum in those days. Another Wykehamist—Nicholas Love, son of a former warden—is said also to have had a share in protecting the college from outrage. Cromwell afterwards appeared before the castle in person, and planted his guns on a hill to the south-west, near St Cross Hospital, still bearing the name of "Oliver's Battery." The great oak doors of "Non-licet" gate, at the corner of "Meads" (supposed to be only opened when a boy is expelled), still bear marks which are shown as the traces of the rebel grapeshot. How the college carried on its work in these troubled times, and whether any temporary suspension took place, are points of great interest, but on which no information seems now recoverable, further than that John Potenger, the head-master, resigned in 1653, in disgust at certain Puritanical innovations; whilst Warden Harris appears to have held on through all changes, political and religious, for eight-and-

* Milner, ii. 415; Woodward, 203.   † Walcott, 172.

twenty of the darkest years of England's history, dying only a month before the Protector, in 1658. One of his eulogists calls him, for his eloquence, the "modern Chrysostom;" but one would think he must also have had a capacity for silence, to have offended none of the various powers that then were.

In 1687, on the eve of another great Revolution, the present schoolroom was finished and opened, which must have been an immense relief to the crowded numbers of college and commoners. From that time Seventh Chamber was converted into what it still remains—the principal dormitory. The new school is lofty and spacious, but the Jacobean architecture is sadly out of keeping with Wykeham's original buildings. It cost £2600; of which Dr John Nicholas, then warden, contributed no less than £1477. Ninety feet long and thirty-six in breadth, it is sufficiently spacious to allow all the "books" to be assembled there without more confusion than is inseparable from the system of teaching so many distinct classes in a single room—an arrangement peculiar to Winchester alone amongst our large public schools. To a stranger the confused sea of sound is rather distracting: but neither boys nor masters make any complaint, and soon learn to concentrate their attention on their own individual work.* Three tiers of fixed seats rise against the wainscoted walls on the east and west,

* The Royal Commissioners have a pertinent remark on this: "It is necessary at the bar, and in other careers, and in the Houses of Parliament, that much mental work of all kinds should be done amidst many outward causes of distraction. It would be matter of regret if public-school life should in any way disqualify boys for the conditions under which they must do their work as men."—Public Schools Report, p. 287.

where the boys are arranged when "up to books," the chairs of the different masters being in front of each. The middle of the room is occupied by blocks of oak benches, with gangways between, upon which are fixed the college-boys' boxes (called in the peculiar school tongue *scobs*—"box" spelt backwards), where the lessons are prepared; each scob having an outer lid, which, when raised, forms a kind of screen, while the inner lid serves as a desk; the books and writing materials being kept below. Against the west wall is fixed a large wooden tablet, on which is painted the well-known Wykehamist device—a mitre and a crosier—at the top, as the prizes of diligence (it must be remembered that all Wykehamist scholars were originally intended for the Church, and all above the age of sixteen were to receive the first tonsure): next, a sword and an inkhorn, pointing to civil and military service for less hopeful students; and the quadripartite rod below, as the last alternative. Under each emblem successively stand, in bold capitals, the warning words, "AUT DISCE—AUT DISCEDE—MANET SORS TERTIA, C.EDI." Underneath is the place of execution, where delinquents are "bibled;" and near it is a socket for a candle-sconce, known as the "nail," under which any boy who has been detected in any disgraceful fault—lying, &c.—is placed as in a sort of pillory to await his punishment; a piece of ancient discipline for which happily there is seldom occasion. On the opposite wall is a similar tablet, containing a code of school regulations in Latin. This schoolroom is almost the only addition to Wykeham's original plan, with the exception of the present warden's house, built by Warden Harmar in 1579 on the site of some old storehouses and other offices, and refronted in 1832 in very questionable taste.

The Revolution of 1688 brought into prominence the names of at least two Wykehamists, whose steadfastness to the allegiance they had sworn, "though to their own hindrance," has won them praise from all honest men of both parties. Two of the nonjuring bishops, Ken and Turner, had been schoolmates in the college before they were fellow-prisoners in the Tower (with a third Winchester scholar of almost a generation earlier—Lloyd of St Asaph), and fellow-sufferers in their deprivation under William. The youngest Wykehamist will point out with a reverent pride the letters "THO: KEN" carved on one of the pillars in cloisters; and not far off may be seen that of his schoolfellow, "Francis Turner, 1655." No profane knife has encroached upon the sacred characters; and though Ken lies buried far from the scenes which he loved with an enduring affection, those few rude letters are memorial enough; no saint who was ever canonised better deserved the title than he who wrote his 'Manual of Prayers for the Winchester Scholars.'

CHAPTER V.

RECENT HISTORY.

The head-masters who followed were Drs Harris, Cheyney, and Burton. The latter, as has been said, gave to "commoners" a permanent establishment, owing to which their numbers rapidly increased, and the school bade fair at one time to rival Eton in aristocratic pupils, especially from the young Scottish nobility. To him succeeded Dr Joseph Warton, the best known of all who have borne rule at Winchester, though by no means the most able or successful of head-masters. He was a man of elegant tastes and accomplishments, of amiable character, dignified and courteous manners; but he was an inefficient disciplinarian, and an inaccurate scholar. He is said to have been deficient in moral courage; which could hardly have been true, if what is told of his collision with Dr Johnson be correct. Warton had ventured on some occasion to express an opinion differing from that of the conversational autocrat. "Sir," said Johnson, "I am not accustomed to be contradicted." "Better for you, sir, if you were; our respect for you could not be increased, but our love might." It need hardly be said that the love between the two doctors was never very cordial afterwards. It might have been supposed that a man who could rebuke Johnson could at least govern schoolboys. Probably it was his defective scholarship, which boys are sharp at detecting in a master, which first weakened his authority. When a stiff Greek chorus formed part of the lesson, Warton always complained of a noise in school; and while he was shouting to the prefect to maintain silence, the passage was allowed to be shuffled over in any way that might relieve him from criticism. For the same reason he was fond of requiring from the boys written translations, in which difficulties could be loosely paraphrased, and which he could, at least, examine and correct at his leisure; and he is said to have liberally rewarded, instead of rebuking, as he should have done, a boy who, when called up to construe a passage in Horace, shut his book and recited Pope's 'Imitation.' His weak though popular administration paved the way for the most formidable rebellion on record in any public school, although the then warden, Dr Huntingford, was the immediate object of the outbreak. It took place on the 3d of April 1793. Strict orders had been issued by the warden that the boys should not attend the parade of the Bucks Militia; that in the event of disobedience on the part of any individual boy, he should be individually punished: but that if any numbers were seen there, the whole school should have their "leave-out" stopped for the following Easter Sunday, when many had invitations to dine with friends. *One* boy only—a prefect—was detected and reported by Mr Goddard, the second-master. The warden not only severely punished the individual, but stopped the leave of the whole school, accompanying this with a quotation more irritating than appropriate,

"*Quidquid delirant reges plectuntur Achivi.*" The boys resented this as a breach of faith; they held a meeting, and after solemnly binding themselves by an oath (in which, however, the younger boys were not allowed to join) to stand by each other in their resistance to the last, they drew up a series of resolutions, of which they proceeded to put the first into execution at once. A Latin note was sent to the warden, submitting to the present punishment, but expressing a hope that in future he would not punish all for the fault of one. To this note Dr Huntingford returned no answer. After three days a second note was forwarded to him, very respectfully worded, but requesting a reply. It was returned with an endorsement charging the writers with "consummate arrogance," and forgetfulness of their position and their duties. Then the storm broke out. The keys of the college gates were seized. Warning was sent both to the head and second masters not to make their appearance in school. The warning to Dr Warton was accompanied by professions of esteem; he was weak enough to comply, and kept away. Goddard (though aware of his unpopularity as the delator of the actual culprit) had a better appreciation of his duty. He was received on entering the school with groans and hisses, and with a shower of marbles from the younger boys—an act censured by the prefects. A summons issued by the warden and masters to the eighteen prefects to appear before them met with no attention; the communication between the warden's lodgings and the rest of the college was blocked up, and the college gates guarded night and day by patrols of the scholars. The cry of "Liberty and Equality" was raised (so contagious were French revolutionary principles), the "red cap" was assumed by all the boys who could procure or contrive one, the bakers' and butchers' shops ransacked for provisions, and bludgeons and swords provided, in preparation for a siege. The warden, having gone out of his own house early next morning to convene a meeting of the fellows at Dr Watson's house (in commoners), was not allowed readmission; and by confining one of the fellows within the college walls, the rebels effectually prevented a *quorum* of four being formed, which is required for any official act of their body. A message was then sent from the warden, to the effect that all the boys might go home; but in that case they were well aware that expulsion of the ringleaders would follow. The warden then applied to the magistrates (who happened to be then assembled to present an address to the King) to put him in possession of his house, from which he was still excluded by the insurgents, by the aid of the civil power. The outer gates of the college had by this time been barricaded, the quadrangle unpaved, and the stones carried up to the top of the tower above, part of the parapet of which the rebels also loosened, to supply them with missiles to resist attack from without. When summoned to surrender by the Sheriff in person, their reply was a threat to burn the college if any attempt was made to force an entrance. Sir Thomas Miller, Mr Brereton, and Canon Poulter, severally did their best to negotiate; but there was such excitement in the town generally, and so much fear of the "roughs" taking part with the boys, that three companies of militia were drawn up under arms in College Street. At last Dr Warton, with one or two of the above named gentlemen, were admitted within the gates; and on their representations the boys agreed to submit the whole question to the arbitration of the magistrates. The matter ended for the time in an entire amnesty, or even more: the warden conceding the original point of dispute by an engagement not in future to punish the community for the sake of an individual. But these terms—plainly far more favourable than ever should have been offered—appear not to have been strictly kept on either side. The authority which failed to assert itself against open violence, sought to take advantage of quieter times, and the result was a most unhappy one. More than one parent at once received a private request to take his son away from the college, at least for a time; and a few days after, one of the prefects was required by his father—it was supposed at the warden's instance—either to beg pardon of the latter, or resign his scholarship. He stoutly chose the latter; and his late companions (a portion of whose mutual engagement had been that no boy should take advantage of another's loss of place in college, in consequence of his share in these proceedings) thought themselves bound in honour to support him. All but one who had signed the oath sent up their resignations to the warden. Nineteen repented the next morning, and asked leave in another note to withdraw them. The only reply was— "The warden and fellows cannot return any answer." A college meeting was held, and twenty-six boys were formally expelled, and others desired to leave. Possibly no other course now remained for the authorities; no government is so bound to severities as a weak one; but the respect which every public-school man must entertain for school discipline, cannot prevent him from feeling some sympathy with the victims. It is not surprising that Dr Warton resigned his head-mastership at the close of the half-year.*

One of Warton's pupils was Sydney Smith, who, with his younger brother Courtenay, entered the college about 1781. If his evidence as to the internal discipline and morals were entirely to be trusted, it would leave on record a very black picture indeed of the Winchester of his day. Even in his old age, says his daughter and biographer, he "used to shudder at the recollection" of it, and speak with horror of the wretchedness of the years he spent there: "the whole system," he used to say, "was one of abuse, neglect, and vice." "There never was enough provided even of the coarsest food, and the little boys were of course left to fare as they could." He declares that his brother Courtenay, who ran away twice, did so because he was unable to bear the hardship. But there are two or three incidental passages in this biography which induce a doubt whether the witty divine's record is altogether an honest one. Master Courtenay Smith, it appears, owed a little bill of £30 in the town the last time he ran away, so that one of his hardships might have been the difficulty of paying it. And when we have Sydney's own testimony that both he and his brothers were, before they went to Winchester, "the most intolerable and overbearing set of boys that can well be imagined," it is easy to conceive that they would not find a public school exactly a bed of roses. Sydney, too, must have enjoyed himself there occasionally, after his own fashion; for Dr Warton found him one day exercising that rough-and-ready mechanical genius which produced the celebrated "patent Tantalus"

* See original narrative in Appendix.

of his after-days, in constructing a catapult in chambers by lamp-light; and commended him highly for his ingenuity, little dreaming that it was intended to bring down a neighbour's turkey, on which the boys had fixed devouring eyes with a view to supper. Both brothers held their own there, at any rate, in point of ability; for the boys, it is said, at last signed a round-robin, refusing to compete for the college prizes if the Smiths were any longer allowed to enter the list, as they were always sure to win them; and Sydney left the school as Captain.

On the other hand, William Lisle Bowles, who left Winchester just as the Smiths were entering, speaks with delight of his school-days, and has no morbid reminiscences of his hardships, even as a junior; and yet Bowles's poetic and somewhat delicate temperament was at least as susceptible to the roughness of public-school life as the more vigorous nature of the Canon of St Paul's. But a Winchester education in those days certainly did imply a considerable amount of this rough training. Independently of very early hours and somewhat coarse fare, it was not pleasant to have to wash at the old "Moab,"* as it was called—an open conduit in the quadrangle, where it was necessary, on a severe winter morning, for a junior to melt the ice on the stop-cock with a lighted

---

* The "wash-pot." Here all the college-boys, within living memory, had to wash in the open air, except that there was originally a sort of penthouse over it, replaced afterwards by a wretched Ionic portico, of which a print appears in Ball's 'Walks in Winchester,' p. 154. The present "Moab" is a convenient room in School Court, containing rows of basins, for which a plentiful supply of water is laid on, with clothes-lockers and other useful appliances. In the same Winton tongue the shoe-cleaning place was known as *Edom*. Other local designations are classical; there is an *Arcadia*, an Upper and Lower *Dalmatia*, and a ditch on the way to "Hills" called *Tempe*.

faggot before any water could be got to flow at all; or for the same unfortunate junior to have to watch out in the cold quadrangle before early lesson (without a hat, for in that sacred enclosure no junior is allowed to wear one), to give notice of the exact moment when the master went into school, so that the seniors might waste none of their more precious time, but make their rush at the last available moment.

William Stanley Goddard succeeded Dr Warton, certainly under very difficult circumstances; but an abler or better ruler never was at Winchester. There was no rebellion in his reign; yet his old pupils know that he governed at least as much by appeals to their better feelings as by fear of punishment. He acted constantly on that assumption of a boy's truthfulness and honour, which has always been found a successful principle of government in judicious hands, and which has been somewhat unfairly claimed as an entirely modern notion, so far as public education is concerned. But he did not hold his office very long; he resigned in 1810, comparatively a young man, living thirty-seven years afterwards, and always retaining the strongest attachment to the college. He showed it by a remarkable act of munificence, ten years before his death, when he invested £25,000 of his private property in order to provide stipends for the masters in the college, on condition of their giving up their claim to "gratuities" from the boys, which had hitherto formed their chief remuneration. This claim was plainly in contravention of the statutes, though it had been authorised by the Visitor; and it had always been, as Dr Goddard declared, "a distress of conscience" to him to receive the money. In fact, up to this time the expenses of a college-boy at Winchester, far from being gratuitous, as Wykeham had intended, amounted, including bills and extras of one kind or another, to something like £80 per annum. Now, it need not exceed £18 or £20. A commoner's charges amount in the whole to an average of about £116. The "Goddard" scholarship for proficiency in classics, the blue ribbon of Winchester, was founded in honour of this liberal benefactor in 1846, the year before his death, superseding the prize which had for some years been given by Sir William Heathcote.

The Rev. Henry Gabell, who had been appointed second-master on Dr Goddard's promotion, succeeded him again in the head-mastership. He insisted strongly upon that *accurate* scholarship, for which Winchester has never lost its reputation. But his administration was marked by a second rebellion, nearly as formidable as the first, of which it seems to have been a sort of copy. The boys, taking offence at some breach, or fancied breach, of their privileges, wrote up in the school as their adopted motto, "*Maxima debetur pueris reverentia*"—scarcely a less inappropriate quotation than Warden Huntingford's on the former occasion. Again the keys of the college were seized, the court unpaved, and the stones carried up to the tower as ammunition for an expected siege; but this time, the senior prefect and five of his fellow-officers, not choosing to risk the certain loss of their prospects at New College, refused to join in the insurrection. Nevertheless, matters proceeded so far that the Fusilier Guards, then quartered in the barracks, were called out to keep the peace in College Street, where the mob had assembled in formidable numbers. The result was, of course, the discomfiture and punishment of the ringleaders; twelve college-boys, most of them prefects, were expelled, many others degraded from their places in the school, and forty commoners were not allowed to return after the vacation.

It had become almost the rule at Winchester for the second-master to succeed to the head-mastership, and Dr Williams was so appointed in 1824. His reign was quiet, and on the whole successful. There was indeed a trifling disturbance amongst the junior commoners, owing to an alleged abuse of the privilege of fagging by the prefects, which caused some excitement at the time. It was the rule in those days, both in college and in commoners, that no junior should presume to get his own breakfast until the prefects had finished, which usually necessitated a very hurried affair of mere bread-and-butter and cold milk on the part of the former. In commoners they had to sit on a cross bench in hall to be in waiting during both the prefects' breakfast and supper; and certainly those young gentlemen must have been curious in the matter of toast, for each of them (there were only eight at that time) regularly employed two juniors as toasters. It is difficult at this date to discuss the important rights of the junior fifth, on which the whole question hinged; but they claimed, by custom, exemption from the duties of breakfast-waiters. However, as boys came to school better scholars, and were consequently higher placed, fourth-form fags grew scarce, and the junior fifth were ordered, as the phrase was, to "go on hall." One champion stood upon his rights, and refused; the indignant prefect proposed to thrash him publicly; the juniors rose in a body and pinioned the prefects. Fond mammas, and other declaimers against school tyranny, will regret to hear that this spirited resistance was not appreciated by Dr Williams; after a patient hearing of the pleas on both sides, he supported the prefects' authority (it may be concluded that they had not really exceeded it), and six of the ringleaders were expelled. One of them was a brother of a baronet, himself a Wykehamist. Dr Williams was much pressed to reconsider his decision, but steadily refused. He resigned in 1836, and was subsequently elected Warden of New College, Oxford. George Moberly, Fellow and Tutor of Balliol College, succeeded at Winchester. Of his long and successful mastership, which has so recently been brought to an honourable close, this is not the time or place to speak. Highly successful it has been on the whole, although at one period (1856), owing to one of those periodical ebb-tides to which all public schools seem liable, and of which the real causes are not easy to discover, the numbers in commoners had declined from 130, at which point he found them, to as few as 65. But from that time they have risen rapidly; in 1859, for the first time, one of the tutors opened a house for the reception of boarders—"commoners" itself not holding more than a hundred boys conveniently; and there are now as many as 205 commoners on the roll, 98 of these being lodged in tutors' houses, of which there are now three. It must be understood that the numbers in college are never more or less than the original 70.

CHAPTER VI.

PRESENT STATE OF THE COLLEGE.

It has been already said that the original plan of Wykeham's college has undergone little alteration. Almost a copy on a smaller scale of the elder sister in Oxford, it is still, in its arrangements, half a fortress. The visitor who enters the massive gateway feels that he has stepped back at once, as far as all surrounding objects go, into the fourteenth century. Even the college-boy whom he meets with his hands thrust into the depths of modern pockets, hardly interferes with the illusion; his gown, at least, is medieval. You pass through the small outer court, which, though now occupied in part by the warden's lodgings, contained formerly little more than the extensive offices required to make so large a society independent,—through the middle gate-tower (whence St Mary of Winton herself, a very graceful figure, with the Angel of the Salutation and the Founder on either side, looks down upon you), into the main quadrangle of the college. Turn to the right, up that flight of stone steps, and you reach the hall, a noble room, near sixty-three feet long, with a daïs at the upper end, which supposes the presence of the warden and fellows at all public meals, as under the original system, which neither Bancroft's nor Laud's injunctions were able to restore. They only dine there now on special festivals. There are the old louvres still to be seen in the roof, whence the smoke used to escape from the charcoal fire in the middle. If you regret, for a passing moment, that it has been superseded by a stove, and that the smoke now finds its way underground, remember that for those who dine there such modern appliances are not altogether unsatisfactory. Look in at the ample kitchen at the foot of the steps as you return, and be sure that as good fare comes forth from its ranges now as when they cooked "a pair of porpoises" there (of all imaginable delicacies) to feast their visitor the Bishop in 1410. Taste the beer—the college still brews its own—and you will find it excellent. You will not be allowed to pass without being called upon to note the picture on the wall by the kitchen entrance, which you know well enough already from woodcuts and all kinds of illustrations, the "Trusty Servant"—*Probus Famulus*—in his blue-and-red livery; that strange figure, a compound of all the virtues, such as these degenerate days have never seen. He has the pig's snout, to signify that he cares not what he eats; a padlock on his lips, for silence; ass's ears, for patience; hind's feet, for swiftness; a right hand open, for honesty; a left hand grasping all manner of implements, to show that he can turn his hand to anything; and a sword and shield, to fight his master's battles. What wages would such a treasure expect? But in modern service you are as like to meet the literal monster as the paragon whom he symbolises. The origin and date of the figure are obscure; and (as may be seen from old prints) it has undergone alterations in the details in the process of repainting from time to time: but it is not peculiar to Winchester; a similar figure was not uncommonly painted in dining-halls in France during the sixteenth century. The Latin verses underneath are probably from the hand of Christopher Johnson.

Through a low ambulatory under a portion of the hall is the entrance to Wykeham's beautiful chapel, with its vaulted wooden roof of Irish oak and exquisite stained windows. Let us not utter, in such a place, an anathema against Warden Nicholas, though he did take up the brasses in the chancel, and cut away the beautiful stonework of the stalls and reredos, in order to set up his Ionic wainscoting of oak; especially since the reredos has been admirably restored by the liberality of a modern Wykehamist, Sir William Erle. Besides, even Warden Nicholas's work is good of its kind, and has had no expense spared on it: he was only acting according to his lights, and was a liberal benefactor to his college in many ways. Nor let our enthusiasm for the past make us forget that there are devotion and heroism even in our own utilitarian age; do not let us criticise too strictly that arcade of floriated work in the ante-chapel, or pass unread that touching inscription underneath, the tribute of Wykehamists to their thirteen brethren whose names are there recorded as having died "in their harness" in the Crimea: "Think upon them, thou who art passing by to-day, child of the same family, bought by the same Lord: keep thy foot when thou goest into the house of God; there watch thine armour, and make thyself ready by prayer to fight and die the faithful soldier and servant of Christ and of thy country."

"Child," it should be remarked, is the kindly term used by Wykeham for his scholars, and long retained in use by the Wykehamists of early days: Ken always employs it in his 'Manual.'

The new stained window in Warden Thurburn's chantry is also interesting, not for its beauty, but as the tribute of gratitude from scholars and commoners to Charles Wordsworth (now Bishop of St Andrews) on his resigning office as second-master. Adjoining the chapel are the cloisters, surrounding the "garth" or burying-ground, in the middle of which stands the beautiful chantry built by John Fromond, priest, steward to the founder. There was to be sung a mass for ever for the souls of himself and his wife, who were interred within. Suppressed, so far as its original purpose went, at the Reformation, it has been since used as the College Library, and contains some curious and valuable MSS. The small room above was probably at first used as a *scriptorium;* it had been converted into a granary in 1570. In the quiet square within, and under the pavement of the cloisters, many a Wykehamist, old and young, sleeps his last sleep. Some few years ago fever was exceptionally fatal in the place; as many as eleven recent tablets may be counted on the cloister walls, bearing the names of young scholars thus early removed—in many cases, where the hope of future excellence was brightest. Yet Winchester has never been reckoned unhealthy; Warton, in his notice of the college, speaks of there having been "scarce an instance of death there once in twenty years." The infirmary, or "Bethesda," as it was termed by its builder, Warden Harris, stands in a piece of ground adjoining

Meads, and thither every case of illness is at once removed.

Years have worked fewer changes at Winchester than at any other of our public schools. Until the last few years, it maintained some curious primitive arrangements which many an old Wykehamist will regret now to miss. The black jacks (still to be seen in the cellar and kitchen) have not long disappeared from hall, and tea has quite lately taken the place of beer. The hour of rising (5 at all seasons) had never altered from the founder's day until, in 1708, Sir John Trelawny, Bishop of Winchester, in his capacity of Visitor, suggested and obtained from the college authorities the modification that from Michaelmas to Lady-Day it should be 6, and that the scholars should be "relieved from the servile and foul office of making their own beds, and keeping their chambers clean."* There are still the original number of eighteen prefects in college. The first ten are "in full power," as it is termed; the Latin form of admission to their office being—"*Esto præfectus cum plenâ potestate.*" Besides the responsibility of maintaining discipline, these have a general privilege of fagging all below them, with some few privileged exceptions, both in chambers and out. The five seniors—not invariably appointed from their standing in the school, but "with reference to their character and influence for good"†—are "officers:" 1. Prefect of hall, who has a general superintendence over the school, and is the recognised organ of communication between boys and master; 2. Prefect of library; 3. of school; 4 and 5. of chapel. These ten have also power

---

* Walcott, p. 196.
† See Dr Moberly's admirable 'Letters on Public Schools,' p. 97.

over the commoners, so far as discipline is concerned, but not to fag them; that being the right of the commoner prefects only, of whom there are at present thirteen— the number being always proportioned to the number of boys in commoners. The remaining eight college prefects (called in Winchester tongue *Bluchers*) have a more limited authority, confined to chambers and the quadrangle; the form of making these is—"*Præficio te sociis concameralibus.*" At least two prefects are located in each of the seven chambers,—one from the first seven in rank, and one from the next seven; the juniors are also divided into ranks of seven, and out of each rank the prefects, according to their seniority, choose one each to fill up the numbers in their own chamber; so that each chamber has, to a certain extent, ties and associations of its own.

At present the hour for chapel is 6.45 in summer, and 7 in winter (sometimes, in very cold weather, 7.30 by special licence); "first peal" always ringing three-quarters of an hour beforehand, when the junior in each chamber has to get up at once; but a senior seldom turns out before "second peal," which leaves him some fifteen minutes for a hurried toilet. The chapel service lasts half an hour, and first school begins at 7.30; after which comes breakfast, served in hall. Middle school is from 9 to 12, comprising two distinct lessons, one in classics, the other in mathematics or modern languages. Third school is from 3 o'clock until 6—also for two lessons, as before. Tuesdays and Thursdays are half-holidays, or, as the Winchester term is, "half-*remedies*,"* when there is no third school; but an hour in summer and two hours in winter (from 4 till 6), called "books-chamber time," is expected

* *i. e., Remissionis dies.* Saints' days only are called "holidays."

to be employed in working under the superintendence of the "Bible-clerk,"* as the prefect in weekly "course" is termed, who is responsible for a decent amount of order and silence at these hours. Whole "remedies" are occasionally given on a Tuesday or Thursday, at the request of the prefect of hall; when, in accordance with ancient custom, the head-master intrusts him with a ring, which he keeps for the day, and the motto on which—*commendat rarior usus*—is a hint that such request is not to be made too often.† On these days four hours are employed at "books-chambers." Saturday, by a singular exception to the practice of almost all schools, is not a half-remedy; but the afternoon school ends at five, at which hour there is chapel. On Sundays there is morning chapel at 8, breakfast at 9, and at 10 the whole school attends the service (litany and a sermon) at the Cathedral, where place is allotted them in the choir, two oaken arm-chairs forming seats of honour for the two senior prefects. There is a Scripture or Greek Testament lesson at 4, and evening chapel at 5. On the afternoons of half-remedies, when the weather allows, the whole school in pairs, each boy with his *socius* (according to the founder's rule—*sociati omnes incedunto*) under the command of the prefect of hall, start from college at 2 p.m. for "Hills;" the breezy downs about a mile south-east of the college, called St Catherine's Hill, which has always formed the supplementary playground for Wykehamists. Here Whitehead used to lie and read his favourite 'Atlantis,'

---

* He has a *scob* appropriated to him in school, near the door, with the inscription, ΤΩ ΑΕΙ ΑΝΑΓΝΩΣΤΗ. His original office was to read the Bible at meals.

† The ring which had been in use for many generations was unfortunately lost a year or two ago.

put the finishing touches to his comedy (written at sixteen), and compose abundant poetry perhaps not much worse than in his laureated days.* Here also, in days within the memory of many, a badger-bait was the great excitement provided for less poetic spirits, on extraordinary occasions; but now the time, which has been extended to three hours, is usually spent in walks in the adjoining country within certain bounds, with an occasional paper-chase or game at football. At other times a college-boy is more strictly confined to bounds than is the case at any other public school; the gates being kept strictly locked, and no exit allowed except into "Meads" —the playground at the back of the college, containing about two acres, with good football and cricket-ground, and fives-courts—or into College Street as far as the bookseller's. The present warden has given a degree of liberty which is much valued—"leave out" to the whole school from 12 to 1, within certain bounds which do not include the city; for any business which a boy may have in the streets, special leave has to be obtained. Supper —consisting of bread and cheese, or beef (on alternate nights) and beer, for prefects; bread and butter and tea for inferiors—is served out at 6; which leaves the services of the juniors at liberty if required for toasting, &c., at the "prefects' mess" at 6.30; those official personages enjoying the privileges of having tea, coffee, &c., made for them by their "valets" in chambers from that hour until 7.30. When the prefects have finished "mess," the valets are allowed to regale themselves on the remains; which repast is known as "*sus*," probably a short form of "sustenance." From then until prayers at 8.45 is

* Nichols's Lit., Anecd. iii. 193.

"toy time"—presumed to be occupied in preparing the work for the next day, under the superintendence of the prefects, who usually maintain very strict order. All the chambers are supposed to be quiet by 9 o'clock. A certain quantity of bread is given out in hall at 6.30 for use in chambers, but there is no regular meal after the six o'clock tea or supper; though there are often surreptitious cookings of tea and coffee, and other accessories, on the "half-faggot" on the hearth; not less enjoyed, because liable to sudden interruption and punishment by the second-master, if he makes, as he is supposed occasionally to do, a round of inspection. It was at such little suppers that Tom Warton (who *ought* to have been a Wykehamist), when living with his brother the Doctor, delighted to assist; hiding himself, like a great boy, when Dr Warton happened to come round; and doing the "impositions" of Latin verse inflicted upon his young fellow-culprits. Bed-time is 9.15 for the juniors; for the prefects, 10. In commoners the hours are much the same. It will be found on calculation that the average day's work expected from a boy at Winchester is rather more than seven hours; quite sufficient, if fairly employed. But when working for "standing-up time," or election-day, a zealous boy will give up a good deal more time than this.*

* At these times a good deal of extra reading is done, and strange devices are adopted to secure early waking in the morning. One very original alarm—known as a "scheme"—is of venerable antiquity, and deserves notice, though not very easy to describe. A hat-box, or some such article, is hung by a string over a boy's head as he lies in bed, the string being fastened to the wall, and a rushlight so arranged as to burn it through at a certain hour; when down comes the hat-box on the sleeper's head. The boy who wishes to be called may probably be a prefect; but it need hardly be said that the head upon which the hat-box descends is a junior's.

DINNER.

Dinner is now at 1.15, for which only half an hour is allowed. It is rather singular that, in this respect, a step has been made backwards, so far as modern habits are concerned. In the last generation, Wykeham's scholars dined more fashionably; the old "supper" at 6, consisting of roast mutton and bread (no vegetables), had become virtually their dinner—the original dinner of hot boiled beef at 12.45 being looked upon in the light of an early lunch;

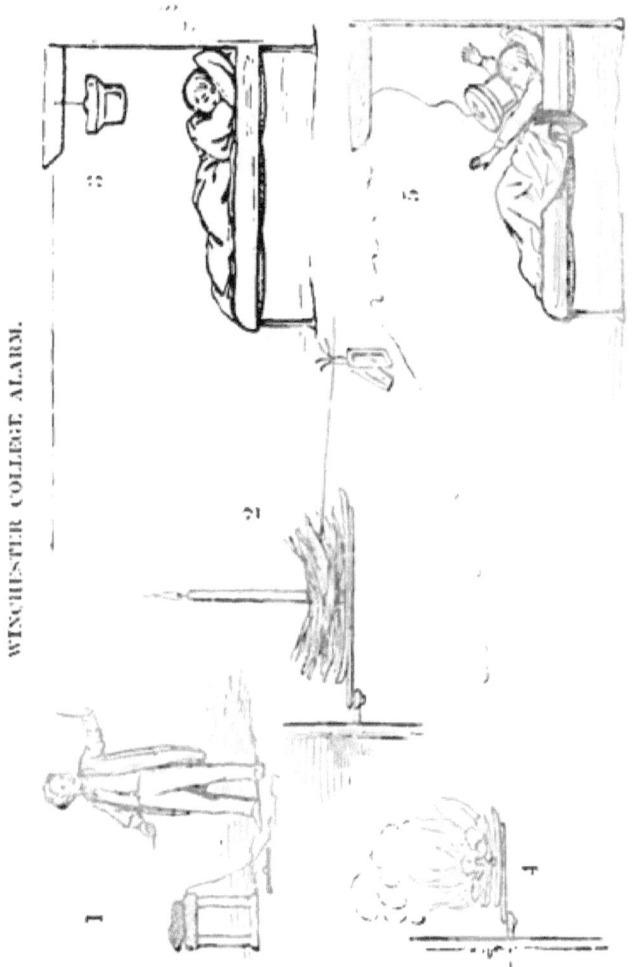

WINCHESTER COLLEGE ALARM.

1. Cutting the hours (an inch of candle is allowed per hour). 2. The *functior*, or candle sconce, to which the string is tied. The rushlight burns down to the bundle of loose paper, which burns the string. 3. The "scheme" arranged. 4. The paper burning. 5. The "scheme" calls.

and since they then breakfasted so late as 10 o'clock, the appetite was not keen enough to relish a dish which is always found to be distasteful on constant repetition, so that commonly the plates of boiled beef went into the "tub" before-mentioned, and served to mend the fare of the prisoners in the county jail, while the boys made their luncheon on bread and cheese. Now, meat is only served once in the day, at the early dinner; beef on Mondays and Thursdays, and mutton on the other days, with the ordinary vegetables, bread, and cheese; and pudding twice in the week. The choristers still wait at table— the only representatives of that class of poor scholars, "servitors," whom our schools and universities formerly maintained. They are now usually the sons of tradesmen in the city, and have a separate school of their own in College Street, though they still stand on the college roll as "*Secunda Classis;*" but formerly they seem to have been of somewhat higher grade, were eligible to scholarships, and in the roll of 1683 several of them appear in fifth and fourth book. Their little grey dresses are furnished them from a legacy of good John Fromond aforesaid.

CHAPTER VII.

ELECTION — GAMES.

The Election-day, both for Winchester and New College, is on the Tuesday next after the 7th of July (St Thomas Beckett), when the Warden of New College, Oxford, with two of his fellows, called the "posers" (or at one time "supervisors"), arrive at the college, where they are received with a Latin oration "*ad portas*" by the senior scholar. Two other speeches are delivered in school just before their arrival: 1, "*Elizabethæ et Jacobi Laudes*" (commonly known as "Elizabeth and Jacob"), by the second senior prefect: 2, "*Fundatoris Laudes*," formerly assigned to the senior "Founder's kin" scholar, but now spoken by the third prefect.

In old times, the New College electors always rode down from Oxford with their servants behind them, making Newbury their half-way house, where they seem to have supped upon a very liberal scale. A regulation of the founder provided that they should not bring with them more than six horses. Presents were usually made to them by the Winchester society; for instance, in 1417, a scarlet cape for the warden, and a "hurry" (or cap) for each of the posers; and they, in their turn, complimented "the warden and Mrs Harris," and "Mr and Mrs Schoolmaster" (in 1633) with Oxford gloves.* In the year of the plague, when Winchester was infected, the Election was held at Newbury; the electors from the two colleges meeting there. The practice of riding down on horseback was continued by Dr Gauntlett, Warden of New College, until 1822, when he was in his 70th year; he also slept at Newbury by the way, and gave a dinner there to all the Wykehamists who chose to attend.

The Oxford visitors, on their arrival, proceed at once to "Election Chamber," to hear any complaints which the boys may have to prefer. This is called the "scrutiny;" the seven senior prefects, and the seven juniors in chambers (one from each chamber), are separately questioned; but complaints are seldom made. Next morning the examination for election of scholars to New College begins—no longer in the renowned "Election Chamber" itself, but in the long "Warden's Gallery," as more convenient for the purpose; all prefects who are of standing to leave the school are examined, with any others who choose. As a rule, none can be elected who are over eighteen on the day of election; all others are superannuated. Boys, however, who bear a good character, and have passed a creditable examination at the election before their eighteenth birthday, can stand again next year. The vacancies used to be about nine in two years, but the uncertainty attending this was the cause of many severe disappointments; now, six scholars are elected every year, and the competition is opened to the commoners. This examination usually ends on Saturday evening, and on Monday the "roll" comes out with the

* Walcott, 251, &c.

names of those elected to Oxford; on Tuesday the election to fill vacancies on the Winchester roll begins. This is now entirely a matter of competitive scholarship; all boys from ten to fourteen are eligible, the candidates being subjected to two gradations of examination, according to age. There are, on an average, about fourteen vacancies in college in the course of the year; and a more than sufficient number of boys are placed " on the roll," in the order of merit, to succeed to these vacancies as they occur. Exhibitions of fifty pounds a-year, to be held by commoners, are also awarded at this examination to the most deserving candidates.

The scholarship at Winchester has always ranked deservedly high, even in the days when the system of election at New College, by which a boy once admitted there as a scholar succeeded as a matter of course to a comfortable fellowship for life, left very little stimulus to industry after the first important step was gained. The statutable exemption from University examinations, which New College long enjoyed and voluntarily surrendered, was also a manifest disadvantage and discouragement. Yet even then, Winchester men obtained their fair share of such distinctions as were open to them. They were always known as good Latin verse writers—an accomplishment to which they are trained early and carefully in the school. The successes of the Wykehamists at Oxford in 1866 were very remarkable: they carried off all three of the Chancellor's Prizes, as well as the Gaisford Prize for Greek verse—a triumph which probably no other school can boast; while they counted no less than ten first-class men in the honour lists.

Election-day is the great college festival—both wardens,

the posers, and resident fellows, all dine on the daïs in hall, the boys sitting at their tables below, supplied with somewhat better fare than ordinary, especially one ancient dish, a kind of mince-meat, highly popular under the name of "stuckling." One table, by a curious traditionary custom, is called the "children's table"—the electors present each choosing one of the junior scholars for their "child," and presenting him with a guinea and a luxurious dinner at this privileged board.

The games at Winchester, as at most public schools, are almost entirely confined to cricket, football, and fives. The annual matches with Eton and Harrow, formerly played at Lord's, have made cricket the most popular and historical.* The first match on record, as played against any other school, was their victory over Harrow in 1825, on Lord's ground, when the two brothers Wordsworth were captains of their respective elevens. Next year they beat Harrow and Eton successively at Lord's; on the whole, the laurels have been pretty evenly divided amongst all three schools, Eton having rather the best of it, as, from their great superiority in numbers, it would be only reasonable to expect. College and commoners join, of course, to form the Winchester eleven. Of late the authorities have thought it undesirable, for many reasons, that these matches should be played in London, but the Eton and Winchester elevens have been allowed to meet alternately on each other's ground and keep up

* The great William Ward, long known as the finest gentleman-player in England, was a Winchester commoner, though whether he was remarkable as a player at school is not recorded. He made the second highest innings on record in any match (278) in 1820. Two of his sons have played in Winchester elevens. Sir Frederick Bathurst was also a Wykehamist.

the friendly contest. One of the largest innings on record in any Public Schools match is that of E. B. Trevilian, who played in the eleven four years running, and finished with 126 to his name, against Eton, in 1862. None showed more enthusiastic interest in these matches than the late excellent warden, Robert Speckott Barter— loved and respected by all who knew him, from the time that he was a boy in college (whence he was elected to Oxford, over the heads of many seniors, at sixteen), and whose death in 1860 was a public loss to Winchester. He had seldom missed a match at Lord's from the time he played in the school eleven himself. He was a tremendous hitter in his day; and the remarkable punishment which he dealt out to the ball, when he was lucky enough to catch it on the "half-volley," has given to a long hit of this character at Winchester (and even elsewhere) the name of "a *Barter*." His hospitality to the stranger eleven, when they came down to Winchester to play, endeared him to many Etonians in only a less degree than his own Wykehamists. Kindly and gentle as his nature was, beaming out from every line of his joyous face, he could be rather terrible upon just occasion. He was travelling outside the Oxford coach while quite a young man, when a fellow-passenger persisted in using language of gross profanity, undeterred by his quiet remonstrance. At last that powerful arm seized the ribald by the collar, and, holding him out over the coach-wheel, Barter vowed to *drop him* if he did not promise to be silent. Such maintenance of order and decency by the strong hand falls in exactly with the humour of all honest-hearted schoolboys; and the story did as much for their warden's popularity with the successive generations of Wykehamists as the hardest "drive" he ever made on the cricket-ground. A memorial of him, such as he would most have desired, has not long been completed, in the taking down and rebuilding, with scrupulous care and good taste, the beautiful tower adjoining the chapel, built by Warden Thurburn about 1480, which had long become so ruinous that the fine peal of bells contained in it were never suffered to be rung. In joint memory of Warden Barter of Winchester and Warden Williams of New College, the restored tower is to be known in future as "The Tower of the Two Wardens:" but this new designation involves, it must be admitted, an apparent injustice to the memory of the older warden who built it.

The Winchester football game is peculiar. It is played "in canvass," as it is called. A portion of Meads, some 80 feet by 25, is marked off by screens of canvass on each side, within which the game is played, the two open ends forming the lines of goal, across which the ball is to be kicked. It is placed in the middle of the ground to begin with, and a "*hot*" formed round it, by the players stooping down all close together, with their heads down, and at a given signal trying to force the ball or each other away. The canvass screens answer to the Rugby "line of touch." When the ball escapes over these, it is returned into play by juniors stationed for the purpose, and a *hot* is formed afresh. But no verbal description could give an adequate notion of the game. Matches are usually played with six only on each side: and in this respect the Winchester game differs entirely from the exciting scene of the Rugby matches, where a hundred players, in their parti-coloured caps and jerseys, may be seen carrying on the struggle at once. But the game is fierce enough after its own fashion, a broken leg being no rare occurrence during the season. The great annual match is that between the " first sixes" of commoners and college, played on " egg-flip day," as the founder's commemoration day (the first Thursday in December) is popularly called. But the more attractive match, at any rate to a stranger, is between twenty-two of each, on the 5th of November. Owing to the increasing numbers of commoners, the college has now enough to do to hold its own in these matches. Great exertions are being made, just at present, to effect some kind of adjustment of football rules in general, so as to adopt one universal code, under which matches between the different schools may be played, as in the case of cricket. The success of any such movement, however, is very doubtful.

The breaking-up ceremonies at Winchester are peculiar and interesting, though much of their picturesque medievalism has disappeared of late years. Some, of intermediate date, are perhaps less to be regretted. The scholars no longer rush out of gates after early chapel on the last dark morning of the winter half-year, each with a blazing birch broom, up College Street and along the wall of the close up to the old White Hart Inn, where a sumptuous breakfast used to be prepared, before the chaises started for their various destinations. This curious torch-race (in which the burning birch must have had a symbolical meaning), long the terror of old ladies who lived on the line of the course, gave place subsequently to a race of the senior boys in sedan-chairs. Top-boots are now no longer considered, by young gentlemen of twelve, "your only wear" to go home in; although the term for them—*gomers* (*i.e., go-homers*)—still survives in the Winchester vocabulary. Great were the struggles of the happy possessors, with the aid of soap and other lubricators, to get into them: and the bootmakers were always in attendance on that morning to assist in the operation. Still greater must have been the difficulty in some instances, when boys from a distance had travelled two days and a night on the top of a coach, to get them off again. Railway stations and cabs have destroyed much of the poetry of "going-home." But the beautiful old hymn, "*Jam lucis orto sidere*," is still sung in procession round the "sands" of chamber-court, on the last morning of the summer half-year, on coming out of chapel, by the whole collegiate body; the head and second masters, followed by the grace-singers, leading the way. On the six last Saturdays, just before going to hills, the old Wykehamist melody, which all schools have borrowed from them in some form or other, "Dulce Domum," is poured forth lustily in hall. But the great "Domum" festival is on the evening of Election-day, when visitors in great numbers from the neighbourhood, as well as old Wykehamists from all quarters, are hospitably welcomed, and the song is sung in Meads, in Chamber-court, and in Hall, over and over again, until the singers—if not the audience—are tired. The old "Domum tree," round which it used to be solemnly chanted, has long since disappeared. It was on the bark of that tree, according to the old legend, which one can but hope was a fiction, that an unhappy boy confined in college during the holidays—or forgotten by cruel parents, for both versions are given—carved those longing words, and composed in his solitary hours the melody to which they are still sung; dying, says the story, of a broken heart, just as the holidays were ending. Wykehamists must have a taste for the sensational, for they have a "haunted" place in commoners, and a "bloody hand," distinctly visible on the wall of seventh chamber (probably the cognisance of some young baronet), about which little college-boys are told a terrible tale; how, in days gone by, a tyrant prefect in that chamber made the lives of two young brothers so miserable, that the elder resolved to deliver himself by taking the oppressor's life. Armed with a sharp knife, he stole one night to his bed-side, and, feeling for the sleeper's breast, plunged in his weapon to the heart; and found, to his horror, that he had killed his brother, who for some reason had been made to take the prefect's place. But we are getting back again into the boundless domain of legend, and it is time for us, too, to "break-up."

APPENDIX TO WINCHESTER COLLEGE.

REBELLION OF 1793.

(Statement drawn up at the time by one of the expelled prefects.)

On the — day of April the warden sent down a note to the scholars intimating that they should not go up to the militia parade; but in case they should transgress his rules, he sent out the following edict: "If one individual is peccant, he shall be severely punished; but if numbers are seen, the whole school shall be punished, by being refused leave to dine with their friends." A short time afterwards, one of the scholars was seen at the parade; that individual was severely punished; but the warden, not content with punishing him, inflicted the same penalty on the whole school, which he declared he would have done had numbers been seen. It may be alleged against us, that the warden, by not giving us leave out, only deprived us of an indulgence which it was in his power to refuse or grant at pleasure. But had we considered it only as the deprivation of an indulgence, we never should have proceeded to those measures which were afterwards adopted; but by the warden's express words, we were led to consider it as a direct punishment, for upon being informed that an individual (a prefect, one whom it was not in the power of any scholar to keep within bounds) was peccant, he immediately said, "Then the boys shall not have leave out to-morrow," accompanying it with this quotation, "*Quidquid delirant reges, plectuntur Achivi;*" by which it is clear he inflicted it as a punishment. We submitted to it without murmuring; but on that evening we held a consultation, when, after great debating, the following resolutions were proposed and unanimously agreed to: "That a civil and respectful Latin note be sent to the warden, to beg him in future not to punish the whole community for the fault of an individual;—That if the warden did not think fit to comply with our request, a note couched in more positive terms should be sent. If he granted their request, the assembly should esteem their point gained, but by no evasive answer;—That we should not proceed to violent measures till every lenient one was tried in vain;—That if one or more boys should be sent for and interrogated by the warden, he should answer plainly and concisely, and avow his sentiments;—That if any number be sent for, the rest shall be ready to attend if called upon;—That no boy should be suffered to be punished in any way whatsoever on account of these proceedings;—That no boy should receive any profit or emolument whatsoever arising from the downfall of another, particularly in the election chamber;—That if one or more boys be expelled, the rest shall resolutely demand them to be recalled, and not cease till they themselves are expelled;—That the assembly shall subscribe their names to this paper, and keep their plighted faith, as they will answer for it at the tribunal of Almighty God." To these, then, having taken a solemn oath to maintain, aid, and abet them to the utmost of our power, we, the forty-one seniors, subscribed our names. As it was a thing of great importance, we agreed not to suffer the remaining thirty to take the same oath, as on account of their age we deemed them incapable of knowing what a serious act they would otherwise have performed; but nevertheless they promised to stand by us to the last. Having done this, we immediately set about performing those things which we had agreed. On that same evening we sent a Latin note to the warden (which, as well as the other note, I have translated into English) couched in the following terms:—

"Reverend Sir,—We grieve that for the sake of one individual all should be deemed culpable, all should be punished. By your late edict we understood that if numbers were seen the whole community should suffer, if *one* was culpable *he* should be severely punished. One was unwarily detected, one whom it was not in our power to restrain. In this we have implicitly obeyed you, nevertheless we hope that in future you will not punish *all* for the sake of *one*."

To this letter we received no answer, having waited with anxious expectation for three days. Despairing then of receiving an answer to our first note, we sent up the following :—

"Reverend Sir,—Relying upon your kindness, we thought it fit to write to you, to which letter we have anxiously waited for an answer in vain. Therefore we hope and trust that by your silence you will no longer keep us in suspense."

The next morning we received, written on the back of our note, the following answer: "When scholars are so forgetful of their rank and of their good manners, as to insult their warden by a letter of the most consummate arrogance and extreme petulance, he can give them no other answer, than that he shall continue to refuse them every indulgence till they behave with propriety."

What then could we do? Our note, which was couched in terms as respectful as possible, was deemed consummate arrogance and extreme petulance. By that we clearly saw our point could never be gained by lenient measures; to recede was impossible. We were therefore forced to proceed to violence. We then held a consultation, and sent a detachment to secure the keys of the college. However, at that time we could only procure two or three of the principal ones. As we had proceeded to such lengths, we could not of course go into school that afternoon. Therefore a verbal message was sent to Mr Goddard, to say we would not trouble him to come into school. He came, however, and met with that treatment which he must naturally have expected.* He no sooner appeared in the school than he was saluted by a universal hiss and most astonishing noise; he commanded silence, but finding some marbles rattling about his ears, he retired. We had previously determined not to offer him any other indignity, but solely to hiss, but some of the lower boys could not restrain their hands. We then wrote a letter to Dr Warton, telling him how much we esteemed him, and begging him to absent himself from school; but, upon the supposition that he would come, we previously determined to walk out regularly two by two, and not create the least disturbance. He did not come, but joined the other masters who were assembled at the warden's house. About an hour afterwards the senior prefect received a summons from the warden and masters to appear before them; this he, at the desire of the rest, refused to comply with. The masters, finding he did not appear, sent down a summons for the eighteen prefects to appear at 5 o'clock; but, as inevitable expulsion would have followed our complying, we refused to go. The warden then sent an express to the fellows, desiring them to meet at 9 o'clock the ensuing day, before whom we were again summoned to appear, which we previously determined not to do. That same evening we got possession of the remaining keys of the college. We then, by stopping up the passage which communicates between the warden's and the masters' lodgings, kept Mr Goddard prisoner in the warden's house that night. As we had not the key of the middle gate, we placed patrols there the whole night. The next morning the warden went out of his lodgings into the town; we judged it expedient to prevent him returning, and to that end closed the outer gate. Finding he could not get in, he went to Dr Warton's, where all the fellows who were outside were convened; however, by keeping one of the fellows within the college, we hindered them from calling a house—a house consisting of four fellows besides the warden, without which number they cannot decide

* Mr Goddard was the master who had caught and reported the prefect who was present at the militia parade.

on any material point. These therefore, by keeping some within and some without the college, we divided. About 12 o'clock we received a message from the warden, saying "we might all go home;" but we well knew what we might expect, so took no notice of the message. The warden, finding he could not procure admission to his house, applied to the county magistrates (who were assembled to offer up an address to his Majesty) to reinstate him in his lodgings. Of this we were apprised, and having barricaded the gates, we took possession of the tower over the gateway. Having filled this place with stones, &c., to defend ourselves with, we there set a watch, determined, if the civil power came against us, to defend ourselves to the last. Soon after, one of the magistrates, attended by a great crowd, came to the gates; but he only came in a friendly manner, to treat with us in the name of the warden, as they were very unwilling to proceed to violent measures. Him therefore, after some deliberation, we admitted, and by his persuasive eloquence he prevailed on us to open the gates, and we referred our cause to be judged by the magistrates. They came then, with the warden and fellows, and adjourned to the warden's house. Soon after, one of the magistrates proposed to us in the warden's name to lay down our arms, and deliver up the keys of the college. The first we complied with, but refused to do the last till we saw the issue of the matter. This being told the warden, he with the masters, after some deliberation, sent down the following propositions: "The warden in future promises not to punish the community for the sake of an individual, and to grant a general amnesty, provided the keys are delivered up." To these terms, which were such as we never could have expected, we consented; the keys were delivered up, and peace again restored. During this disturbance, which was carried to such a height, we did not injure the college in the smallest degree, or vent our rage against the harmless windows; and though we had the keys of the college, we did not open the doors. We chiefly owed our reconciliation to the efforts of Sir Thomas Miller and Mr Poulter, who exerted themselves greatly in our behalf, and their humanity deserves the highest encomium.

Here, then, you may naturally expect to behold us once more in peace, and even showing every submission to the warden on account of his humane behaviour. But, alas! the flame broke out again, and through our indiscretion we involved ourselves in ruin. Though an amnesty was granted, it was repeatedly infringed. We were not treated as before, and the masters were continually hinting at our late behaviour. The warden frequently said we might go home, that, as I suppose, he might regain his lost dignity and power, which he could not had we remained. We had every reason to suppose the warden had written to our friends desiring them to take us away for a short time, as some boys were daily sent for by their parents. Some time after, one of the senior boys' fathers came down in haste to Winchester, and having concerted with the warden, told his son he must beg the warden's pardon or instantly resign. He refused to comply with the former, so was obliged to accede to the latter. The reason of his father's coming, we afterwards heard, was occasioned by his receiving an anonymous letter with the Winchester post-mark, stating that if he did not immediately take his son away from college he would inevitably be expelled. This was looked on as a compulsory resignation, and little better than expulsion, therefore we thought ourselves bound to espouse his cause and follow him. To confirm us in our opinion, we received a letter from the boy himself, informing us he thought himself expelled or forced to resign, which amounts to the same; moreover, he said, he had every reason to believe the anonymous letter was written by the masters. He looked upon himself as having fallen a victim to our proceedings, and as such we were bound to follow him. Therefore in evil hour, having previously sent up a note to the warden to acquaint him with our design, we carried up our resignations, and from that moment forfeited our places as scholars in that illustrious seminary. The next morning nineteen of us, being the remainder of those who had left Winchester, being made sensible of our error, sent up our names to the warden to acquaint him that we were sensible of our error, and would retract our resignations if he would permit us. To this note we received the following: "The warden and fellows cannot return any answer."

This document (which shows considerable ability) must, of course, be taken, as an *ex parte* statement; but the main facts are sufficiently corroborated by a paper drawn up by one of the college authorities. Dr Warton's injudicious policy after the suppression of the outbreak receives additional confirmation from the following extract from a letter written by a friend to the father of one of the ringleaders:—

"*April* 11*th*, 1793.

"I am glad I had not sealed this letter before Mrs Warton arrived. She brings me a confused account of the most dreadful and formidable riot at the college ever known. The warden had forbidden the scholars appearing at the militia roll-call, and because some of them disobeyed this order, one was caught and punished. This was followed by an absolute refusal of any of them going out of college to dine with friends on Easter Sunday. In consequence of this, 'Liberty and Equality' became the cry; and the red cap was worn by all who could procure or contrive one. They laid in provisions, taking them by force—bread from the baker, one whole sheep from a female butcher, swords, bludgeons, &c. —and mounting the tower of the chapel, they loosened the parapet to provide ammunition against any who should attack below, locked the warden out of college, and Goddard the second master, having taken an oath not to submit or quit each other. Dr Warton appeared, and to him alone would they open the gates; he was received with a general hurrah of applause, but when he attempted to speak of peace, not a word would they hear—they would lose their lives for him, but no peace with the warden or Mr G., whom they mentioned with every opprobrious epithet. Two thousand people gathered round the gates, and it became necessary for Dr W. to speak to some gentlemen below to go to the Town Hall (it being the county meeting to form an address) and request the sheriff and all the men of consequence to come down, which they did in a body; but this had not the least effect. The boys swore that they had laid in faggots and combustibles, and would instantly apply them if in any sort attacked. This lasted on Thursday, and all the night until noon on Friday; matters then subsided. Expulsion was violently proposed of forty boys, but this was overruled both by Dr W. and the county gentlemen, as destructive of the scholars and injurious to the college. I have not time to be more particular, but it is most wonderful that not one person was hurt. Some of the ringleaders have been taken home, to undergo the remonstrance of parents, and divide the insurgents. Others have, and more will have, very serious letters and corrective admonitions from their parents. I am to write to B—— when enough in spirits to undertake so disagreeable a task. It was impossible for any one boy to decline; he must have left the college next hour if he had not joined, or perhaps have fallen a victim to the fury of the day. Some foolish people without proposed firing through the gates among the boys. All was quiet soon after Friday, and remains so now, though no apology or submission has been made. Dr W. means to be silent and placid for some days longer, and will then begin to remonstrate, and take on him the 'Informator;' and many a hard imposition will be appointed, which will keep the young men at hard study for many days."

WESTMINSTER SCHOOL

The chief printed authorities are—

Widmore's History of Westminster.
Welch's Alumni Westmonasterienses [with notes by C. B. Phillimore].
Lusus Alteri Westmonasterienses.

WESTMINSTER SCHOOL.

CHAPTER I.

THE FOUNDATION.

WESTMINSTER claims to be the oldest school in England. If this only means that there was a school in Westminster from time immemorial, it may be so far true; though the same claim might be made with equal justice for Winchester, and probably for other less distinguished cities. There is, indeed, one very circumstantial piece of autobiography, purporting to be by a Norman monk, secretary to the Great Conqueror, in which he speaks of his own education at Westminster in the days of Edward the Confessor; and records how Queen Edgitha sometimes met him as he came out of school, and after "posing" him in grammar and verse-making,* sent him off rejoicing with "three or four pieces of money from the hand of her maidens," and an order for some good things in the royal refectory. But remorseless historical

---

* " De literis et versu meo *opponebat*."

sceptics have overthrown all faith in Abbot Ingulph's history; and the schoolboy days of this very "old Westminster" must, however unwillingly, be considered as more or less mythical.

No doubt a school was attached to the Abbey at Westminster, as to other religious foundations. Probably Stow is right in concluding that St Peter's was one of the three great schools whose scholars (according to Fitzstephen) were accustomed on the days of their patron saints to challenge each other to a contest of grammar and versification*—a custom which Stow speaks of as existing in his own days with very little alteration:—

"I myself, in my youth, have yearly seen, on the eve of St Bartholomew the apostle, the scholars of divers grammar-schools repair to the churchyard of St Bartholomew, where, upon a bank boarded under a tree, some one scholar hath stepped up, and there opposed and answered, till he were of some better scholar overcome and put down; and then the overcomer, taking his place, did like as the first, and in the end the best opposer and answerer had rewards. . . . I remember there repaired to these exercises (amongst others) the master and scholars of St Paul's, London, and St Peter's, Westminster."

* The passage is curious, as containing apparently the earliest form of what was afterwards developed not only into the Westminster "Challenge," but into the Eton "Montem:" "Pueri diversarum scholarum versibus inter se conrixantur, aut de principiis artis grammaticae vel regulis praeteritorum et supinorum contendunt. Sunt alii qui epigrammatibus rhythmis et metris utuntur vetere illa triviali dicacitate, licentia Fescennina socios suppressis nominibus liberius lacerant, *salibus* Socraticis sociorum, vel forte majorum, vitia tangunt."
—Fitzstephen, Descript. Lond.

But all this was long anterior to the foundation of the present collegiate school of Westminster. This can only date its existence at the earliest from 1540, when the monastic house was dissolved, a bishopric founded out of its confiscated revenues, and a school for forty scholars, with an upper and an under master, established by charter of Henry VIII. There is no doubt that the school was in active operation, since the names of its earliest masters have been preserved. John Adams, who was first appointed, was succeeded by Alexander Nowell, well known among the Reformers, and subsequently Dean of St Paul's. He taught through Edward's short reign; but under Mary the whole reformed establishment—bishop, chapter, and school—was swept away, and Nowell only escaped the stake by taking ship for Germany.

Elizabeth, almost immediately upon her accession, restored her father's foundation in every particular, and gave to the college the statutes which are more or less observed to this day. Besides the forty scholars on the foundation, these statutes provide for the admission of eighty others to be taught in the school, under the names of *pensionarii*, *oppidani*, and *peregrini*. Of these three classes, the *pensionarii* answered to the old *commensales* of Eton and Winchester. They were to be not more than eighty in number; to be lodged with some of the authorities of the college, who were to be responsible for their conduct and to guarantee their payments; and to dine with the scholars at their table in hall at a certain fixed charge. The dean was allowed to have six of these boarders (who would probably be boys of superior rank, like the warden's *com-*

mensales at Winchester), the head-master four, the usher and each of the prebendaries two. The *oppidani* would comprise all those boys who lived in the city with their parents or friends, sufficiently within reach of the school to attend as day-scholars; and the *peregrini* were those who might be sent from a distance for education, lodging, and boarding, as was the early custom at all great schools, with any neighbouring householder who might be induced to undertake such a charge.

The election of the forty Queen's scholars was to be after the manner of Winchester and Eton. The candidates were to be examined by the Dean of Christ-Church, Oxford, and the Master of Trinity College Cambridge, with the assistance of a Master of Arts from each college (called "posers" or "electioners") and the head-master of the school. A preference was to be given in the election to the sons of tenants of the chapter estates, and the choristers, who were originally taught in the school, were also to be preferred as scholars if found competent; but it is doubtful whether even in the earliest times this provision was ever attended to. "A child's place" at Westminster, both in the days of Elizabeth and of the Stuarts, became commonly a matter of favour which secretaries of state, and even monarchs themselves, were not ashamed to ask for their friends, and which deans and chapters were very ready to bestow. Promotion by merit, though unquestionably it existed in theory, was very little known in practice in the primitive age of scholastic foundations. The scholars had their board and instruction entirely free, with an allowance for "livery"—now a gown and college waistcoat—which no doubt, in those earlier times, covered the greater part of their expenses for dress. After four years' residence, a certain number of these boys were to be elected annually either to Christ-Church as students, or to Trinity, Cambridge, as scholars on the foundation : three to each, if there were vacancies enough in the college, and if so many were found eligible ; and more, if it could be done conveniently.*

Thus, as at Eton and Winchester, a complete course of liberal education was provided for a boy of industry and ability, without cost to himself or his parents ; for a studentship or scholarship at either university was intended to be a sufficient maintenance for its holder, and was so to a youth of quiet and studious habits. And, as in the case of Wykeham's and Henry VI.'s foundations, the stewards of the founder's liberality were to be those in whose hands the interests of learning and the rights of the scholar were held to be safest—the elder collegiate body of scholars and divines to which the school was attached.

In early times, at least, the trust was well discharged. More than one Dean of Westminster was a nursing father to the school. Gabriel Goodman (of whom Fuller says, "Goodman was his name, and goodness was his nature"), who was appointed to the deanery the year after Elizabeth's reconstitution of her father's foundation, and continued in the dignity for nearly forty years, did everything to promote the comfort and welfare of the "Queen's scholars." Some of the old monastic buildings had been allotted for their accommodation ; but he is said to have first collected them into the large schoolroom now in use,

* "Sex ad minimum." "Plures autem optamus, si ita præfatis electoribus commodum videbitur."

which had been the ancient dormitory of the Benedictines. Holding the prebend of Chiswick, he procured the conveyance of the "college-house" there to the chapter as a pesthouse (or, as it would now be called, a sanatorium), in which the whole body, prebendaries, masters, and scholars, might take refuge in case of contagious sickness reaching Westminster; and he planted a row of elm-trees there with his own hands, some of which are said to be still standing. It will be seen that at a future time this retreat was taken advantage of.* The excellent Lancelot Andrewes succeeded Goodman in the deanery, and in his hearty love for the school. He exercised a fatherly superintendence over masters and scholars—fulfilling, in fact, the theory of the statutes, that the dean should be to the whole community "*quasi mens in corpore;*" not only taking care that the best classical authors were read in the school, and having the exercises of the boys brought to him for commendation or correction, but even, as a grateful pupil tells us, "frequently in his own person supplying the place of head-master and usher for a week together." He often had the elder boys with him in the evenings at the deanery, and there gave them private instruction in the elements of Hebrew, as well as in Latin and Greek; and when he walked out, as he often did by way of recreation, to his prebendal house at Chiswick, it was very seldom, says the same quaint writer, "without a brace or two of this young fry" as

* "To this day a piece of ground is reserved in the lease to the sub-lessee as a play-place for the scholars."—Faulkner's Hist. and Ant. of Chiswick, p. 293. Freind and Nicoll, when head-masters, occasionally resided there during the summer holidays. In 1853 the house was occupied by Whittingham's celebrated "Chiswick Press."

his companions; "and in that wayfaring leisure he had a singular dexterity to fill those narrow vessels as with a funnell."*

Dean Williams (subsequently Archbishop of York and Lord Keeper to James I.), who succeeded a few years afterwards, also took a lively interest in the welfare of the Queen's scholars—an interest which did not cease after he had become Bishop of Lincoln, still holding the deanery *in commendam*. He increased the royal foundation by the addition of four boys (to be chosen either from his native Wales or from his diocese of Lincoln), who were to be educated gratuitously, and to be boarded with the Queen's scholars, and lodged in a special chamber; to wear gowns of violet colour, and to go off as exhibitioners to St John's College, Cambridge. But, unluckily, Bishop Williams neglected to provide sufficient funds for these benevolent purposes; and though the "Bishop's boys" received their violet gowns and their free education, they had to board themselves with the town-boys; and their university provision, such as it was, after a while was lost to them entirely. The low numbers of the school for many years having furnished no candidates for the St John's scholarships, the University Commissioners of 1856 seized upon this fact as a pretext for suppressing them altogether. The coloured gown, which had become anything but an honourable distinction, has now been given up, and the four Bishop's boys, who are still elected, have no other privileges than the remission of the usual school-fees, which the dividends of the foundation just suffice to pay.

* Hacket, Life of Archbishop Williams, p. 45.

The first Westminster scholars were elected to the universities in 1562—two years only after the refoundation of the school by Elizabeth—when one was sent to Oxford and one to Cambridge. During the next ten years, sometimes two and sometimes three were elected to each university. But Christ-Church was not at first eager to welcome the Westminster students. Of the three elected in 1554, the college would only admit one—pleading in excuse the want of room. In 1575, two of those elected were refused admission as students by Dr Piers, then dean. But the claimants, Carow and Ravis, pleaded their own cause manfully. "*Non mea solum, sed totius Westmonasterii res agitur*," said Carow, with equal truth and spirit, in a letter to Lord Burleigh.*
The remonstrance was successful, and Ravis, in future years, rose to be himself dean of Christ-Church, and to maintain in that capacity the rights of Westminster.

Some difficulties also arose a few years later with the Cambridge authorities. Whitgift, as Master of Trinity, complained that Westminster filled so many of his scholars' places, that there was no roof left for other deserving youths. It was settled that in future two only should be sent to each university, except in every third year, when three might be elected.† But a more liberal arrangement was subsequently adopted.

The first master of the school after Elizabeth's reconstruction was Nicholas Udall or Uvedale, who appears to have been appointed in the previous reign, when the

---

* Strype, Ann. II., i. 553-56.
† Lord Macaulay (Essay on Lord Bacon) speaks of Whitgift as having thus "saved the noblest place of education in England from the degrading fate of King's College and New College;" but there seems to have been no great risk of any such result.

school was all but in abeyance. Though he is said to have been an excellent scholar, his reputation in other respects is by no means a creditable one. He had been dismissed some years before, when a very young man, from the head-mastership of Eton on a charge of theft, and even of worse misconduct, which appears, from one of his own letters, to have had at least some foundation.* Of his conduct in his new position there is no record, nor is much known of his immediate successors—Randall, Browne, and Howlen. Edward Grant, the next head-master, had been educated on the foundation, and was apparently the first Westminster scholar who held the appointment. He published, for the use of the school, the first attempt at a Greek Grammar by an Englishman; and upon this foundation his successor at Westminster constructed what became afterwards better known, somewhat unfairly, as the 'Eton Greek Grammar.' This successor was William Camden, who had for some years been second-master, and during that time, in his holidays and leisure hours, had produced his great work 'Britannia;' he was promoted to the head-mastership upon Grant's resignation in 1593. Camden's name belongs not more to Westminster School than to the history of English literature; but the account which he gives himself of his mastership (in a letter to Archbishop Usher) must be quoted, for the light which it throws upon the early history of the school:—

"God so blessed my labours that the now Bishops of Durham, London, and St Asaph, to say nothing of persons now employed in eminent places abroad, and many of especial note at home of all degrees, do acknowledge

* Letters of Eminent Men (Camd. Soc.)

themselves to have been my scholars. Yea, I brought there to Church divers gentlemen of Ireland, as Walshes, Nugents, O'Railys, Shees, the eldest son of the Archbishop of Cassilis, Peter Lombard, a merchant's son of Wallingford, a youth of admirable docility, and divers others, bred popishly."

These young Irish gentlemen, sent over to England for education, were no doubt *pensionarii* with Camden as head-master. A letter from Sir Robert Cecil, about the date of which Camden speaks, curiously illustrates his account of these Irish pupils, and at the same time shows that the dean's privilege of receiving boarders was at least occasionally exercised in the case of youths of rank. Cecil is speaking of David Barry, son of Lord Barry, afterwards second Earl of Buttevant :—

"I have placed him at the Deane's at Westmynster. I have provided bedding and all of my own, with some other things, meaning that for his dyet and residence there it shall cost him nothing." *

The conversions to the Reformed faith among these boys probably implied a little pressure on the part of the Westminster authorities; for Cecil begs in a subsequent letter that young Barry may not "be *distrainedly* dealt with, though he refuse to go to church."

Camden resigned his mastership in 1599, devoting the rest of his life to historical studies. Besides his appointment as Clarencieux king-at-arms, he had, as he says, "gathered a contented sufficiency during his long labours in the school."

It is probably to the period of his successor, Richard

---

* Sir R. Cecil to Sir G. Carew, August 2, 1600. Letters, &c. (Camd. Soc.).

Ireland, that we must refer the following curious and interesting account of the internal economy of the school, preserved amongst the state papers of 1630, but without actual date or signature. A copy in the possession of the present head-master has the following note endorsed: "The handwriting I recognise to be that of Abp. Laud. —G. H." But Laud is not known to have been educated at the school.

"This course was in my time taken by the schoolemr. of Westminster, specially for those of the 6th and 7th forms, wherein I spent my time there.

"About a quarter of an hour after 5 in the morning we were called up by one of the Monitors of the chamber (with a '*surgite*'); and after Latin prayers we went into the cloysters to wash, and thence in order, two by two, to the schoole, where we were to be by 6 of the clock at furthest.

"Between 6 and 8 we repeated our grammar parts (out of Lilie for Latin, out of Cambden for the Greek); 14 or 15 being selected and called out to stand in a semicircle before the Mr. and other scholars, and there repeate 4 or 5 leaves in either, the Mr. appointing who should begin and who should go on with such and such rules.

"After this we had two exercises that varied every other morning. The first morning we made verses extempore, Latin and Greek, upon two or three several themes; and they that made the best (two or three of them) had some money given them by the schoolmr., for the most part. The second morning, one of the form was called out to expound some part of a

Latin or Greek author (Cicero, Livie, Isocrates, Homer, Apollinarius, Xenophon, &c.), and they of the two next forms were called to give an account of it some other part of the day; or else they were all of them (or such as were picked out, of whom the Mr. made choice by the fear or confidence discovered in their looks) to repeate and pronounce distinctly without book some piece of an author that had been learned the day before.

"From 8 to 9 we had time for Beaver, and recollection of ourselves, and preparation for future exercises.

"Betwixt 9 and 11, those exercises were read which had been enjoined us over night (one day in prose, the next day in verse), which were selected by the Mr.; some to be examined and punished, others to be commended and proposed for imitation. Which being done, we had the practice of *Dictamina;* one of the 5th form being called out to translate some sentences out of an unexpected author (*extempore*) into good Latin; and then one of the 6th or 7th form to translate the same (*extempore* also) into good Greek.

"Then the Mr. himself expounded some part of a Latin or Greek author (one day in prose, another in verse) wherein we were to be practised in the afternoon.

"At dinner and supper times we read some portion of the Latin Bible in a manuscript (to facilitate the reading of such hands): and, the Prebendaries then having their table commonly in the Hall, some of them had oftentimes good remembrances sent unto them from thence, and withal a theme to make or speak some extempore verses upon.

"Betwixt 1 and 3, that lesson which out of some author appointed for that day had been by the Mr.

expounded unto them (out of Cicero, Virgil, Homer, Euripides, Isocrates, Livie, Sallust, &c.) was to be exactly gone through by construing and other grammatical ways, examining all the Rhetorical figures, and translating it out of verse into prose, or out of prose into verse, out of Greek into Latin, or out of Latin into Greek. Then they were enjoined to commit that to memory against the next morning.

"Betwixt 3 and 4 we had a little respite: the Mr. walking out and they (in beaver-times) going in order to the Hall, and then fitting themselves for their next task.

"Between 4 and 5 they repeated a leaf or two of some book of Rhetorical figures, or choice Proverbs and Sentences, collected by the Mr. for that use. After, they were practised in translating some *Dictamina* out of Latin or Greek, or sometimes turning Latin or Greek verses into English verse. Then a theme was given them, whereupon to make prose or verses, Latin and Greek, against the next morning.

"After supper (in summer-time) they were three or four times in a week called to the Mr.'s chamber (especially they of the 7th form), and there instructed out of Hunter's Cosmographie, and practised to describe and find out cities and countries in the maps.

"Upon Sundays before morning prayers in summer they came commonly into the school (such as were King's scholars), and there construed some part of the gospel in Greek, or repeated part of the Greek catechism. In the afternoon they made verses upon the preacher's sermon, or epistle and gospel.

"The best scholars in the 7th form were appointed as Tutors to read and expound places of Homer, Virgil,

Horace, Euripides, or other Greek and Latin authors, at those times (in the forenoon, or afternoon, or after beaver-times) wherein the scholars were in the school in expectation of the Mr.

"The scholars were governed by several *Monitores* (two for the Hall, as many for the Church, the School, the Fields, the Cloyster—which last attended them to washing, and were called *Monitores immundorum*). The Captain of the School was over all these, and therefore called *Monitor Monitorum*. These Monitors kept them strictly to speaking of Latin, in their several commands; and withal they presented their complaints or Accusations (as we called them) every Friday morning, when the punishments were often redeemed by exercises, or favours shown to boys of extraordinary merit, who had the honor (by the Monitor Monitorum) many times to beg and prevail for such remissions. And so, at other times, other faults were often punished by scholastical tasks, as repeating whole orations out of Tullie, Isocrates, Demosthenes, or speeches out of Virgil, Thucydides, Xenophon, Euripides, &c.

"Upon play-days (within an hour after leave granted and the *oppidales* dismissed) the scholars of the house were often called in again for an hour or more till they had briefly despatched the task of that day.

"There was a writing in capital letters within the school, which the Mr. was wont to show strangers as a testimony how he was restrained for leave to play. When Plumpe-walkers [*] came in (*i.e.*, such as strived to hold

---

[*] A "Plump" is a close body, or party of men; the term here used may mean such as walked the streets in knots or parties the idle loungers of the day.

the Mr. in long discourse) the Mr. would call out some of his scholars to show what verses they could make on a sudden, upon a theme to be given by them, if they were scholars.

"Every Friday they had *Repetitions* of what was learned the former part of the week. Upon Saturdays they pronounced their *declamations* in Greek and Latin, and the Prebendaries did often come in to give encouragement unto them.

"All that were chose away by Election took their leave in a public oration to the Dean, Prebendaries, Master, Usher, and Scholars, made in the school."

Some of these school terms (as, for instance, the titles of the monitors and the parting "oration") remain almost unchanged to this day; the "speaking of Latin" during school-hours still survives in certain cases, as will be noticed hereafter; the Friday "Repetitions" have only lately been discontinued; and of the general system of teaching it may fairly be said, that modern deviations from it have not always been improvements.

The next head-master of whom we have any definite history—for of Ireland and Wilson, who intervened, little more has come down to us than the names, except that the latter "had a faculty more than ordinary for instructing youth"—was Lambert Osbaldiston, or Osboldstone, student of Christ-Church, who succeeded in 1622. He was an able and diligent teacher, and it was during the sixteen years of his rule that Westminster began to take high rank among the great schools of England. It was said that, at the time of his expulsion from his office, there were no less than "fourscore doctors in the two universities" who had been educated under him—when a doctor's degree was somewhat more of a reality than at present. He had too tender a conscience for the days of fierce religious and political strife in which his lot was cast. For some alleged offence against the royal prerogative, the Star Chamber condemned him to be dismissed from his mastership and his prebend at Westminster; to have his ears nailed to the pillory in Dean's Yard in the presence of his scholars; to pay a fine of £5000, and to be imprisoned during the royal pleasure. From this cruel sentence he escaped by flight, to be restored again to his prebend by the Long Parliament in 1641, and to be again sequestered by the same party a few years afterwards, because he boldly protested against some of their violent proceedings.

CHAPTER II.

BUSBY.

In 1638 a head-master succeeded to Westminster, whose name for more than half a century was identified with English school education and discipline. Richard Busby had been born in a comparatively humble station in life, and had been a King's scholar at Westminster. Elected to a studentship at Christ-Church in due course, he was too poor to pay the fees for his degrees, which were advanced to him by the vestry of St Margaret's, Westminster. They were gratefully repaid when he rose to riches and honour, and he added an endowment for the parish school. He held the head-mastership of Westminster for fifty-seven years, resigning his beloved office only with his life, when nearly ninety years old, and even at that great age a vigorous and able master. His name has passed into a proverb for severity—probably not without good reason. His rod, he used to say, was the sieve which sifted the wheat of scholarship from the chaff. He certainly made sound scholars, showing in many cases considerable acuteness in discerning latent talents, and spared no pains in teaching wherever he saw promise of excellence. And, in spite of his vigorous discipline, he retained through life the esteem and respect of his old pupils, as is plain from many of their letters to him which have been preserved. At one time he could boast that sixteen of the bishops then on the bench had been taught by him — an honour which assuredly no head-master of any school could ever have claimed before or since. He had a great dislike (in which some of our best modern teachers will fully sympathise) to the ordinary "notes" by which classical authors are illustrated, for the supposed benefit of the learner, and forbade the use of such editions in the school. To the religious training of his scholars he was conscientiously attentive, teaching them, as one of them tells us, "not only by precept but by example." *

More fortunate than his contemporaries in office at the other great public schools, Busby held his mastership at Westminster throughout the troubles of the Great Rebellion. Partly, no doubt, this was owing to his high reputation; partly also to some interest which he appears to have had with the Parliamentary Commissioners.† An attempt was made to shake his supremacy at Westminster in 1657 by the second-master, a young man named Edward Bagshawe, a violent republican, who was supported in the attack by Owen, Dean of Christ-Church, who is reported to have said that "it would be never well with the nation till Westminster School were suppressed." Bagshawe had been one of Busby's favourite scholars—one of his "white boys," as the others called

---

* Giles Oldisworth, in an unpublished treatise called 'The Westminster Scholar a Pattern of Piety.'—(MS. Bodl. Libr.)

† A Commission to visit Eton, Westminster, Winchester, and Merchant Taylors' Schools was issued by ordinance of the Protector, Sept. 2, 1654.

them—and it had been at his special request that he accepted the second-mastership. But they could not agree in their new relations. Probably Busby was somewhat overbearing. An impartial witness (Dr Pope) says that the late second-master, Vincent, had been Busby's "servitor at Oxford, and little better at Westminster;" and he had warned Bagshawe that possibly he might not find the position of a subordinate quite to his taste. But Bagshawe was a troublesome fanatic. He thought fit to bear his testimony by sitting with his hat on in the Abbey Church, for which Busby very properly rebuked him. He also made no secret, by his own account, of "not overvaluing Mr Busby's Greek Grammar,"* which was just published, and had superseded Camden's in the school—an offence which no author could be expected to overlook. The actual quarrel was owing to an order which Busby obtained from the Governors (that is, the Parliamentary Commission, of which "Lord" Bradshaw was the head) for the enforcement of the old statute under which the fourth form was included in the upper school, which would bring it under the head-master's teaching, instead of the second-master's—in spite, as Bagshawe alleged, of "sixty years' usage to the contrary;" and he complained that he was now set to teach "the puny boys" in the first and second forms, which had hitherto been under the care of an usher. Not only this, but Busby had removed this usher—"his minion Mr James," as the angry complainant calls him, but who was certainly a young man of remarkable abilities—to assist in the teaching of the upper forms; thus placing

* Narrative of the Differences between Mr Busby and Mr Bagshawe, 1659.

him virtually above the second-master. No doubt this was hard to bear; but it was an arrangement quite common to all public schools in which the second-master, by the foundation statutes, had the distinct charge of the lower school, and the assistants were merely the head-master's deputies, paid by him (as was the case with Mr James), and employed to teach such forms as he might assign them. Mr Bagshawe, in his wrath, took the strong measure of desiring his boys not to pay Mr James the customary compliment of rising when he entered the school. They enjoyed the partisanship, and carried it still further by ignoring in the same way the great Busby himself—with what consequences may be guessed, though they are not told. Bagshawe even went so far as to rebuke one of the monitors for rising in Mr James's presence; and when told that it was by Mr Busby's order, desired him to "write that down on his bill;" a proceeding equivalent, as Mr Busby declared, and as Westminster and Eton men will perhaps agree, to ordering the head-master up for corporal punishment. For these acts of contumacy, Busby lodged a formal complaint before the Commission, which Bagshawe was called upon to answer. He did not mend matters by a personal taunt against his chief at the outset of his defence. He called him an "Actor."*
The fact was that the great schoolmaster had first brought himself into royal favour by his clever acting

---

* "It is very well the cause was not weighty, for I am sure the *Actor* hath not been wanting."—(Narrative of the Differences between Mr Busby and Mr Bagshawe.) In this Narrative he pretends to regret Busby's having so mistaken his words. "I meant it innocently," he says, "for an Actor in a cause, not an *Actor* (sic) of *Crotander*." The innocence is obvious.

of *Cratander* in 'The Royal Slave'—a play written by William Cartwright, also a Westminster scholar, and acted by the students of Christ-Church before Charles I. and his Queen; and the applause he then received is said to have bred in him such a passion for the stage, that he declared he would have adopted it as a profession, had not the Rebellion broken out. Bagshawe had reckoned too much, in his opposition to his superior, on the support of the Lord President Bradshaw and some others of the Commissioners; Busby had his friends among them too —he "ploughed with the same heifers," as Dr Pope expresses it,—and the majority supported him, and suspended Bagshawe from his office. Either in disgust, or anticipating dismissal, he resigned next year. His subsequent career shows that Westminster was well rid of him. He returned into residence at Oxford, and there was strenuous against the wearing of caps and gowns, and distinguished himself by such violent abuse of all ecclesiastical authorities, after the Restoration, as to earn for himself imprisonment at different times in the Tower and in Newgate.

It is asserted that another attempt was made to deprive Busby of his office about this time, and that one Mr Owen Price, Master of Magdalen College School in Oxford, hoped to succeed him. But Mr Price's letter, addressed to the Secretary of Cromwell's Privy Council,* rather shows that it was the *second*-mastership to which he aspired, on Bagshawe's resignation, with which event the date (1658) corresponds. For he endeavours to make some conditions as to the appointment: specially, that he should not be obliged "to be constant with the

* Printed in Peck's Desiderata Curiosa, p. 502.

gown-boys at bed and board any more than the late master was;" and this superintendence has always been the *second*-master's duty. He wishes also "that the schoolmasters should have leave to pray each in their turns, not using the same forms;" a privilege quite unnecessary for a head-master to ask under a Puritan Commission, but which it would be very difficult for a subordinate to secure under the orthodox Busby. Mr Price's letter makes some amusing complaints of the delay in the matter of the appointment. He cannot think "what the *remora* is;" he challenges any one who "would be so uncivil as to call his abilities in question" to "make a trial of his boys" at Magdalen School, where in eight years he boasts that he has "raised more godly men and preachers than some that keep greater noise." He goes on:—

"There appears very much of God in this unexpected providence of bringing me to this place, but there appears more of the divell in keeping me out of it; in that he is so aroused as to incense all his agents, both here and at Westminster, to set all their wits to conspire against me."

Among the "divell's agents" he would probably have included Mr Busby, who secured the second-mastership for a man of very different character—Adam Littleton; who, though he had been ejected by the Puritans from his studentship at Christ-Church, was allowed to accept and retain this office unmolested. He was an excellent oriental as well as classical scholar, and under him the King's scholars gathered that smattering (it could hardly have been more) of Chaldee and Arabic of which South boasts in his school-days. Charles II., to whom Littleton was subsequently appointed chaplain, granted him the reversion of the head-mastership after Busby; but he experienced the truth of the old proverb about "waiting for dead men's shoes," for though he lived to nearly the Psalmist's measure of years, he left his old master still vigorous at his desk.

Busby saw more serious troubles than these at Westminster during his long administration. In 1642, the Puritan rabble of London attacked the Abbey in their zeal for the expurgation of Popery, intending to make a clearance of all images, organs, and other ornaments of the Church. They had actually "forced out a pane of the north door, and got entrance;" but meeting with a stout resistance "from the scholars, quiremen, officers, and other servants, they were driven out." The leader of the attack—"one Wiseman, a knight of Kent"—met with the fate of Abimelech; he was killed by a tile which some one of the defenders launched upon him from the battlements. During the civil wars which followed, all the members of the collegiate chapter were expelled from their preferments, with the single exception of Osboldstone, the late head-master, who had just been restored to his prebend. It was perhaps owing to the good offices of this able and conscientious man that his old school escaped the fate of most other ecclesiastical foundations. As having been a sufferer for conscience' sake, he would deservedly have much influence with his party. The annual elections, indeed, were more than once suspended; no scholars were sent to Cambridge in 1643 or in the following year, and in 1660 there was no election either to Oxford or Cambridge, "on account of the unsettled state of the kingdom and universities." But, with these exceptions, the business of the school appears to have suffered no interruption in those times of national trouble.

Certainly it was not because the Westminster scholars had much of the spirit of the Vicar of Bray. The loyalty of the school was strong enough to justify the bitter words of Dean Owen. "In the very worst of times," says South, "we were really King's scholars, we were not only called so." He was captain in 1651; and records, to the lasting honour of the school, that King Charles was prayed for there by name, in the usual form, on the morning of his execution. Among all the loyal hearts in Oxford, none were more loyal than the Westminster students of Christ-Church. Fell, the Dean, with Dolben and Wall, canons of the house, refusing to recognise the visitation of the Parliamentary Commission, were deprived of their preferments. The two former were among the little band who, when the Common Prayer was proscribed, met at Dr Willis's in Merton College, and there used it, with surplices and all due solemnities, on Sundays and holidays, until the Restoration. Rare were the cases in which even the younger students did not prefer their principles to their places. Robert Waring, the Professor of History, James Croft, Matthew Llewellyn, and David Whitford, served either as officers or privates in the Oxford garrison; William Cartwright was one of the King's Council of War. Robert Mead, already a rising physician, gave up the lancet for the sword, and commanded a company during the siege of Oxford, and at the relief of Abingdon. Some of the wilder wits among the juniors, when summoned to appear before the Commissioners, even broke jests upon that formidable body. "I profess unto you," said John

Carrick, imitating the sanctimonious snuffle of his interrogator, "I will not submit; yea, verily, I will not submit." Robert Whitehall, being required like others to give his answer in writing, replied in this doggrel:—

> "My name's Whitehall (God bless the poet);
> If I submit, the King shall know it."

Richard Gale, who had somehow escaped the general expurgation of the house (the undergraduates seem to have been little interfered with), drank the King's health in hall, during the following Christmas holidays, upstanding and bareheaded, with his whole table, and was expelled therefor. One is sorry to learn, though impartial history is obliged to record the fact, that he was " a notorious sot and evil liver," and would probably have drunk Oliver's health if he had good liquor to wash it down. Of James Quin, his fellow-student, a story is told which shows that convivial qualities may sometimes be turned to better account. He too had been deprived of his studentship as an obstinate malignant; but he could sing a good song, and some friend put him in the way of exhibiting his gifts in this line before Cromwell. The Lord General was charmed, and asked the young man what he could do for him. Quin promptly suggested that he might be restored to his student's place, and his request was granted. Samuel Speed, after his expulsion from Christ-Church, engaged in some unsuccessful plots against the Protector's Government, and was obliged to fly the kingdom. He was not heard of for many years, and was said to have turned buccaneer. He returned from his foreign wanderings, whatever they were, after the Restoration, became chaplain to the Earl of Ossory, and was on board his ship in that capacity in the sea-fight in which the Duke of York commanded against the Dutch. His behaviour on that day gave some colour to the reports of his previous adventures; for he is said to be the hero of the lines in Sir John Birkenhead's ballad—

> "His chaplain he plied his wonted work,
> He prayed like a Christian, and fought like a Turk,
> Crying—'Now for the King and the Duke of York!'
> With a thump, thump, thump." *

Nor were the scholars of Trinity College in Cambridge less constant in their loyalty, in most cases. Abraham Cowley, William Beale, Robert Crighton (afterwards Bishop), and several others, suffered deprivation rather than acknowledge any allegiance but to the King.

But there were noble spirits too amongst the nurslings of Westminster, who took the other side in that terrible national struggle—men who were neither revolutionists nor fanatics, though they could not conscientiously be King's men. Such a man was Nathaniel Hodges, whom the Parliamentary visitors brought from Trinity, Cambridge, to fill one of the vacant studentships at Christ-Church. He practised physic afterwards in London; and when the plague was at its worst there, and all medical skill seemed hopeless, and the scared physicians (the great Sydenham included) fled before it, he continued his work of charity, and, though twice attacked by it, escaped with his life. Escaped, indeed, only to die at last in great poverty in Ludgate prison;

---

* Welch's Alumni Westmonasterienses. To the copious and interesting notes to the new edition, by Charles Bagot Phillimore, Esq., these pages are much indebted.

there is the more need that Westminister posterity should make his memory such amends as it may. The same true heroism is recorded of Thomas Vincent, another student of the Puritans' appointment, who, says Antony Wood, "continued all the time of the plague in the city, doing all the good he could, visiting everybody who sent for him, and publickly preaching every Lord's-day and holiday at some great church." Among his school contemporaries, too, was Philip Henry, a gentle studious boy, going with his mother to attend those terrible morning lectures at the Abbey, delivered by members of the Assembly of Divines, where he sometimes sat from eight o'clock in the morning until four in the afternoon. He had a special dispensation from Busby for these attendances, which must have interfered seriously with school lessons: but he was always a favourite with the great master, as he deserved to be. He had been chosen into college captain of his election —" partly by his own merit, and partly by the interest of the Earl of Pembroke" (even Puritans liked a little job)—and was clever and diligent, getting up to read in the dark hours of night or early morning; a practice still characteristic of hard workers at Westminster, and peculiar (as a habit) to this alone of public schools. One anecdote is told of him which shows that Busby had a gentle side to his character, less known to modern chroniclers than his severity, but which accounts for the affection which so many of his scholars bore to him in after-life. Young Henry, while holding the responsible office of "monitor of chamber," got into trouble for not stopping some irregularities among the juniors. When reported to the head-master, Busby said to him reproachfully, "Καὶ συ, τεκνον!" (Thou too, my son!) which must have been sorer to the boy than the copy of Latin verses set him as a punishment—for Busby does not seem to have had the heart to flog him. Henry's biographer makes kindly mention of another Thomas Vincent, the hard-working usher of the fourth form in those days— "so much grieved at the dulness and non-proficiency of his scholars that, falling into a consumption, I have heard Mr Henry say of him that he 'killed himself with false Latin.'" It is fortunate for all schoolmasters and tutors that this kind of malaria is not commonly fatal.

There is one story connected with these days of trouble which is undoubtedly authentic, and bears pleasant witness to the kindly feeling which bound together the Westminster scholars, even when they found themselves ranged on hostile sides in the great national struggle. A curtain formerly was drawn across the school, dividing the upper forms from the lower. One day a boy was so unlucky as to tear it; and Busby's known severity left no doubt of the punishment that would follow. The offender was in despair, when a generous schoolfellow volunteered to take the blame upon himself, and suffered in his friend's stead accordingly. The boys grew up, and took different sides in the civil wars. John Glynne, who was the real culprit, became a sergeant-at-law (and eventually Chief-Justice to Cromwell), and sat as one of the commission to try the prisoners who had been taken in Penruddock's unsuccessful rising in the King's cause at Salisbury, in 1654. Among others who were sentenced to death, Sir John Glynne saw one face which struck him as familiar; he found upon inquiry that it

was no other than that of his old schoolfellow, William
Wake, now a Royalist colonel, who had taken his flogging at Westminster. He said nothing at the moment,
but took horse and went straight to the Lord-Protector,
and obtained his friend's life as a personal favour.*

The great schoolmaster was scarcely past the prime
of life when England rang once more with the old loyal
watch-cries. He had the honour of carrying the ampulla at the coronation, when Charles II. came to his
own. He had also what he would probably consider
the greater honour of escorting his Majesty over his
royal school at Westminster; which gave occasion to
the well-known anecdote of his apologising for keeping
on his hat in the King's presence, on the ground that it
would never do to let the boys believe there was a
greater man in the world than himself—a joke which
no one would enjoy more than King Charles. In
truth, Busby's tenure of his dominion there was far
more secure and lasting than that of the unfortunate
Stuarts. He lived to see another of them deposed,
without any serious interruption to his own reign at
Westminster. During the brief ascendancy of the
Romanist friends of James, which led to this second
revolution, he met one of his old pupils, now the
well-known Father Petre, one day in St James's Park.
Petre accosted his old master: Busby declared he could
not recognise him in that dress, and Petre mentioned
his name. "But you were of another faith, sir," said
Busby, "when you were under me—how came you to

* There has been some doubt whether the judge might not have
been Robert Nicholas, one of the Barons of Exchequer; but it seems
tolerably certain that Glynne was the man.

change it?" "The Lord had need of me," replied the convert. "Need of you, sir? Why, I have read the Scriptures as much as any other man, and I never read that the Lord had need of anything but once, and then it was an ass." Many others of the foremost men on both sides during and after the Revolution had been under his stern rule at Westminster :—Charles Montagu, afterwards Earl of Halifax, whom a great modern historian ranks as not inferior to Pitt in the intellectual qualities of a statesman, but wanting Pitt's honour and magnanimity; and Francis Atterbury, perhaps the ablest and by no means the worst of the intriguing politicians of his time, though the character was more of a scandal in the great churchman than in those whose vocation was exclusively secular. Whatever his faults, he was true to Westminster, and Westminster was true to him. As Dean of Christ-Church, or as Bishop of Rochester, he never lost his kindly interest in the school; and it is pleasant to read that, when he was hunted to ruin by his many enemies, with his brother bishops at their head (for whose bitter hostility Lord Bathurst could only account by the sarcastic supposition that, "like the Indians, they thought when they destroyed an enemy they inherited his powers"), the King's scholars, too young and chivalrous to care for the unpopularity of their hero—perhaps worshipping him all the more because of it—paid him frequent visits during his imprisonment in the Tower.

Very many of the young nobility were entered at the school under Busby, and most of them were boarders in his house. In some cases they seem not to have been profitable scholars, and to have left their names on the head-master's books in more senses than one. An original note-book of Busby's (now an heirloom of the head-master's) has the following curious entry—probably of the date 1661:—

"Lord Maidston left two beds and furniture of chamber, but paid nothing for himself or man, either entrance, boord, schoole, or attendance in time of sickness at Nursery." *

In the same pages it stands recorded that, in 1664, William, Henry, and Daniel Finch† (sons of Heneage, first Earl of Nottingham), owed respectively for five, four, and three years' board and tuition, and that "Lord Colchester and his brother owes for all their time." The charge for board in those days was thirty pounds per annum. Of the numbers we can only learn that in 1656 they were, in the first quarter, 241, of which 37 were boarders, and at Christmas 203, the boarders being 38—most likely all with the head and other masters.

More than one personal record of school life at Westminster under Busby has come down to us. It must be remembered that his rule continued for fifty-seven years, and that he taught, in several cases, the grandsons of his earlier scholars. South, as has been said, was captain of the school in 1651, and has left us a copy of Latin elegiacs (written probably while a student of Christ-Church) which give us some insight into its state as he knew it. There were some three hundred boys, divided into seven forms (the old Winchester and Eton arrangement), under three masters only. He

---

* Alumni Westm., Append., p. 571.
† Lord Maidstone was of the same family son of Heneage Finch, second Earl of Winchelsea.

corroborates the traditions of Busby's penal discipline :—

> "Consurgit crescitque puer, velut hydra, sub ictu;
> Florescitque suis sæpe rigatus aquis."

If the common anecdote be true, South spoke from considerable personal experience. "I see great talents in that sulky boy," said the old master, "and my rod shall bring them out of him." William Taswell, rector of Newington in Surrey, whose Latin diary has been translated by his grandson, tells us how he was entered at Westminster as a town-boy in 1660. In three years' time he was sufficiently advanced to be admitted by Busby "above the curtain"—that is, into the fourth class, the lowest in the upper school. Of this class, however, he says the head-master "took little or no care;" but as he rose into the higher forms he found the teaching more satisfactory. The system of election into college, and the hardships of a junior's life, were as characteristic of Westminster two hundred years ago as they have continued to be until a very recent date. It was not till he had been seven years a town-boy that Taswell got elected on the foundation; and his account of his experience as a junior might serve for that of more than one of his successors within living memory. "Extremely maltreated during my seven months and two weeks' servitude as junior by the monitors;" "employed chiefly in performing the menial office of a servant; in consequence of this, diverted from my studies, and even when freed from this state of slavery, could scarce return to them, indulging a lazy disposition." In 1665, in consequence of the prevalence of the plague, Busby removed with his scholars to the house at Chiswick, where he carried on the school for a few weeks; but the infection spreading to that neighbourhood, he called the boys together, and "in an excellent oration," took credit to himself that "for twenty-five years he had never deserted the school until now," and so dismissed them to their several homes. Memorials of this migration of the Westminster scholars were still to be seen in the old collegehouse at Chiswick, while it was in the occupation of the Miss Berrys and their father, in the names which the boys had written up upon the walls; among them was that of John Dryden the poet, and Charles Montagu Earl of Halifax. Taswell was kept at home for the next ten months, during the whole of which time it would appear that the school remained closed. He was present at the great fire of London in 1667, and records an instance of gallantry on the part of the dean of Westminster, which shows at the same time the fatherly relation in which, like so many of his predecessors, he stood towards the King's scholars. The dean was John Dolben (afterwards archbishop of York), himself a Westminster student of Christ-Church, "who in the civil wars had frequently stood sentinel," says Taswell (he had, in fact, not only served in the garrison at Oxford, but carried a pair of colours at Marston Moor), and now held the deanery together with the bishopric of Rochester. He "collected his scholars together, marching with them on foot to put a stop, if possible, to the conflagration. I" (continues the writer) "was a kind of page to him, not being of the number of the King's scholars. We were employed many hours fetching water from the backside of St Dunstan's-in-the-East, where we happily extinguished the fire." The next evening young Taswell stood on Westminster Bridge to look at the fire, which was still raging, with his little pocket edition of Terence in his hand, which he could see to read plainly by the light of the burning city. He was elected student of Christ-Church in 1670; on which occasion he records that the Cambridge electors made choice of two scholars whom Oxford had previously rejected as of unsatisfactory moral repute, though they stood high at the examination.

Taswell lived to see three of his sons elected on the foundation at Westminster. It was while he himself was at school there that Mr Evelyn paid his visit, which he has very much obliged that section of posterity who are interested in these details by recording :—

1661, *May* 13*th*.—" I heard and saw such exercises at the election of scholars at Westminster School to be sent to the University, in Latin, Greek, Hebrew, and Arabic, in themes and extemporary verses, as wonderfully astonished me in such youths, with such readiness and wit, some of them not above twelve or thirteen years of age. Pity it is that what they attain here so ripely, they either do not retain, or do not improve more considerably when they come to be men, though many of them do. And no less is to be blamed their odd pronouncing of Latin, so that out of England none were able to understand or endure it. Any that would helped to pose."

Another of Busby's pupils, who came a full generation after Taswell, has left an account of his school-days, which, though unfortunately bare of personal anecdote, is very minute in some of its details, especially in the matter of school fees and expenses. Francis Lynn, afterwards Secretary to the Commission for Sick and Wounded Seamen, entered the school as a home-boarder in 1681.

It was the year in which, as Antony Wood briefly records, "the Westminster boys" (tired, we may presume, of the old feud) "burned Jack Presbyter instead of the Pope." Young Lynn kept a diary in a methodical fashion very unusual with schoolboys of any date. He took his place as the very lowest boy, and passed out of every form as "captain." He paid ten shillings a-quarter for school-fees, making a present besides, every Christmas, of a guinea to the head-master, and half-a-guinea to the usher. Such was the old system in every public school; the masters were entirely dependent for any income beyond their statutable salaries on the liberality of the parents of those boys who were admitted as "commoners," or "oppidans," or under any other designation; and by degrees these gratuities became matter of recognised custom and claim. In 1689, having been now eight years at school, he got his election into college—still as captain, by which he escaped the "servitude" in his first year as junior, of which Taswell makes such heavy complaint. But the items of his expenditure show the existence of the same elaborate system, in the relations between seniors and juniors among the scholars on the foundation, which has all the prestige of an immemorial antiquity to recommend it, and perhaps little besides. He had to pay "to the eight seniors for his freedom as captain of election," the sum of £8, 12s. He also expended 7s. to entertain his schoolfellows—"an usual custom." On Shrove-Tuesday he had the privilege of paying another 10s. "for tarts, to treat, as free-boy." The same sum was paid to some college official, "for putting up his name in gold letters;" an honourable distinction conferred upon the captains of each year's election, who are still thus recorded on the wooden tablets on the walls of the dormitory. The fees to the masters appear to have increased as boys rose into the higher forms: he paid to Dr Busby for a year's schooling, in 1690, £4, 6s. The whole cost of his Westminster education, for ten years, was £70, 15s.; and of this more than half, £39, 17s., was incurred in the last year and three months, from his election into college until his election to Cambridge.*

Some minor abuses had crept into the foundation even in these early days. It is clear that any payment to the masters, from scholars on the royal foundation, was such; and Lynn had to purchase for himself a bed, bolster, blankets, table, and mat, and to pay for candles. The punishments for speaking English in hall or school, which have been before alluded to, were strictly enforced in his days in the way of fines, called "admonishing money," which figure occasionally in his account. The custom was for the second boy of the second election to act as a sort of monitor for this purpose, and to deliver to any boy who so offended a "mark" or tally, with the words, "*tu es custos;*" this mark he had to pass in turn to the first whom he could detect in a similar slip, and the boy with whom the mark remained when hall broke up incurred a fine. Charles Dryden, son of the poet, thought himself so hardly used by being made *custos* three days running (by some unfairness, as he conceived), that the father wrote a strong letter on the subject to his old master, Busby, and was very nearly removing the boy from school.†

---

* A copy of this diary was sent by Mr Lynn's representatives to the 'Evening Mail,' Jan. 1834.
† See Nichols's Illust. of Lit. History, iv. 298.

CHAPTER III.

HEAD-MASTERS KNIPE—FREIND—NICOLL.

Busby was succeeded by the second-master, Thomas Knipe, a man of high character and good scholarship. His pupil, Dr Robert King, speaks highly of the religious training which boys received under him, and Mattaire, whose word on points of scholarship ought to have great weight, gracefully admits that he owed everything to his teaching—"*cui se sua omnia debere fatetur.*" Busby is said to have undervalued Knipe's powers as an assistant; perhaps it is difficult for a master to conceive that a boy who has been under his own training may rise to be his equal or superior in his own line in after-life. The school certainly rose in numbers under Knipe's government; for in the list of 1706 there were 353 names, apparently without including those of the King's scholars, which would bring up the total to very nearly 400. Under his successor, Dr Robert Freind, they rose (in 1727) to 434; and this is the highest tide of numerical prosperity of which any positive record seems discoverable, though Bishop Newton says that in his time (under Freind and Nicoll) there were "not less than 500" boys in the school. Dr Freind was an able master, and something more. He had a very extensive literary and political acquaintance; his house is said to have been "the resort of all the wits and statesmen of the time." Some of them celebrated his promotion in the following tolerable epigram:—

> "Ye sons of Westminster, who still retain
> Your ancient dread of Busby's awful reign,
> Forget your fears at length, your panic end,
> The monarch of this house is now a *Friend*."

His were the palmy days of Westminster in every way. Under his auspices began the annual dinners on the Foundress's day, under the stewardship of noblemen and gentlemen of degree who had received their education in the school. (These were distinct from the dinners at the Election, which, under the statutes, were to be on the Monday, Tuesday, and Wednesday after the Conversion of St Paul, Jan. 25th,—subsequently changed by Dean Goodman for the same days in Rogation week.) The first of these gatherings was held in 1726-7, when the Duke of Devonshire, the Earl of Oxford, Henry Pelham and William Pulteney, Esquires, and Dr Freind, were the stewards. A Latin speech was recited by one of the boys before the dinner, and an English one afterwards; and then the electors and visitors were entertained with a series of epigrams composed—or at least recited—by some of the more distinguished aspirants. The names of some of these, who spoke at the next year's dinner, will give some idea of the popularity of the school as a place of education for the young nobility. There were the young Earl of Holderness, Viscount Harcourt, Lord Middlesex and his brothers Lord John and George Sackville (sons of the Duke of Dorset, an old Westminster, and one of the next year's stewards), Lord

Danby, Lord Clifton, Lord Cranbourne, Lord Henry Gray, Lord Vere Bertie, the Honourables W. Fitzwilliam, Geo. Dawnay, T. Coote, James Noel, John and Robert Hay, Spencer Cowper, S. Masham, J. Hamilton, Randall and Charles Vane, W. Leveson Gower, and W. Boscawen; Sir Edmund Thomas, Sir Danvers Osborne, Sir Edward Newdigate, Sir Herbert Palmer, Sir William Burdett, and Sir Hugh Wrottesley. Dr Freind probably brought forward on this occasion the whole effective strength of his more aristocratic pupils, since many of these boys were in the lower forms; but it is a titular list which certainly the rival Eton could not have paralleled in those years. The epigrams were, it must be confessed, poor enough in most instances to have been the genuine compositions of schoolboys. They were *de rebus omnibus*, some in English and some in Latin, commonly turning upon some subject of the day; one or two here and there are amusing enough for this reason. The following, for instance, suggested by the accident of the then popular "Count" Heydegger having fixed one of his entertainments for the evening of the dinner, illustrates also the old school discipline applied in more cases than one to individuals who brought down upon themselves the wrath of the Westminsters. It was spoken in 1730-1 by Vane, a son of Lord Barnard:—

> "Without respect to Westminster at all,
> Has Heydegger this night proclaimed a ball;
> But should he interrupt our learned sport,
> Or rob us of one guest, we'll swinge him for't:
> The Count shall for his modern arts be thanked—
> Here's Pitt * and I will toss him in a blanket."

---

* Son of the Earl of Londonderry.

The well-known punishment of Curll the bookseller was still fresh in the memory of the school and its friends. It had taken place a few years after Freind's accession to the head-mastership. A letter bearing date August 3d, 1716, which was circulated in print at the time, gives the correct details of a story often told. When Dr Robert South, a name held in honour by all Westminster scholars, died in the course of that year, his remains, after lying in state for four days in the Jerusalem Chamber, were carried into the college hall before interment, and a funeral oration spoken over them by the captain of the King's scholars. Curll had surreptitiously got hold of a copy and published it. The letter tells the rest.

"A certain bookseller near Temple Bar did, without consent of Mr John Barber, present captain, publish the scraps of a funeral oration spoken by him over the corpse of the Rev. Dr South, and being on Thursday last fortunately nabbed within the limits of Dean's Yard by the scholars, there he met with a college salutation: for he was first presented with the ceremony of the blanket, in which, when the skeleton had been well shaken, he was carried in triumph round the school; and after receiving a grammatical correction for his false concords, he was reconducted to Dean's Yard, and on his knees asking pardon of Mr B. for his offence, he was kicked out of the Yard, and left to the huzzahs of the rabble."

This piece of Lynch-law was commemorated in various ways. It forms the subject of one of the Christ-Church *Carmina Quadragesimalia.** A print was also engraved,

---

* The "Lent Verses" spoken annually in the College. Those here

representing in three compartments the three several punishments, with the following lines from Martial: *—

> "Ibis ab excusso missus ad astra sago:
> . . . . . .
> Etherias, lascive, cupis volitare per auras;
> I—fuge; sed poteras tutior esse domi."

That the boys should have cordially enjoyed the thing is perfectly intelligible; but there is also evidence that it was looked upon as a rather laudable act of retribution by some of the authorities. Mattaire (who had been second-master, though he had resigned before this took place) mentions, in a letter dated Oct. 21, 1736, Curll's "impudent way of dealing with dead authors' works, and sometimes with those of the living," and goes on to say—"Your Lordship by this may see how much this saucy fellow deserved that correction which was inflicted on him at that school."

But this was the iron age of public schools, so far as order and discipline went; when the fights with the

alluded to were probably spoken in 1717. The thesis is "An causæ sint sibi invicem causæ?"

> "Authore invito tenues mandare libellos
> Furtivis solitus Bibliopola typis
> Ultores pueros, deceptus fraude malignâ,
> Sensit, 'ab excusso missus ad astra sago.'
> Nec satis hoc; mensâ late porrectus acernâ
> Supplicium rigidae fert puerile scholae;
> Jam virgæ impatiens pueris convicia fundit,
> Vicinique crepat jurgia nota fori;
> Flagra minas misero extorquent repetita; minasque
> Quo magis ingeminat, vapulat ille magis."
> —Vol. i. 118, 119.

* Lib. I. 4.—The first line was long in use both in the dormitory at Westminster and in Long Chamber at Eton, whenever an unfortunate victim was tossed in a blanket. It was chanted in a rhythm appropriate to the ceremony—"Ibis ab excusso" (here came the preparatory heave) "missus ad astra sago" (up he went to the ceiling).

*skies*** were long and obstinate, and head-masters turned their eyes the other way. The 'London Evening Post' gives an account of a "customary" warlike exercise about this date, which helps us to understand how Westminster trained such good soldiers a couple of generations afterwards :—

"It being customary at this season of the year for the youths of Westminster School and the other schoolboys in the liberty of Westminster to attack one another with clubs and staves, the former were apprehensive that the latter would be too hard for them, and hired the apprentices of Bridewell Hospital as auxiliaries, who went down to their assistance last Tuesday night, and made their masters victorious wherever they came; for which services they were so bountifully rewarded that they afterwards got into an alehouse in King Street, where they became drunk and quarrelled with the Constables and the Watch, and wounded several of them, causing such a riot and disorder that the Guards came from Whitehall, and seized fifteen of the Bluecoat boys, † who were secured in the gate-house, and this day carried before the bench of Justices to be examined."— [May 9th, 1728.]

The annual dinners at Westminster ceased in 1732. But after that, for many years, the old members of the school were wont to meet together at Cambridge, on Nov. 17th—the day of Queen Elizabeth's accession. The banquets were jovial, and somewhat uproarious, as was the fashion of the day. On one occasion, the noise

---

* Current Westminster for plebeians; said to be an abbreviation of *Volsci*, the outer rabble of invaders upon the territory of Dean's Yard, belonging of right to the *gens togata* as Romans.

† Westminster Bluecoat School, founded 1688. There are also Black, Green, and Grey coat Schools.

was so great, that the University authorities paid the party a domiciliary visit, and insisted on their dispersing. Franklin, then Greek Professor, who had been an usher in the school, was the chairman of the evening, and stood upon his rights against the proctors. He was summoned before the vice-chancellor, but the dispute seems to have ended in a war of printed letters and pamphlets.

It has been said that this was the great era of the school. Bishop Newton writes of the election days which he remembered—

"There was something august and awful too in the Westminster elections, to see three such great men presiding—Bishop Atterbury as Dean of Westminster, Bishop Smalridge[*] as Dean of Christ-Church, and Dr Bentley as Master of Trinity; and 'as iron sharpeneth iron,' so these three, by their wit, learning, and liberal conversation, whetted and sharpened one another."

Bentley was sharp enough to be disagreeable occasionally. The mode of election — each University choosing one from among the candidates alternately, and not at all necessarily those who best acquitted themselves at the examination—led almost of course to some jealousy between the two bodies of electors; especially since the Trinity scholarships were of very inferior value to the studentships at Christ-Church. Bentley says that in fact the friends of the candidates continually wrote to him to beg as a favour that he would

[*] Smalridge was an admirable Latin scholar. The election of 1682, when he went off with others to Christ-Church, was known as the "Golden Election," from the great ability of the successful candidates. He succeeded his schoolfellow, Atterbury, as Dean of Christ-Church —"like a bucket of water," as he said, "to put out fire:"—so much offence had Atterbury given there.

not choose them to Trinity; though he made some amends for the poverty of his scholarships by usually procuring the election to a fellowship of the senior Westminster scholar of his house. For the Oxford studentships, on the other hand, all possible interest, regular and irregular, was made with the Dean and other electors at Christ-Church. In 1688 there was a regular fight between the two Universities for the person of a most desirable candidate (as was then thought), Edmund Smith, or Neale, which was his real patronymic. Christ-Church got him, and found him by no means such a prize as they had bargained for. He turned his wits, which were very considerable, to lampooning Dean Aldrich and other college authorities, and was highly irregular in his habits besides. They bore long with him, in consideration of his promise of distinction, but at last he was expelled. He lived a slovenly disreputable literary life about London afterwards, known to his familiars as "Captain Rag," and was honoured— for what reason Dr Johnson only knows—with a place in the 'Lives of the Poets.' The great Master of Trinity would occasionally step out of his way to *disoblige* the friends of a student who were specially anxious to get him off to Christ-Church. At one election, according to Lord Bolingbroke, he "leapt over eight boys" purposely to take Robert Prior (nephew of the poet), and, " with all the good-breeding of a pedant, remained inflexible." Once, in his war with some of his fellows, touching the removal of Sergeant Miller from his fellowship, Bentley had an idea of making use of the Westminster men to serve his own purposes in the college. He suggested to Zachary Pearce (afterwards Bishop of Rochester) that " being a Westminster scholar, he might bring a body of students educated at that school, among whom a great *esprit de corps* existed, and block out the Sergeant by manual force."

In 1716, during Freind's head-mastership, William Murray, son of Lord Stormont, was sent from Scotland to Westminster School. The future Earl of Mansfield (for it was he) rode the whole way, attended by an old servant of the family, on "a Galloway pony," which caused some delay by falling lame upon the road. They reached their journey's end, however, at last, and the pony was sold in London by the help of a Scotch apothecary who had known the family in "auld lang syne." Young Murray was put to board at a dame's, Mrs Tollet, in Dean's Yard, where he paid for three quarters (including extras) the sum of £20, 10s. 4d. The fees to the head-master continued the same as in Lynn's latest account—four guineas annually; but in Murray's bill the same amount is also paid "to the other masters." Some of the items of his outfit would now seem curiously out of place for a schoolboy; he paid a guinea for a sword, and 4s. 4d. for two wigs. But at that date, and indeed long subsequently, a young gentleman of any consideration was hardly considered full-dressed without these appendages. Wigs were in use for many years afterwards among the Westminster scholars, and the old ones were occasionally utilised by being turned into nightcaps—if we may take the evidence of an old school epigram said to have been written by Sir Elijah Impey about 1745. The theme given was "*Decus et Tutamen;*" and Impey's application of it to his wig gained great applause—

" Hæc coma, quam spectas, duplicem mihi servit in usum
 Tutamen capiti nocte, dieque decus.'

Murray distinguished himself considerably at Westminster. He gained admission into college, head of his election, in 1719, and went off as captain to Christ-Church. A story is told of his having been found one day by Lady Kinnoul, at whose house he was spending a holiday, busy composing epigrams for a school exercise. She asked him what the subject was, and he answered with a laugh—"What is that to you?" Her ladyship was considerably shocked at his rudeness; but he explained to her afterwards that he had really only given her a literal translation of the Latin thesis—"*Quid ad te pertinet?*" After he had risen to his judicial honours, as long as his strength permitted him, he was one of the most constant at the play and at the annual meetings.

Freind held the head-mastership for two-and-twenty years, when he resigned, and was succeeded by Dr John Nicoll, who had already been for twenty years undermaster; a careful and conscientious teacher, whose memory should at least be held clear from the prevalent modern assumption, that the public schools of former generations ignored any religious training. We have the strong testimony of Cowper (no prejudiced witness in favour of public education) on this point:—

"I must relate one mark of religious discipline which in my time was observed at Westminster. I mean the pains which Dr Nicoll took to prepare us for confirmation. The old man acquitted himself of this duty like one who had a keen sense of its importance; and I believe most of us were struck by his manner and affected by his exhortations."—Letter in Southey's Life, i. p. 13.

There was another branch of training, too, which has been much too loudly claimed as the peculiar honour of modern schoolmasters, the value of which Nicoll seems to have perfectly understood; "he had the art," says another pupil, "of making his scholars gentlemen."

"There was a court of honour in that school, to whose unwritten laws every member of our community was amenable, and which to transgress by any act of meanness that exposed the offender to public contempt, was a degree of punishment compared to which the being sentenced to the rod would have been considered an acquittal or a reprieve."*

Cumberland mentions more than one instance of the recognition of this high tone both by master and boys. A case of dishonourable conduct was once laid before the seniors by Dr Nicoll, and their opinion asked as to what punishment it seemed to deserve. Their answer was, "The severest that could be inflicted." "I can inflict none more severe than you have now given him," said Nicoll, and so dismissed the culprit. So again, when Cumberland himself was called up for judgment on a charge of being concerned with others in some disturbance at a Quakers' meeting, and the master saw a confession of guilt and penitence in his face, he let him off with a quotation from his favourite Terence—"*Erubuit —salva res est.*"

One of the ushers under Freind and Nicoll was Pierson Lloyd (afterwards second-master), a fine scholar, and something of a humorist, who worked in the school for forty-seven years, and died universally beloved and lamented—

"Senex amabilis,
Quo non fuit jucundior,"

---

* Cumberland's Memoirs, p. 53.

as he is described in the beautiful ode upon his death written by Dr Vincent,* and translated by Cowper, who speaks of him in terms of great affection. Another was Cowper's favourite, "Vinny" Bourne—"the neatest of all men in his versification, and the most slovenly in his person;" "so good-natured and so indolent," says his pupil, "that he made me as idle as himself." His good-nature was an irresistible temptation to schoolboy jokes; and we are told how the future Duke of Richmond set a light to his greasy unkempt locks, and then boxed his ears, with an eager apology, to put out the conflagration. His Latin verse has perhaps been somewhat overrated by enthusiastic admirers, but it is remarkable for ease and grace, and Westminster was indebted to him for many a successful epilogue and epigram. Bourne was quite sensible of his own weaknesses, and conscientiously refused to take holy orders, for which he felt himself unsuited, though he had good prospects of preferment in the Church. A memorandum which he left behind him shows the humble spirit of the man: "If any surviving friend will show his love to my memory by a small tablet, I desire that this, and this only, may be the inscription :—

> Pietatis sinceræ
> Summæque humilitatis,
> Nec Dei usquam immemor
> Nec sui,
> In silentium quod amavit
> Descendit
> V. B."

---

* Vide Lusus Alt. Westm., p. 286.

CHAPTER IV.

MODERN HEAD-MASTERS.

Dr Nicoll was succeeded in the head-mastership by William Markham, a great scholar and successful teacher, under whom the school continued to flourish during the eleven years of his rule. His taste in Latin versification was especially happy, and he won the attention of his scholars by the appropriate anecdotes and illustrations with which he constantly enlivened the lesson. He was made Dean of Rochester soon after his resignation in 1764, and became afterwards in rapid succession Dean of Christ-Church, Bishop of Chester, and Archbishop of York. For this last promotion he was indebted perhaps not so much to his unquestioned merit, as to the fact of his having been chosen preceptor to the Prince of Wales (George IV.) and the Duke of York. Dr John Hinchliffe, the next head-master, held the office only a few months, when he resigned on the plea of ill-health. A letter from a Westminster boy of his day gives the only hint of his character which seems now recoverable: "Our new master, Dr Hinchliffe, is, I believe, very good-natured; he did not flog any one for the first week, but has gone on at a good rate since."*

* Lusus Alt. Westm., i. p. 285, note.

He was a man of humble origin (his father kept a livery-stable in Swallow Street), and of no very remarkable merit, but fortunate in his patrons; he rose, some years afterwards, to be Master of Trinity College, Cambridge, and Bishop of Peterborough; and as he held both these offices together, it must be supposed that his health had considerably improved. Dr Samuel Smith, his old schoolfellow, who filled his place at Westminster, and ruled there for the next twenty-four years, seems to have been a man of no great mark. "Very dull and good-natured," George Colman calls him; but he could be energetic upon occasion, for in a rebellion of some kind which took place under his government, he knocked down one of the ringleaders—no less a person than Sir Francis Burdett—with a stick which he had brought into school. Sir Francis, among others, was expelled for this outbreak. On Smith's retirement, William Vincent, the under-master, was promoted into his place. He passed twice through every form in Westminster School as pupil and master, a fact which he has thus modestly recorded:—

"My own success in life has not depended upon talents, but labour, steadiness, and perseverance: I have twice passed through the school, from the lowest form to the highest; first as a boy, and secondly from the lowest usher to the office of head-master. . . . I have been rooted to the spot from eight years old till now, my seventy-second year."*

As an under-master, Vincent's reputation for severity had been almost equal to Busby's. He was not even content with the regulation punishment, but boxed the

* Letter to Nichols, Lit. Hist., iii. p. 771.

boys' ears and pinched them; against which Colman protests, as most public-school boys would, as an unwarrantable indignity. "A pedagogue," says he, "is privileged to make his pupil red in the proper place with birch, but he has no right to squeeze him black and blue with his fingers." He left off this practice when he became head-master, though still his discipline was anything but mild. There was a caricature of him in the Westminster print-shops, the work of some young Hogarth among the boys, with the Latin verse underneath—

"Sanguineos oculos volvit, virgamque requirit."

It may be pretty safely ascribed to James Hook (brother of Theodore, and afterwards Dean of Worcester), who was the humorist of the school, and whose vagaries were sometimes too much for even the stern gravity of Dr Vincent. On one occasion he dressed himself up as an old woman, and in that character begged half-a-crown from Vincent at the gate. A few minutes afterwards, the Doctor was shocked at seeing the unfortunate object of his charity held under the pump in Dean's Yard by Harley, the future Earl of Oxford, Carey (head-master and bishop), and another schoolfellow. He rushed to the rescue in natural indignation; but detecting Hook's physiognomy, he wisely turned away and laughed.

Dr Vincent's love of study was almost excessive. For many years of his life he rarely took any kind of exercise, except such as he obtained by walking up and down in front of his form in school—"like a captain on his quarterdeck"—as was his constant habit while hearing a lesson, and enlarging upon it in his own forcible language. This sedentary life made him a great sufferer from gout. But no student could be less of a recluse; the society of his friends was his favourite relaxation. His love of all that belonged to Westminster led him to make a rather singular display on one occasion, when he pronounced a funeral oration over the grave of Richard Cumberland, the dramatist, his friend and schoolfellow. The following characteristic reminiscence of him is from an anonymous pamphlet:—

"I see him now, gently rebuking a fault, or eagerly catching at an opportunity to enlarge upon some merit, so that his phrases might vivify a hitherto torpid emulation; I see him as he used to pace to and fro, swinging himself on the boards, which creaked beneath the pressure of his ample buckled shoes, while he rolled out a full-mouthed Atticism, or transfused into kindred English, by his own copious diction and majesty of enunciation, the seemingly untranslatable magnificence of some ecstatic chorus. Or yet again, when kindling with a deeper and more solemn energy, he brought to our knowledge and our affections the things belonging to salvation."

It was in these years that the only attempts were made at Westminster to set up a school periodical. The success of the 'Microcosm' at Eton roused at once the emulation and the jealousy of the rival school—for rivals, and not always amicable rivals, they were in those earlier days. A magazine called the 'Trifler' was set on foot by a few young aspirants, of whom the chief were John Hensleigh Allen, W. H. Aston (ninth Lord Aston), Robert Oliphant, Taunton (afterwards Sir William), and the Hon. Thomas James Twisleton. It was not remarkable for ability; perhaps the cleverest thing connected with it was a caricature by James Hook, in which Justice was represented as weighing the 'Microcosm' in a pair of scales against the 'Trifler,' when the former was made to kick the beam, in spite of the heavy body of King George III. being thrown in as a make-weight. The court-patronage which Eton received in his reign was always a sore subject with the Westminsters. The sketch was engraved, though not exactly published; the boys were expected to subscribe for it at a shilling apiece. It produced from the Etonians a rejoinder which was at least as good as the attack :—

> "What mean you by your print so rare,
>   Ye wits, of Eton jealous?
> But that we soar aloft in air,
>   While ye are heavy fellows."

Dr Smith did not encourage the publication of the 'Trifler;' and on its first appearance set as a subject for the weekly exercise what he intended as a hint to its writers—"*Scribimus indocti doctique.*" It did not live through more than a few numbers. But it was nearly containing the first poetical effort of Robert Southey, then one of the younger boys, who sent in to the editors some verses on the death of his sister, which they "declined with thanks." He was afterwards a contributor to a second periodical published in the school, got up chiefly by himself and his friend Grosvenor Bedford, and called the 'Flagellant.' Vincent was now head-master, and his fondness for the rod suggested both the title and a good deal of such wit as it contained. Vincent's wrath was excessive; he took the rather undignified step of commencing an action for libel against the unfortunate publisher; and Southey, who was the writer of the specially obnoxious article, came forward and confessed the authorship. The avowal might perhaps in these days have been met by more generous treatment; but no doubt the offence was grave, and the future laureate had to leave the school at once.

The younger Colman has left some characteristic memoranda of his own school life. He tells us how he and a schoolfellow kept for their private use a phaeton and pair—of donkeys—in what was then Tothill Fields (now Vincent Square), in which they took drives in state, to the great admiration of their schoolfellows; occasionally riding the unfortunate animals (sometimes double) by way of change: and how he was saved from drowning by his schoolfellow, George Cranstoun, and brought back to consciousness, when the case seemed after all very doubtful, by the tender attentions of Jack Roberts * the waterman, who employed a remedy unknown to the Humane Society—the blade of an oar applied smartly to what was considered the most sensitive part of a young Westminster's person. The Duchess of Kingston's trial for bigamy was going on in those days; and though the hall was crowded, the Westminster boys contrived to squeeze in, and were much disappointed when they found her Grace's plea of "privilege" admitted in bar of "corporal punishment"—a penalty which they understood only as inflicted by Drs Smith and Vincent, and were curious to see carried out.

* This family have held the appointment of watermen to the College for above a century. "Dicky Roberts," the old school Charon, who died in 1816, was the subject of a clever epigram spoken that year. See Lusus Alt. Westm., p. 311.

Dr Vincent rested at last in the well-earned ease of the Deanery, where still his delight was to visit and encourage the school. There he died; still "rooted to the spot," his whole life from infancy (with the exception of his four years at Cambridge) having been spent within the precincts. His successor in the mastership, Dr Wingfield, held the office little more than three months. Then came Dr William Carey, an excellent scholar and popular headmaster. He owed all his success in life to the early patronage of Cyril Jackson, Dean of Christ-Church. His father kept the old wellhouse at Malvern; and Jackson, while staying there, employed young Carey to carry the botanical and mineralogical specimens which he was fond of collecting in his rambles. He was so much struck by the lad's intelligence that he offered to take charge of his education; and finding that his *protégé* justified his anticipations, placed him on the foundation at Westminster, chose him in due course for a studentship at Christ-Church, and finally recommended him for a bishopric. As headmaster of Westminster, Carey showed remarkable administrative tact, and firmness without severity, which gave him great influence with his boys. He was an especial favourite of the Duke of York, who used to recommend all his military friends to send their sons to Westminster. This might partly account for the fact that the school in those days became the great nursery for the army. The Duke of Wellington is said to have declared that Westminster men infallibly made good officers. The names of Paget, Somerset, Cotton, Bentinck, Byng, Lennox, Cadogan, Wilson, and many others, were as well known in the battlefields of the Peninsula as in the cloisters of St Peter's. A few years ago, five out of eight field-marshals (two of the remaining three being princes) were Westminster men—Lords Anglesea, Combermere, Strafford, and Raglan, and Marshal Grosvenor; and it was remarked that when our troops embarked for the Crimea, the commander-in-chief, the chiefs of the artillery and cavalry, and the quartermaster-general, had all been educated at the school.* But it would be a great mistake to suppose that, in the presence of this military spirit, the more liberal studies were neglected. Carey's were perhaps the palmy days of Westminster scholarship. He encouraged a system of what was called "private studies," probably peculiar to the school. It will be best described in the words of one of his most distinguished pupils. Every boy in the sixth and in the next form below—the shell—was expected to apply for permission to read, out of school hours, some particular books :—

"The head-master watched over this private study. . . . He went round every Saturday with a pen in his hand, and made marks on the pages of the book which the boy was reading, comparing it with a similar entry made the previous week. He had the boys up one by one for examination. It came round to each boy once a-

---

* Lord Raglan, Sir W. Cator (Artillery), Lord Lucan, and subsequently Lord George Paget (Cavalry), Lord de Ros (Quartermaster-General). The motto of Westminster men in those days might have been "*Ubique*." An English officer, on his return from India, came down the Nile, and at Thebes had to procure the *visé* of the Bey of the district. After some preliminary compliments on each side through the dragoman, the Bey intimated that he had been in Europe, and hinted at some former acquaintance with his visitor. The latter saw only a stranger in the bearded Oriental before him. "Why," said the Bey at last, in good English, "surely you are little S——, whom I remember in the Fourth at Westminster?" It was so; but the Bey's own history was an unhappy one.

fortnight, and he questioned him for about three-quarters of an hour, in order to ascertain whether the progress which he professed to have made was real and true. He conducted the examination entirely himself; and the result was that at the time I was a boy there I had read the 'Æneid' of Virgil twice over, the 'Iliad' and 'Odyssey' of Homer twice over, Xenophon's 'Anabasis,' the 'Cyropædia' of Sophocles, about twelve of the tragedies of Euripides, the 'Tusculans' of Cicero, and Sallust. You will probably think that those who did that were unusually willing readers, but I assure you there were many such cases. . . . It was but an average case, showing the working of the school."*

Dr Carey's advent to power was marked by a serious disturbance, consequent upon the suppression of certain acts of licence which had grown out of the celebration of the 5th of November; but he put down the incipient rebellion with a firm hand, and the remainder of his reign was peaceful, and on the whole successful. He became Bishop of Exeter, and subsequently of St Asaph; and Page, the under-master, succeeded, but only lived five years to enjoy his promotion.

Dr Goodenough (a very accomplished scholar), and then Dr Williamson, followed, the latter having been a town-boy—the first instance for two hundred and fifty years of a head-master who had not been a King's scholar. It was now that the school began to decline rapidly in numbers and reputation. In Carey's time there had been an average of about 300 boys; the numbers fell off in the later days of Goodenough. Dr Williamson found 226 in 1828; in 1841 there were only 67. Mr Liddell, now Dean of

* Public Schools Report, Westm. Evid., 887, 891.

Christ-Church, raised them to 147 on his accession to the head-mastership in 1846, and they have continued at about the same point under his successor, Dr Scott. Several causes contributed to this decline. That there were faults in the internal administration is undeniable; but these chiefly affected the boys on the foundation. The decrease in the number of town-boys was partly due to the influence of fashion, which had now set in with a full tide towards Eton and Harrow. The late Duke of Richmond continued to send his sons there to the last; but for nearly half a century the names of most other noble families who were once hereditary Westminsters have disappeared from the roll. The rapid progress of building, which had covered with houses even the swamp in Tothill Fields, where the future Duke of Richmond used to shoot snipes in the present century, had no doubt confined the boys more to the limited area of Dean's Yard, though Vincent Square was still preserved as a playground; but, in point of fact, modern improvements have very much opened the immediate neighbourhood of the college, and swept away some of the worst of the old localities. What these were may be imagined from the complaint of Cumberland, when boarding as a town-boy, in 1748, with a private gentleman in Peter Street, two doors out of College Street, that he was kept awake at night "by the yells and howlings of the crew of depredators that infested that infamous quarter." Nor, perhaps, was there really much to regret in the free range of Tothill and Battersea Fields, which had been open to the past generation; though the ditches which intersected the latter certainly formed an admirable leaping-ground, and it was no objection to schoolboys that they were stagnant and green. St David's Day was the great anniversary of ditch-leaping, and such as were too wide to leap the boys would actually swim. The great ditch known as "Spanking Sam," immortalised by "Bingham's* leap," is still fondly remembered by old Westminsters. But the days were now past when Colman could drive his donkeys in Tothill Fields, or Lord March keep a covey of *tame* ducks there in a pond, upon which to practise the new art of shooting flying. The truth is, that the choice of a school is very much a mother's question; and, as the late Sir James Graham (who was fag to the said Lord March) told the House of Commons, the ladies object to the situation of the school. They think that London— and Westminster is now London—is an unwholesome atmosphere for their sons. They have a "prejudice," as one of the masters loyally phrases it, in favour of country air. They shudder also at the hardships of the college juniors, and fail to see in them that preparation for the roughing of actual life which used to be considered one of the advantages of a public-school training. As a stanch old Westminster puts it—"Spartan mothers are not to be found under modern crinoline." One Westminster witness, however, gave it as his opinion (which the Commissioners were bold enough to print), that this conjugal influence is "on the wane." Whether the old prosperity of the school could be recovered by its removal to the college estate at Chiswick, as has been suggested, or elsewhere into the country, is a point which discussion has as yet failed to settle, and upon which the best friends of the school are hotly divided.

* General Richard Bingham. The ditch was subsequently leapt by James Agar (brother to the present Earl of Normanton).

The place was certainly a rough nursery in the days of Carey and Goodenough, and the boys had the credit of being the most pugnacious young gentlemen in the kingdom. Not content with "feeling each other's might" by way of recreation, like the knights of the old Round Table, they waged battle with every "ski" who crossed Dean's Yard, then unenclosed. It was all done on the most honourable principles. If the outer barbarian was tall and stout, one of the bigger boys attacked him; if he was smaller game, a junior was selected, about his match in size and weight, and "fagged" to fight him. This reception of strangers, in fact, was not intended to be of a personally hostile character, but a national law and custom of Dean's Yard, to which all plebeians were subject. On the other hand, a boy could hardly go outside the gates without being attacked in his turn by some of the blackguards who inhabited "Thieving Lane" and the "Little Sanctuary"—purlieus which lay close to the Abbey, and are now happily swept away. If any real offence was given to the school, the discipline of the Pump was had recourse to, as in the ancient precedent of Mr Curll. So late as 1830, it was solemnly inflicted upon a very deserving object. A letter had been received by the captain of the school offering to secure for any senior a scholarship at Cambridge "for a consideration." The letter was answered in due course, and a personal conference suggested. The would-be vendor came to Westminster, and after some pretended negotiation, was invited to see the cloisters, where he was seized by the captain's orders, hauled under the pump, and held there until he was thoroughly well drenched. As he was making his escape, he met Dr

Goodenough, the ex-head-master, to whom he complained of the treatment he had received. A few words from the seniors explained the real state of the case, and the only comfort he received from the Doctor was, "Served you right, sir!" *

* The College Pump in Dean's Yard, alas! is never likely to be an instrument of justice again. Owing to the works of the Metropolitan Railway, or from some other cause, it has entirely failed of late. It was thus lamented in the Prologue of 1865:—

"Illa Hippocrene nostra, fons ille optimus,
Lymphis *Decani* qui rigabat *Arena*,
Qui vestram et proavûm toties sedavit sitim,
Jam siccus, eheu, deficiente aqua jacet."

CHAPTER V.

THE PLAY.

THE most interesting and peculiar feature of Westminster is, of course, the Play. Perhaps no old custom connected with Public Schools, dating from Queen Elizabeth's days, has gone on with so little interruption, and enjoys such undiminished vitality as the Latin Comedy —an entertainment perfectly unique of its kind—which is presented annually in the dormitory of St Peter's College. The Eton Montem and the Harrow Shooting Butts are things of the past. The old Shrewsbury Play (which during Ashton's head-mastership was probably on a more magnificent scale than the Westminster performance, and drew Elizabeth herself many miles to see it) gradually degenerated into ordinary English amateur theatricals, and even these have long been discontinued. The Latin plays with which the Universities were wont in former times to entertain their royal visitors, and which grave divines thought it not derogatory to compose for such occasions, would be voted "a bore" by the impatient spirits of our generation; though it may be doubted whether the fancy balls and other entertainments which have replaced them are not even more dreary affairs to many of the company, while certainly they are far less suitable to the associations of the place. But Terence and Plautus hold their own at Westminster; and if any one doubts whether they still preserve their old attraction for the audience, he will best solve the question for himself by getting a ticket for the next representation.

The performance of these Latin Comedies in the school at Christmas is enjoined by the Elizabethan statutes. But dramatic entertainments of some kind had probably been customary at Westminster, as at Eton and at Winchester, before that date. The preference of Terence's pure Latinity to the barbarisms of medieval dramatists is due to the good taste of Nowell, who, when head-master, introduced the use of the book into the school, five days in the week, "for the better learning of the pure Roman style." The statute also required that the master of the choristers should take care that his scholars presented an English play at the same time; but this practice, if it ever prevailed, soon fell into abeyance. Once only, so far as any known dramatic records of the school extend, an English afterpiece followed the Latin Comedy: it was in 1727, when an adaptation of Molière's 'Scapin' was performed exclusively by the juniors and "second election." The little Prince William (better known afterwards as the Duke of Cumberland of Culloden), then only six years old, was present; and this performance of the younger boys was perhaps intended for his special amusement. English plays have been got up on some few other occasions, but these were probably quite independent of the statutory custom. Dryden's 'Cleomenes' was performed in 1697—most likely in compliment to the author as an old Westminster—when Lord Buckhurst spoke the prologue. Congreve's 'Mourning Bride' was put upon the stage in 1718; and in 1725, the town-boys, in rivalry of the histrionic triumphs of the King's scholars, acted 'Julius Cæsar' for four nights at the French Theatre in the Haymarket. The juniors in college, some few years ago, were in the habit of getting up an English farce on their own account, a week or two before the Play; and the town-boys occasionally did the same in the boarding-houses. This practice was put a stop to, owing to a boy having narrowly escaped being burnt to death in·woman's clothes at one of these latter performances.

But the legitimate drama at Westminster has always been a Latin Comedy. Of the earliest performances little or no record is to be found. Queen Elizabeth seems to have been present on at least one occasion, and to have contributed liberally to the "*cap;*" for she is recorded to have paid, in January 1564, the sum of £8, 6s. 8d. "for certain plays by the grammar school of Westminster and the children of Powle's." Barton Booth, the great tragedian, says that he took a part in one of Seneca's tragedies when a Westminster scholar in 1693. But from the beginning of the next century (since which time an almost continuous record has been recovered) four of Terence's comedies—'Andria,' 'Eunuchus,' 'Adelphi,' and 'Phormio'—have kept almost exclusive possession of the stage; of late years, in regular succession in the order named. Plautus has now and then been substituted; his 'Amphitryon,' 'Aulularia,' and 'Rudens' have had their turn; and, in 1860 and 1865, the 'Trinummus' was acted, and seems to have been now promoted to permanent rank in the series, vice 'Eunuchus,' cashiered in deference to modern scruples as being somewhat "*contra bonos mores.*" But Plautus will never be as popular, either with actors or audience, as his more lively and vigorous rival.

These performances take place just before the Christmas holidays. The play is repeated three times, on fixed nights in the second and third weeks in December. The acting has usually been of a much higher order than might be expected from the very limited choice of actors; for the cast is strictly confined to the forty scholars on the foundation. But the play has always been made a point of honour at Westminster; and immense pains have been taken, and are taken still, both by masters and boys, in the preparation. Practice, in this as in other things, makes perfect: the juniors have the opportunity, year after year, of studying the performance of their seniors, and are eager to emulate the popular heroes of the stage when their own turn comes. Details of stage business, and points in the dialogue, become traditional, and are handed down from generation to generation. Many of the old actors, who were stars in their little hour upon the stage, have long passed into oblivion; some few have been more fortunate in being preserved to fame in the notices of their contemporaries. The character of *Ignoramus* was so admirably performed in 1730 by George Lewis, that not only was a fourth night demanded, but the actor found his reward in the ambiguous compliment of being distinguished thenceforth from others of his name as "*Ignoramus* Lewis." At the first of these performances the young Duke of Cumberland was again pre-

K

sent.* The play was revived in 1747, and was again a great success. Hamilton Boyle (sixth Earl of Cork and Orrery) was the hero, and the whole performance was so good, that the scenes were left standing over the Christmas holidays, and an additional night was given after the return of the boys to school. The cast of the 'Phormio' of 1749 is remarkable for the well-known names which it contains. George Colman, the elder, soon to become famous in the real drama, was the *Geta*; George Hobart (brother to the Earl of Buckinghamshire, and afterwards president of the Italian Opera) played *Antipho*; and among the other actors were Samuel Smith, the future head-master, and Robert Lloyd, the eccentric but accomplished usher, whose clever Latin verses so often enriched future prologues and epilogues.† Garrick was present at the 'Andria' in 1765, and was so delighted with the acting of John Eckersall as the

* He seems to have been put forward at this time as the popular patron of schoolboys; he was present at the "Hunting of the Ram" at Eton in the same year, and at the Montem of the year following.

† He was the son of Pierson Lloyd, already mentioned as undermaster. He wasted brilliant talents, and lived a dissipated and improvident life, which ended early. His great friend and school-contemporary was Charles Churchill. These two, with Bonnell Thornton, George Colman, Joseph Hill, Cowper the poet, and one or two other Westminster men, composed the "Nonsense Club." Lloyd always hated his work as usher, and soon resigned it. He describes himself as—

> " Still labouring with incessant pains
> To cultivate a blockhead's brains;
> Still to be pinioned down to teach
> The syntax and the parts of speech;
> To deal out authors by retail,
> Like penny pots of Oxford ale."

The Oxford ale was certainly more to his taste. His Latin translation of Gray's 'Elegy' is very beautiful; a poem called 'The Actor' has also considerable merit. (See his Poems, London, 1774.)

comic slave *Davus*, that he presented him with a free admission to his theatre. He also highly complimented the actors in the 'Phormio' of 1769. In 1796, Robert Stevens, the present venerable Dean of Rochester, played *Euclio* in the 'Aulularia' with singular ability.

In more than one instance besides the Colmans, elder and younger, the mimic stage at Westminster either generated or encouraged a dramatic talent which developed practically in after life. If Busby himself did not go upon the public boards (which his enemy Bagshawe insinuated would have been his proper sphere), he was accused of having sent some of his pupils there, by the applause and encouragement which he bestowed upon their acting. Barton Booth, the cadet of an old Lancashire family (some of them were Earls of Warrington), had been intended for the Church, but his early dramatic triumphs in the dormitory of St Peter's fixed his future vocation. At the early age of fourteen his performance of *Pamphilus* in the 'Andria' was the delight of Busby's declining years. At seventeen he ran away from the school, and joined a company of strolling players in Dublin; to the intense mortification of his father, who had a horror of the stage, and declared that old Busby "had poisoned the boy with his dying breath." In his first public appearance, however, as *Oronooko*, he narrowly escaped a ridiculous breakdown; for the lamp-black on his face came off in streaks with his exertions, and nothing could have carried a young actor through such a trial but the good-humoured hilarity of an Irish audience, who applauded even more loudly than they laughed. He became subsequently a pupil of Betterton, and rose to be one of the most refined and classical of our English tragedians. Westminster men were proud of him. In a prologue to one of the annual performances which took place after he had established his fame, he was honoured with a special couplet as one of the rising celebrities of the school:—

> " Old Roscius to our Booth must bow;
> 'Twas then but art—'tis nature now.

Poor David Ross (not a King's scholar, however, but a town-boy), also took to the boards professionally, and was disinherited by his father in consequence. He reaped but poor compensation in a second-rate reputation as a comedian—a reputation which might, however, have been higher but for his improvidence and indolence. The lazy style in which he sometimes went through his part is satirised by his old schoolfellow and friend, Churchill, whose bitter verse spared no man for any thought of "auld lang syne":—

> " Ross—a misfortune which we often meet—
> Was fast asleep at dear Statira's feet."

It should not be forgotten that the difficulties in which Ross's own imprudence involved him were materially relieved by the generosity of an old Westminster schoolfellow—Admiral Barrington—who paid him for some years an annuity of £60. The gift was anonymous, and it was only by accident that the donor became known.*

Bridge Frodsham, of an old Cheshire family, of rather

---

* So the late Right Hon. Charles Wynn for many years paid an annuity to his old schoolfellow Robert Southey, when he stood in need of such help; which the poet accepted in the spirit in which it was offered, without any feeling of humiliation. These are not the only instances in which Westminster men have acted on the principle of their favourite author—" *Communia amicorum sunt inter se omnia.*"

later date, ran away from the school twice—the second time, like Booth, to join a company of strolling players. He acted at Leicester and at York, where he was known as "the York Garrick," and had a considerable provincial popularity. Such was his overwhelming conceit, that he employed his only interview with Garrick in giving him his own conception of the proper way to act Hamlet, to that great actor's considerable astonishment, though he recognised undoubted talent in his provincial rival.* In the case of another Terentian actor, the Hon. Thomas Twisleton, a friend and contemporary of Southey's at Westminster, a boy of great promise, and remarkably handsome, the histrionic tastes which were there called into play affected his future life in a different fashion. He fell in love with a young lady with whom he acted in some private theatricals during the holidays, and eloped with her instead of going back to school. He went out to the Colonies, and subsequently became Archdeacon of Colombo.

The boys were authors as well as actors. Ben Jonson was a pupil of Camden when head-master, but whether in his schoolboy days he gave any foretaste of his abilities as a dramatic writer does not appear. But Cowley wrote a masque called 'Pyramus and Thisbe' when he was but ten years old, and 'Constantia and Philetus' two years

* A contemporary satire (quoted by Tate Wilkinson in his 'Wandering Patentee') illustrates both his style of acting and his self-conceit:—

"With arms and legs outstretched like a Pantine,
Lo! Frodsham roars or whispers through the scene;
He rants, he splits the tasteless groundling's ears,
And Herod's self out-heroded appears;
Above mankind in his own mind he soars,
Himself the idol he himself adores."

later, which last he dedicated to Osbolston, as headmaster. So Charles Saunders, while yet a King's scholar, wrote a piece called 'Tamberlane the Great,' which was actually performed at Drury Lane Theatre, and also at Oxford before Charles II.

The College Theatre is fitted up at the further end of the long dormitory, some dozen beds having to be dismantled for that purpose. Where the unfortunate occupants retire to at night during the six weeks of preparation and performance is a mystery to all but the initiated. In former times some slept under the stage, which must have been uncomfortably close quarters; and even now a curious stranger, who peeps under the ascending flight of seats constructed for the audience, may see the limited amount of chamber furniture which contents a Westminster junior arranged here and there under the feet of an unsuspecting public. The pit and galleries will hold in all about 350 comfortably; but the issue of tickets is liberal, and sometimes nearly 500 contrive to squeeze in. Some kind of scenery appears to have been always in use, at least since the erection of the present dormitory; but it was of a very rude character, and the dresses were modern; it must be remembered, however, that the same bad taste prevailed on the regular stage, where Booth himself acted *Cato* in a full-bottomed wig. In the 'Eunuchus' it was usual for *Chærea*, who is described as being on garrison duty—"*custos publice*"—to appear in the full-dress uniform of an officer in the Guards. In 1758 a new set of scenes were given by Dr Markham, then head-master. They were designed by James Stuart—better known as "Athenian" Stuart—and represented, as now, a street or public place in

Athens, with "practicable" houses on each side. It was remarked as a singular coincidence, that Edward Salter spoke the prologue as captain on the first occasion of their use, and that his son enjoyed the same distinction fifty years afterwards, in 1808, when they made their appearance for the last time, and made way for a new set, supplied by the liberality of another head-master, Dr Carey. The very pretty scenery now in use (which was specially admired by the late Prince Consort) is from the designs of an "old Westminster" artist, C. R. Cockerell. The dresses, though their fashion underwent some change from time to time, continued to be more or less incongruous down to the days of Dr Williamson's head-mastership. He introduced the present classical Greek costumes, publishing at the same time a little treatise of considerable research upon the subject.* They were indebted for much of their richness and elegance, which improved from year to year, to the taste of Mrs Williamson, and of the ladies of succeeding head-masters, who have taken the greatest interest in the "Play."

On at least two occasions the comedy was enlivened by the introduction of a Latin song. In the scene in Terence's 'Andria' where Mysis takes up Glycerium's baby (who has always been one of the most popular comic characters at Westminster), Dr Smith assigned her a sort of nursery ditty,—a translation of Swift's "O my kitten, my kitten"—which was sung as she dandled the little stranger, to the great delight of the audience. In 1798, when the 'Rudens' of Plautus was performed, the fishermen in the second act sang a Latin glee, which was accompanied by one of the party, Robert Bligh, got up

* 'Eunuchus Palliatus.'

as a wooden-legged fiddler. The words were a liberal paraphrase of the old ballad, which begins—

> "Had Neptune, when first he took charge of the sea,
> Been as wise, or at least been as merry as we," &c.

It may perhaps be questionable how far a Latin jingle in the medieval style harmonised with the verses of Plautus; but there can be no doubt as to the cleverness of the adaptation.* It was from the pen of the well-known "Jemmy" Dodd, who was usher of the school for thirty-four years, and took great pains with the plays, composing several of the best prologues and epilogues. He was the son of a London actor, who is said to have adopted the stage as a profession from his own successful performance of *Davus* in the 'Andria' when a boy at some school in Holborn. Dodd was an intimate personal friend of the great Porson, and resembled him in some of his eccentricities as well as in his scholarlike tastes. The fine construing and rigid parsing of the text of the 'Iliad,' in which he drilled the fifth form for many years, is not yet forgotten by those who were under his rule. He was long known as one of the most convivial guests at the dinners of the Roxburghe Club, where he sang "Robin Hood" ballads with great applause.

The prologue to the Play has for many years been invariably spoken by the captain of the school, in full

* "O Neptune, si fecisses
    Maris undam vinum,
  Biberemus sicut pisces
    Laticem marinum.

"Hauserimus, tale nacti
    Gaudii suasorium.
  Piscatores pisces facti,
    Totum vas æquoreum.

"Piscatores, Piscatores,
    Vinum coronemus!
  Liberi feliciores
    Genio libemus!

"*Chorus*—Bene, Bene," &c.

—Lusus Alt. Westm., p. 178.

Queen's scholar's costume — black knee-breeches, silk stockings, buckles, and long bands. It is usual to introduce briefly the chief events of the year which have affected the interests of the college, the public honours won by distinguished scholars, or the death of any old Westminster of remarkable eminence. It was amidst rounds of cordial applause that the captain of the past year referred to the fact that the foremost places in Church and State were both then filled by Westminster men—as Archbishop of Canterbury and Prime Minister.* The epilogue is now always in Latin Elegiacs, and from time immemorial has been more or less in the comic vein, treating of some of the public events of the year, or some fashionable folly, in a burlesque travesty, often with admirable humour. Of late years it has assumed very much the form of a short Latin farce; the chief characters of the comedy re-appearing in a modern dialogue, in the costume of the day; and the clever way in which classical idioms are twisted to express modern English ideas is not the least amusing part of the performance. It would be difficult to give any fair idea of the humour by any selection of passages, and the reader who remembers enough of his Latin to enjoy it may do so thoroughly in the pages of the 'Lusus Alteri Westmonasterienses.'† The highest

---

* Archbishop Longley and Earl Russell.

† Some brief taste of their quality may find place in a note. It may be remembered that, in 1779, Mr Adam (M.P. for Gatton) challenged Fox in consequence of some remarks made by him in the House, touching, among other things, on the peculations of Government contractors. Fox was hit, but the bullet hardly penetrated his waistcoat. Adam hoped he was not much hurt. "Oh! no," said Fox; "there's no harm done—it was *only Government powder*." The Westminster Play that year was 'Phormio;' and the epilogue was

talent of the college has been employed ungrudgingly from time to time in these playful compositions. Vincent, Carey, and Page contributed frequently when head-masters; and others less publicly known, but not less elegant scholars, have gladly lent their wit and fancy to do honour to their old school.

The chief *dramatis personæ* are distributed amongst the seniors; the arrangement is in the main their own, but the list is revised by the head and under master, who make any desirable alterations in the cast. The minor parts are allotted to boys in the lower elections, who thus obtain an early familiarity with the College stage.

Let us borrow an old actor's vivid description of the scene "within College walls on a play night." The year is 1855, but the sketch would suit the 'Phormio' of 1864 equally well. A note has been added here and there for the benefit of outsiders.

"Juniors in every degree of heat, seniors in every

spoken by Phormio himself in the character of a contractor, who has tried gunpowder as well as other speculations :—

"Quæstus erat mihi pulvis tormentaria,—deque hoc
  Tranquillæ (Dis est gratia) mentis ero;
Namque ita curavi mistam cauteque paratam,
  Monstrum esset, cuiquam si nocitura foret.
Quin cum privatis certetur ubique duellis,
  Nemo perit—*pugnat pulvere quisque meâ.*"

The clever turn of the jest drew shouts of laughter alike from Westminster Whigs and Tories. In 1860, the 'Trinummus' was put upon the stage—the plot of which turns upon the sale of a house, under the floor of which a treasure is known to be concealed. In the epilogue, the Ghost of Busby is introduced, who hears with horror that there is a talk of removing the school into the country, and selling the old premises. He warns them that he has buried a *treasure* underneath. They proceed to dig to discover it,—and a gigantic ROD is found.

"En tibi Busbeius quas sepeliret opes!
  Aurea virga tibi est, portas quæ pandit honorum!"

degree of excitement, Third Election and Second Election in the stiffest possible white ties and the glossiest possible black trousers, the captain ruefully contemplating the knee-breeches in which it is his painful duty to encase himself, and vainly trying to look as if he had been accustomed to buckles all his life; Stoker* and his assistants giving an extra hammer at the green baize, the gasman attempting to get the lights into order, so as to avoid the violent crack which invariably takes place in the most pathetic scenes, as if the lamp-glasses were overcome by their feelings; add to this, College John † wandering about as if he were making himself generally useful (which he is not), and an occasional glimpse of the under-master with some final instructions for the captain, and farewell hints about the epilogue—and you will have some faint idea of the confusion worse confounded which heralds in a second night's performance.

"But at length Demipho has accomplished the more than Herculean feat of compressing the largest possible of legs into the smallest possible of fleshings, and a last brush has been given to the hair, and a last look has been taken at the tie, and Under-Elections walk up and down college with their caps on, and fancy they are seniors. A rushing noise is heard, as of a party of inebriated whirlwinds coming up college, and the *Di Superi* (in vulgar parlance 'the gods' ‡) make their ap-

---

* The college carpenter.

† The porter and factotum of college—invariably so called, whatever his name may be.

‡ The juniors, who occupy a back gallery. A proposal was made in 1792 to exclude them from the performance on the grand nights, which, however, was successfully resisted.

pearance. Now is the time to see the 'god-keeper'* in his glory, in kid gloves, cane, and commanding voice: 'Here, Jones, go up closer.—Room for three or four more in that corner—tumble up, Davis.' Now small boys, who have never before been in such an exalted position, get into a tremendous state of mind, and fail lamentably in their attempt to look as if they were enjoying themselves; now mightily triumphant look those lucky dogs who, through the favour of some monitor, have obtained the doubtful privilege of sitting on a couple of inches of window-ledge, with their legs dangling down as if on the verge of dissolving partnership with the bodies to which they belong, and setting up on their own account in the 'Ladies' Pit.'

. . . . . .

"And now, at about five minutes to seven, the gods go off into a succession of claps, the young old Westminsters stand up, and everybody in the house imitates their example, to welcome Mrs Headmaster, who appears leaning on the arm of the captain, who for this minute or two looks as happy as any one in knee-breeches and buckles can be expected to look.

. . . . . .

"Five minutes more, and the house again rises, and again the gods clap, and the band strikes up 'See the Conquering Hero comes;' and presently the conquering hero appears in the shape of the head-master and his party, though what connection of ideas associates those gentlemen, mostly in grey heads and expansive waistcoats, with conquering heroes or Judas Maccabæus, no

* A Third-Election boy, who acts as deputy monitor, and keeps the gallery deities in order.

one, as far as my knowledge goes, has ever yet discovered.

* * * * * *

"And now suppose that in the epilogue the usual number of allusions have been made, and that the old gentlemen have all gone off into the usual excited state of uproarious mirth, produced by the comprehension of a Latin joke (for their enjoyment of it is considerably heightened by finding they have not so utterly lost all their classical knowledge as to be unable to construe it); and suppose the worthy canon in the fifth row has understood every word, and translated all the more abstruse jokes aloud for the benefit of the surrounding company; and that Demipho has wound up with a very neat and appropriate *tag* of about twenty lines, and that he has made his bow, and the other characters in the epilogue have made their bows, very gracefully (with the exception of Chremes, whose wig came off), and that the curtain has fallen,—you must indeed be of a very phlegmatic temper if you do not join in the thunders of applause which echo from the gods above, and the old gentlemen below. All vie with one another in their energy; even the ladies join, and amidst a perfect hurricane of approbation the curtain rises once more, and all the characters appear in a tableau.

"A shout of 'cap, cap!' arises, and all available trenchers having been pressed into the service, the captain distributes them amongst the old Westminster portion of the audience, who present substantial proofs of their satisfaction. There is another immense clap (the band keeps up a running fire of 'God save the Queen' during all these proceedings), in the midst of which the head-master and his party pass out; then the 'young old Westminsters' carry the stage by storm, and shake hands frantically with all the performers. . . . Now also do all such as can manage to get hold of a friend to take them behind the scenes, indulge largely in sack-whey,* sundry glasses of which exquisite compound are also conveyed to the ladies, who only want 'a little, just to taste'—but find that taste so satisfactory that they finish their glass."†

The sum collected in the 'cap' has frequently amounted to above £200. After discharging all expenses of the play, the surplus is divided among the performers. But as these expenses have a natural tendency to increase rather than diminish, while the number of old Westminsters present is necessarily fewer than in the more prosperous days of the school, the balance has of late been now and then on the wrong side.

An attempt has more than once been made to suppress the Play, on the ground of the immorality of Terence's Comedies. It would be out of place to discuss such a question here; it may be enough to say that the acting copies are now judiciously castigated, and that few who have witnessed one of these representations would wish to see them discontinued. The performance was actually suspended, out of deference to what was supposed the popular sentiment, in 1846; but the strong memorial sent up next year (headed by the name of the Archbishop of York) against the change, has probably settled the point for some time. Independently of the familiar

---

* The orthodox drink, by immemorial usage, on play nights.

† 'The Westminster Play: its Actors and its Visitors.' Ginger, Westminster, 1855. (By G. Lavie, Esq.)

acquaintance which a boy must gain, in thoroughly getting up a play of Terence, with the most elegant form of colloquial Latin, it is fairly argued that it encourages a wholesome confidence and readiness in the actors, and has a tendency to form good readers and speakers. Sir Robert Phillimore's evidence on this point before the late Commission was decided and emphatic:—

"Such boys as took part in the play soon got accustomed to speak with great fluency. Everybody knows that the Westminster play was always well sustained and acted; and Lord Granville once said that he never understood Terence until he saw the plays acted by the Westminster boys. It was not more the discipline of the boy's mind, which resulted from the study of the play, which was advantageous to him, than the readiness in speaking and replying which it produced. Dr Hawtrey, when Provost of Eton, often said, 'I wish I could get Eton boys to speak as well as the Westminster boys do;' and I have always attributed that fluency and readiness to the discipline and training which the boys undergo in practising the speaking of the lines which they have to repeat at the play."

The college being a royal foundation, the play has always been stopped when a death has recently occurred in the royal family. Such was the case in 1760, on the death of George II.; of the Duke of York, in 1767; Prince Alfred in 1782; and the Princess Amelia in 1786; and at the beginning of George III.'s last illness in 1810. In the memorable '45 there was no play, owing to the panic caused by the advance of the Pretender to Derby. In the year 1791 there was something like a rebellion in the school (under Dr Vincent), and the performance was omitted in consequence. The seniors of 1817 and 1818 were especially unfortunate; there was no performance either year, in consequence of the deaths of the Princess Charlotte and the Queen.

Royal visitors have not been unfrequent. The late Duke of York for many of the last years of his life never missed a play. William IV. was present in 1834, and contributed £100 to the "cap;" and the late Prince Consort attended three performances.

The recitation of the epigrams, which takes place at the annual dinner on Monday in election week, when the electors and such old Westminsters as choose to attend meet together in the College Hall, is another classical exercise peculiar to the school. The subjects for the year are given by the under-master; the theses being usually some terse Latin adage or commonplace, which (or its contradictory) is to be illustrated by some dozen, more or less, of elegiac verses. It is usual for each of the seniors to recite two epigrams, and each "third election" and certain of the juniors, one. These are not necessarily of their own composition; the under-master is considered responsible for the production of a sufficient number which will bear criticism, and he receives contributions, as in the case of the epilogues, from his fellow-masters and from Westminster celebrities of bygone days. After the recitation, a cap is handed rounded to the guests, and the silver which is put into it becomes the property of the reciters. In these *jeux d'esprit*, as in the epilogues, the popular subjects of the day are good-humouredly satirised.*

* For instance, on a late occasion the theses were, "Fors sua cuique loco est," and "Beatus vulnere," treated both affirmatively and negatively. Count Bismark, John Bright, "The Lambeth Casual," and College John, were all utilised—not always in the most complimentary manner—by the writers.

CHAPTER VI.

FAGGING.

THE system of fagging among the Westminster scholars has always been objectionably severe. Its terrors have been exaggerated by indignant parents, and by those rose-water school reformers who would substitute moral suasion for birch, and regulate schoolboy life by the etiquette of polite society; and, on the other hand, disagreeable facts are ignored and explained away by loyal enthusiasts, with whom one cannot help strongly sympathising, who will see nothing wrong in the old school. But from Taswell's day (and most likely long before), down to the day of the late Royal Commission, the life of a junior in college for his first year has been fairly defined as a "servitude." It is admitted so to be by the stern old Latin phrase still in use, when the "captain of the election" into college (the boy who stands first in the examination, and who has the privilege of exemption from the common lot which awaits all his companions) is admitted by the seniors in conclave assembled to the privileges of freedom in the words, "*Esto liber, cæteri servi.*" Much of the hardship of a junior's life arises from the fact of the whole body of collegers being lodged in one large dormitory, and confined to very close quarters for a considerable proportion even of the day-time, so that a younger boy is hardly ever out of the reach of those who have a claim upon his services: and to this must be added the lamentable deficiency in the staff of servants. This is a point upon which the authorities of the school itself are not responsible. Being really a dependency of the collegiate church of St Peter, all the domestic arrangements are subject to the control of the Dean and Chapter; and although this body have of late years shown a spirit of greater liberality in many improvements which have been made, especially under Dean Buckland, yet for many generations they proved but grudging guardians to their scholars; looking upon the school, as was very fairly suggested by a witness before the late Commission, "somewhat as a nuisance, which it was desirable to abate as much as possible." It is not without reason that the Commissioners, in their Report, "invite the serious attention of the Dean and Chapter" to the manifest need of additional servants to relieve the junior boys from some of the menial offices which almost of necessity fall to their share.

At the date of the Commissioners' visit, each junior in turn had to call his masters—it might be even so early as four o'clock, for Westminster boys have a habit (very little known at other schools) of early reading, at times when preparation for the Play interrupts the regular work, or when an examination is impending; he had then to rake the cinders out of the grates, to light the fire, and boil water for an early breakfast. A considerable part of what ought to be his leisure hours had to be spent in going on his master's errands, or on "station"—that is, either attending the games in the "Green" in Great Dean's Yard, or, on a rainy day, in college. One junior—called the "watch"—has to remain in college during play-hours to answer inquiries, receive messages, and so forth, performing, in fact, the duties of a servant; and another again is detailed for duty during the regular school hours, who remains on guard at the door of the college as a sentinel, to see that no suspicious characters find their way in. This functionary is known as *monos**—i. e., *monitor ostii*; and no doubt the office has a very high antiquity, if that is any satisfaction to the modern holders. There was an officer of the same kind among the college-boys at Winchester, who bore a similar name—*ostiarius*. But in point of fact, the post of *monos*, carrying with it, as it used to do, an entire exemption from all lessons for the day, was apt to be only too popular with the idly disposed among the juniors. In the evenings, after locking-up, which in winter is at a quarter before six, a junior is liable to a good many interruptions, which may be—and certainly have been in past days, if not now—made very harassing and vexatious by the caprice or tyranny of the seniors. No tea was provided as a regular meal; only a supper of cold meat, bread and cheese, and beer in hall; and a Westminster senior, perhaps for that reason, affected tea to an extent which would

* These school terms are terrible stumbling-blocks to biographers and their printers. Even Frederick Reynolds (the dramatic author), though himself a Westminster boy, allows this officer's name to be printed *Minos* in his amusing Memoirs—"I was stopped on my entry into school by the Minos." The title of "Conduct," by which the chaplains of Eton College are known, was for many years ludicrously misprinted by the successive editors of Horace Walpole's Letters, who make him talk of "standing funking over against a *conduit* to be catechised."

shock that mysterious brotherhood who advertise themselves as the "Anti-teapots." Twice—and occasionally three times—a fag would probably have to prepare this cheerful beverage to solace his master's studies through the long winter's evening, happy in the reversion of the teapot for his own benefit. From about 8 o'clock to 10 (the hours vary with the season of the year) he is supposed to be at work, in a sort of common-room assigned to the juniors collectively, preparing his lessons for next day; but the call of "*Election!*" which signifies that the services of one of the junior election are required by one of the seniors, used to be frequent enough to be a very serious interruption. It is admitted that these demands upon a junior's time have commonly been such that "a boy who is tempted to be idle, as most of them are, finds very considerable difficulty in doing his work." In order to check these interruptions as far as practicable, a late regulation has made all fagging unlawful during these evening hours of work.

But of all the services required of a Westminster junior, the most remarkable and original is that which was exacted of him up to the date of the Public Schools Commission, and which supposed him to be a walking treasury of small conveniencies for his seniors' use in and out of school.* He wears, as has been said, a college waistcoat of peculiar pattern; and the pockets of that waistcoat used to contain a store which would have put to shame even the miscellaneous treasures which our

---

* The present head-master has, amongst other judicious reforms, abolished this custom *in toto*. The duties of "Monos" are now almost nominal; "Watch" is only on duty during the summer half-year; no doors are opened, and no juniors allowed to get up, until 6 A.M.; and only one general tea-making is now allowed in hall.

great-grandmothers were wont to produce from the depths of some similar receptacle. He had to carry about with him, and produce instantaneously upon legal demand (the items are recorded in the published Evidence), two penknives, two pieces of india-rubber, two pencils, two pieces of sealing-wax, two pieces of pen-string, two "dips" (little globular ink-bottles), two dip-corks, two wedges, two pieces of gutta-percha (for putting on the points of foils), and any number of pens. Besides this, he had to carry with him into school a portfolio containing a sufficiency of "quarterns" of paper. All or any of these articles he was supposed to supply, upon requisition, to any boy of the "upper election." He was not expected, indeed, to furnish all this miscellaneous stationery out of his own private purse; for his lawful senior, and commonly his second and third elections as well, allowed him to obtain from the booksellers' the usual half-year's supply in their names: so that in fact he was little more than the steward of his master's goods in this respect. But it may be imagined that such a responsibility was rather troublesome.

The roughnesses of Westminster life have, however, been considerably smoothed of late years. The dormitory in old times was like nothing known to mortal schoolboys except Long Chamber at Eton. It was all one long open room where the whole forty boys slept in public—the juniors in not much greater comfort than the "casuals" in a modern Union. The windows were continually broken, and never repaired but during a vacation. In the winter time the atmosphere was consequently often at freezing-point; and this was taken advantage of by such seniors as were given to vigorous exercise, to order the fags out of bed, when a frost had set in decidedly, to pour water down the middle of the room so as to insure a practicable slide by the morning: the advance of science had even taught them to use *boiling* water, as freezing more rapidly than cold. This same floor was on one occasion converted into a draught-board. It was chalked out into large squares, and on each square a junior was stationed: two of the seniors, standing on an adjoining table, played a game at draughts with these human pieces; and when a "king" was made, his representative had to carry, by way of crown, a small boy upon his shoulders. The beds were not luxurious at the best; and did not impress visitors very favourably. When George IV., as Prince of Wales, came to the Play, and passed along the dormitory, he said to the master who escorted him—"You don't mean to tell me, sir, that Arthur Paget ever slept in one of those beds?"* But a junior was often obliged to lend his own pillow to improve his senior's accommodation, and to content himself

---

* The rudeness of the sleeping accommodations served to point an epigram more than once;—*e. g.*,

"Hæ latebræ dulces. (1806.)

"Sponda, torusque rudis, pannus lacer unus et alter,
   Pro velo lodix squallida, turpe toral;
Quàm tamen hæc dulces nobis immunda suppellex
   Efficiat somnos, vos meminisse reor:
Tu certè nòsti quàm sit, Pater optime, nobis
   Difficile ex isto surgere mane toro."

"Inest sua gratia parvis. (1810.)

"Hospes si nostrum visat quis forte cubiclum,
   Horret, qualis odor quàm miserique tori!
Infelix, qui non sentit quæ gaudia præstet,
   Quantas delicias iste olor, iste torus;
Iste meus longo jam fecit lectulus usu,
   In nullo ut metuam jam recubare toro."

with the most convenient log he could pick up out of the firewood. Rats at one time almost disputed the right of occupation. Leather braces had to be hung up somewhere out of reach, or there was only a mangled remnant and a buckle or so to be found in the morning. A nobleman now living awoke one night with a rat hanging to his ear; and it is well remembered that a present Archbishop, missing his surplice just before early prayers, found one small corner of it sticking out of a rat-hole, and thus barely rescued it, in such condition as may be guessed, from these indiscriminating marauders. They furnished sport for their enemies, of course, in their turn. Hunts, like those which Porson remembered with such gusto in the Eton Long Chamber, enlivened the nights at Westminster. Traps of all kinds were set; and one ingenious sportsman contrived a small battery of brass cannon, in front of which the victims were tempted by baits of toasted cheese.

The feeding arrangements, until recent improvements took place, were not more satisfactory than the sleeping. The statutes of course provided that the boys should be fed. But, as at Eton, there was no special ordinance about breakfast; that meal being a less formal one amongst all classes in old times than in the present, and very commonly consisting in a piece of bread and a cup of small beer taken standing. No breakfast at all was provided for the King's scholars at Westminster for many generations; up to the year 1846, they resorted for this purpose to the different boarding-houses of which they had been members before their election, and this cost them something like £30 a-year. In the case of any sick diet or nursing being required, they had to betake themselves to the same quarters. But even at the college dinners, the younger boys were never half fed. The recognised allowance was a sheep a-day; and the course of distribution in hall, not many years ago, was this: the four head boys had the saddle, the rest of the senior election the legs; the third election had the shoulders and neck; and the second election and juniors sat looking at a vacant expanse of coarse huckaback, making circles on the table or the pewter plates with their two-pronged forks, till the more fortunate were called up by their seniors to receive a plateful of broken meat, such as might be given to a Newfoundland dog. It was a high privilege to be handed a leg-bone or a shoulder-blade by a senior when he had done with it; and often a boy got no dinner at all. This again, notorious as it was to the authorities as well as to the boys, served repeatedly as the popular point in an after-dinner epigram.* The allowance of meat was supposed to furnish a supper as well, and a joint of some kind was usually reserved for that meal for the seniors; but a junior rarely saw any meat at supper. It is not to be wondered at that this should have led to a considerable expenditure of pocket-money outside the college walls, or that all kinds of extempore meals were cooked by the dormitory fires. Most varieties of cookery which a gridiron will accomplish are pretty well known to all schoolboys; punch made in a washing-basin (ladled out with a tea-cup tied to a toasting-fork) may have been enjoyed elsewhere; but a batter-pudding boiled in a stock-

---

* "Carnem Prima vorat classis; sine jure Secunda
Jus omne; omne sibi Tertia sumit olus;
Interea mensae qui accumbit Junior imae
Vix aurâ infelix vescitur ætheriâ."
—Epigr. 74, Lus. Westm. See also Epigr. 123.

ing-foot was perhaps a delicacy peculiar to Westminster. The result of the hardships which had become inseparable from an initiation into college life was, that a place on the royal foundation—an invaluable boon, as it should have been, to a boy of gentle birth and humble means— was understood to imply an ordeal to which few parents had the hardihood to subject their sons. In some cases a boy broke down under it, and had to be removed. From 1841 to 1847 the scholars were below the statutable number, and in one year there were no less than seventeen unfilled vacancies.

The boarding-houses, where those boys who are not on the foundation are lodged, had always affected more comfort in their domestic arrangements than was to be found in college. What this comfort amounted to, after all, may be gathered from the story told to Her Majesty's Commissioners by an old Westminster witness:—

"I remember hearing of the present Lord Mansfield's brother being very ill in one of the boarding-houses, and his mother, Lady Mansfield, coming there to see him. There was only one chair in the room, upon which the poor sick boy was reclining, and a friend who was with him was sitting on the coal-scuttle. When Lady Mansfield entered the room, the lad who was sitting on the coal-scuttle got up, and with perfectly natural politeness and good-breeding offered it to her ladyship to sit down upon."

CHAPTER VII.

SCHOOL CUSTOMS AND GAMES.

QUAINT old Latin formulæ still continue in use at Westminster, unchanged since its earliest foundation, giving a savour of ancient dignity to its everyday life which no loyal son of the house would willingly part with. While the school is at morning lesson, the *monitor ostii* watches the clock, and at half-past eleven comes to the monitor of school and announces the time. The monitor goes to the head-master's desk, makes his bow, and says, "*Sesqui est undecima.*" At a quarter to twelve he makes the further announcement, "*Instat duodecima.*" When twelve o'clock has struck, he says again, "*Sonuit duodecima;*" at a quarter-past twelve, "*Prima quarta acta est;*" at half-past, "*Sesqui est duodecima,*" at which welcome words books are shut, and the whole school is dismissed. The same formalities, with the necessary variations, are repeated during afternoon lesson. Before dinner the captain calls out two boys of the second election, one to say grace—"*Age gratias,*"—and the other to repeat the proper responses—"*Agite responsa;*" and when dinner is over, before grace again, he pays even the juniors the compliment of asking whether they have had enough—"*Satisne edistis et bibistis?*" to which the compulsory answer is made—in old times too often by hungry lips—"*Satis edimus et bibimus.*" Every night at ten o'clock the monitor of chamber gives the order for the juniors to put out the lights and go to bed—"*Extinctis lucernis intrate lectos.*" It is only within the last generation or two that the rule of speaking Latin exclusively, both by boys and masters, during school hours, has fallen into abeyance. It was certainly in force up to the end of Dr Vincent's head-mastership. One of the neatest of the English epigrams which have been preserved was recited in 1811; the thesis given was "*Crede colori,*" which was thus applied to his portrait as Dean, just painted by Owen:—

> "The tints on Owen's canvass spread
> Are truth itself, no mockery;
> I thought the living portrait said—
> '*Eloquere — eloquere.*'"

This was Vincent's usual exhortation to a boy to "speak out."

The old Shrove-Tuesday custom of tossing the pancake, though now peculiar to Westminster, is said to have been also formerly in use at Eton. The ceremony as at present performed is this. The cook, preceded by the verger, enters the large school, in full official costume, with the hot cake in the pan. He tosses it—or tries to toss it, for it is no easy feat—over the iron bar, which has been already mentioned as having once held a curtain screening off the upper school from the lower. If he succeeds he claims a fee of two guineas. There is a scramble among the boys, who stand on the other side of the bar, for the pancake, and if any boy can secure it whole, which seldom happens, he carries it up to the dean, who presents him with a sovereign. They also claim a right to "book" the performer (*i.e.*, hurl a shower of books at him) if he fails more than once. This right was liberally exercised in 1865, when the wrath of the school had culminated owing to repeated failures in that and the previous year. The exasperated cook replied to the attack with his only available missile—the frying-pan—and a serious row was the consequence. The battle is celebrated in a clever mock-heroic poem, in Greek Homeric verse, attributed to a high Westminster authority.*

With the great highway of the Thames passing almost by their very gates, it would have been strange if the Westminster boys had not taken to boating. But the spirited contests which of late years have enlivened the river are a comparatively modern introduction. In the golden age of Westminster a "racing eight" was unknown. It was not until 1829 that any race took place between this school and Eton. Their opponents were not the regular Eton eight, though most of their best oars were among the number, but a crew made up from the school by the Marquis of Waterford, who pulled stroke. The rival crews—"the Etonians in blue striped Guernsey frocks and dark straw hats with blue ribbon, the Westminsters in plain white shirts and white straw hats" (so say the authentic chronicles)—started from Putney bridge, pulled through Hammersmith bridge, and down again to Putney, Eton winning by about a quarter of a mile. They met next in 1831 at Maidenhead,

---

* ΜΑΓΕΙΡΟΠΑΙΔΟΜΑΧΙΑ. Printed, with an English version, in the 'Carmina et Epigrammata' for 1865.

where the light blue came in again first by about the same distance, in a course of six miles. In this last race the Westminster crew was composed entirely of collegers. In 1836, a mixed crew of collegers and town-boys were again beaten by the Etonians at Staines. But the next year Westminster won, for the first time, at Datchet, after a severe struggle; the excellent steering of their coxswain, Lord Somerton, contributing no little to the result. King William IV. was present, only a month before his death, and with his usual good-nature invited the crew to see Windsor Castle. Westminster won again, more easily, at Putney in 1842; in the four following races, up to 1847, the laurels were equally divided. The Westminster crews of 1843 and 1845 were the lightest that ever pulled in a race of such importance, averaging little more than nine stone in weight. Then followed a long interval, during which, for several reasons—amongst others, the disproportion between the diminished numbers of Westminster and the continual increase of Eton—these contests were altogether suspended. They were renewed in 1860; but the Eton crew were too powerful for their lighter opponents, and won easily, after a gallant struggle, in which the rowing of the Westminster stroke (J. H. Forster) was the admiration of both friends and foes, and gave promise of the reputation which he now enjoys as stroke of the "Leanders," and perhaps the finest oarsman on the London water. Eton had again easy victories in the two following years, since which time there has been no race. In 1865 a challenge was once more sent by Westminster; but Eton, having already been in training for the Henley Regatta, could not give up the time necessary for another preparation. They replied, therefore, by sending an invitation to the Westminster "eight" to join their procession to Surley on Election Saturday. The Westminster crew was received with great honour and hospitality, and with congratulations on a victory which they had very opportunely achieved over the Leander Club on the preceding day.

Cricket began at least as early as at any other public school. The first regular match of which any record or tradition remains was played in 1796 on Hounslow Heath against Eton. It is said to have taken place in defiance of express prohibition on the part of the authorities of both schools, and the elevens were made up, as they best might, out of such adventurous spirits as dared to "skip" roll-calls and "absence" for the purpose. Eton, who were the losers, attributed the fact to the want of their best men in consequence of these difficulties. In 1799 the two schools met again on " Old Lord's" ground. This match was not played out; Eton in their one innings got 47 runs, and Westminster had scored 13, with the loss of five wickets, when the stumps were drawn. It would appear, from the small amount of play, as though there had been again some difficulty or interruption. They played again next year, when Eton won easily in one innings. There is said also to have been a match in 1801, but of which no record seems now discoverable. Since that date Westminster does not appear to have played against any public school, except Charter-House. Amongst the players whom the school has produced none had a wider reputation than Edward Hussey, of the Kent Eleven—" Hussey of Ashford town"—whom Mr Lillywhite's annals celebrate in prose and verse. John Salter (famous as a wicket-keeper), George Parry, Walter Fellows, Edward Drake, and Charlton Lane, of later date; and more recent still, Balfour, Winter, H. E. Bull, and Ashley Walker, have shown that if Westminster sends comparatively few cricketers into the field, the few are good. Vincent Square, an enclosure of some ten acres, within easy reach, is the cricket-ground.

Football is popular at Westminster, as at all English schools, but is now played either in Dean's Yard or in Vincent Square; so that there is no risk of the shade of Addison being disturbed, as he complains that his living meditations once were, by the King's scholars playing football in the cloisters. They have long been shut out from this inappropriate playground, where the Dukes of Richmond of past generations used to rejoice in hoop-races "twice round from Mother Park's." Hoops are as unknown there now as Mother Park herself. Hockey, the great delight of the school-days of our forefathers, is also obsolete. Fives, played with racquets, is almost the only recognised game besides cricket and football, and there is a demand for more fives-courts. In lieu of the cloisters, the Dean and Chapter have made part of the crypt under the schoolroom into a sort of covered playground for the boys; but Westminster reformers maintain that the college gardens were intended at least as much for the benefit of the King's scholars as for the Canons' wives and children, and that they ought to be thrown open for their use, at any rate under some limitations. At present they have the right of entrance there, by immemorial custom, during the three or four days of "election."

CHAPTER VIII.

SCHOOL BUILDINGS AND SYSTEM.

The school-buildings are somewhat unfortunately situated, so far as a visitor's first impressions are concerned. As one passes through Little Dean's Yard, the two boarding-houses in the square, built in the worst style of the last century, have a dingy and gloomy look, and the place altogether shows more of the deformities of age than of its venerableness. But enter the noble schoolroom, nearly a hundred feet in length, and wide and lofty in proportion—the ancient dormitory built by the Confessor for the Benedictines*—with its fine old chestnut roof of later date, like that of Westminster Hall, and your impressions take at once a very different colour. There is perhaps no room in England so well adapted for its purpose. It has a solemn medieval tone, and yet is as light and airy as a modern gymnasium.

---

* "The east, west, and south walls of the school . . . still exhibit portions of the Confessor's masonry, into which more recent alterations have been ingrafted; while externally one of the original windows of the period still remains."—See Appendix to Scott's 'Gleanings from Westminster Abbey:' 'Further Remarks, &c.,' by Rev. T. W. Weare.

Here Busby taught and whipped with all his energies for half a century; and here Vincent paced the old boards in front of his boys, practising his own precept of "speaking out," as he rolled forth his "sounding Atticisms." The walls are as full of history as those of Nimrud—only easier to read. There stand the names of the old scholars of generation after generation; some cut by their own hands, others rescued from oblivion by some pious descendant, and set up legibly in due order, according to date, from the ancestor whom Busby flogged to the young King's scholar who went off to Christ-Church last year: goodly rows of Slades, Phillimores, Vernons, Mures, Madans, Dicks, Lowthers, and many more of the old loyal houses, of whom it is to be hoped that Westminster, in old Hebrew phrase, may "not want a man for ever." In no school, perhaps, has the hereditary tie been so strong; and it was only one remarkable expression of a widespread feeling, when William Dolben, in 1792, was brought to school by his father and grandfather, who both attended prayers in this room on the morning of his admission. It was until very lately the only schoolroom, and in it, as still at Winchester, all the forms were taught together. There was quite sufficient space for the purpose, even in the days when there were above three hundred boys in the school; the benches being arranged against the walls longitudinally in four tiers, still leaving a wide thoroughfare clear in the centre. Of late years two or three class-rooms have been added, in compliance with the modern preference for separate teaching; but many of Westminster's old scholars protest against this innovation, which is still resisted by the authorities at Winchester. There is much truth and good sense in the following remarks by one well known among their number:—

"It was a great and important feature in the old management, that the whole school and all the masters were every day in presence at the same time. The faces and voices of the latter were familiar to all the boys, and they were known to the masters and to each other. The daily proceedings of the whole body were patent and public; it was known who were high and who were low in the forms—who were shown up, and who were flogged. They met at the same hour in the morning, sat together all day, and rushed out like a torrent at the same hour in the evening. To this good custom, in no small degree, is owing that friendly and brotherly feeling and those social ties which bind old Westminsters together in every age and in every quarter of the world." *

At the end of this room there is a kind of semicircular apse, in which the "shell" form were formerly taught, and the shape of which is said to have given rise to this name, since adopted at several other public schools. Behind is the "French room," once known as the "birch room" (in which those useful implements were manufactured and used), where a bench is carefully preserved bearing the name of "John Dryden," no doubt cut by the poet himself, as the style of the letters corresponds with his date.

The Hall, built by Abbot Litlyngton about 1370, was the abbots' refectory, and though now seldom occupied by any guests but the King's scholars (except on election days and other festival occasions), was the common

* Some Account of Westminster School, &c., 1860. By James Mure, Esq.

dining-room in older times for all the members of the collegiate house. It is not the only instance in which the separation of the school from the chapter has worked to the manifest disadvantage of the weaker body. The present Dormitory was built in 1732, from a design given by an old Westminster, the Earl of Burlington. It superseded an older structure which stood in Great Dean's Yard, and is said to have been originally the granary or malt-house of the abbots. It is now parcelled off into separate boxes or "cubicles," an arrangement which checks many of the abuses to which juniors were liable under the old system, when privacy was out of the question. There were three fireplaces—" Upper, Middle, and Under fire"—each of which was the centre of a distinct social circle in winter time. These were the only Lares and Penates of a colleger before the present improvements of studies for the seniors and day-rooms for the lower boys were introduced. Here, each seated on their "locker"—and there was an important contest, under fixed regulations, at the beginning of each half-year, to get a locker near the fire—they read, or did not read, through the long winter evenings. Many were the curious relics and ornaments hung up by the seniors round this public hearth. Once, in the days, now happily gone by, when the carrying off door-handles and knockers was thought befitting sport for young Englishmen, a collection of trophies of this kind—spoils of the neighbouring *Volsci*—was to be seen suspended there, with this classical dedication—

" Æneas hæc de Danais victoribus arma."

It has been already observed that the election of boys

into the number of the forty collegers, though nominally open to free competition, had been—it may be assumed from the very earliest times—really a matter more or less of patronage on the part of the electors.* No doubt a boy of very eminent abilities would find some one or more of the electors inclined to choose him; for it may be as pleasant, and certainly is quite as creditable to an elector, to patronise genius as to favour his own relatives or friends. But on the whole, whether to get into college or be elected off to the university, it was almost necessary to have or make a friend among the seven electors. There was no disguise or secret about the matter; nominations were asked for, and promises made, as a matter of course. The election by open competition, which in the case of the scholars has now prevailed for some generations, is comparatively a modern reading of the statute, and is even now not considered by all Westminster men to be an unmitigated improvement. It is confidently asserted that the students whom the school sends to Christ-Church are not as much distinguished for scholarship now as when Cyril Jackson was dean, who openly avowed that he usually elected

---

* Instances might be multiplied to weariness. In 1604, King James I. "desires" one Moreton to be elected to Cambridge. In 1624, Secretary Conway recommends one Andrews, "according to promise," to be made a King's scholar; in 1628, he writes again in favour of Maplett. In 1662, King Charles II. himself begs a place from the Dean for a son of Capt. Underhill, who had fought in the royal cause. Next year, on the same ground, one George Cockes, who has a son in the seventh form, petitions his Majesty to desire him to be elected to Christ-Church. In 1713, Atterbury, then Dean of Christ-Church, writes to Bishop Trelawney about his son, with whose acting in the 'Phormio' he has been highly pleased,—"Your Lordship may depend upon it, *in whatsoever place he stands*, he shall go first of his election to Christ-Church"—and so he did.

those belonging to old Westminster and Christ-Church families. But it must be remembered, that the recent opening of the foundations at Eton and Winchester draws off many boys of promising talent, who might otherwise be attracted by the liberal bounty of Westminster.

While the social position of a scholar at Westminster entails no sort of inferiority, his solid advantages are very considerable indeed. By the operation of some very wholesome and necessary reforms, he now gets his board (as ought always to have been the case) almost entirely free, although he has still to pay a sum of seventeen guineas a-year for his education.* There can be no question but that this is an abuse which requires to be at once remedied. It is implied by the statutes that the education of the scholars should be entirely gratuitous, and that it should be covered by the stipends assigned to the masters. But while the revenues of the Chapter have very much increased, the surplus seems to have been regularly divided among the governing body, while the stipend of the masters has remained very nearly stationary. The head-master at present receives from the college estates something under £40; a sum which might have made him "passing rich" in the days of Elizabeth, but which is ludicrously insufficient now. There is evidence that the system of receiving fees from the Queen's scholars began at least as early as Dr Busby's time; but these fees were then small, and were no doubt received (as in the similar case of the Winchester scholars) in the way of presents: time, the great nursing mother of abuses, has ripened this system into a fixed

* The whole cost to a Queen's scholar is now about £31 per annum.

charge for every scholar of a sum about equal to what is paid under the head of tuition by *non-foundationers* at Rugby or Shrewsbury. An energetic protest was made upon this point by the father of a Queen's scholar elected in 1860, who went so far as to refuse to pay the sum at all, until informed that his son "would be removed from the foundation" in default; the Chapter pleading the sanction of the Queen, as visitor, to the charge in question. He then paid under protest, and applied to the Home Secretary "to be informed what her Majesty really did sanction;" and in reply was referred to his solicitor. The Royal Commissioners most properly recommended that in future "the Chapter should take upon themselves the whole cost of the tuition of the Queen's scholars," such a course appearing to them to be "consistent with, at least, the spirit of the statutes," although they "do not feel called upon to express any opinion" as to the legal statutory obligation.*

The elections now, both into college and to the universities, are perfectly open. To be a King's scholar, a boy must not be above fifteen years of age, and must have been a member of the school (as a town-boy) for not less than a year preceding. Then, if he thinks proper, he "stands out for college"—or, in the old Latin phraseology, becomes one of the *minores candidati*. He undergoes a very severe examination, called the "Challenge," the form of which must have been preserved from Queen Elizabeth's days, and is the last surviving relic of the old scholastic disputations; those tournaments of Latin and Logic, in which Queen Bess was

* Report, p. 169.

wont to reward a successful champion with a purse of gold from her own virgin hand, and her successor James distributed liberally the more economical guerdon of royal applause and criticism. For six weeks or more, in addition to the usual work of the school, this "challenge" goes on for some hours on fixed days in the week, in certain portions of authors which have been previously set and prepared; each candidate being assisted by one of the seniors whom he chooses for his "help"—who acts, in short, as his special private tutor for the occasion, and to whom, if successful, he makes a present of books. The candidates question each other in turn, according to an elaborate but well-understood system, the head-master sitting as moderator to decide on the fairness of the questions and the correctness of the answers, and lose or gain places each day accordingly; the "helps" standing by to "watch the case" for their "men." A keen competition between two boys who were closely matched has been known to last, with little interval, from early morning to nine o'clock at night. Those who stand at the head at the conclusion of the last challenge are elected into college, according to the number of vacancies. The "captain" of election —the boy who gains the first place—has the privilege of being almost entirely exempted from the fagging incidental to his junior year, and has his name painted on the election board in gold letters. These tablets, fixed up in the dormitory, go back as far as 1629; and among the names of the "captains," besides Lord Mansfield, as already mentioned, may be read those of Markham, Warren Hastings, Cyril Jackson and his brother the Bishop, Randolph (Bp.), Abbot (Speaker), Longley, &c.

The captain has also the perilous honour of being "chaired" on the college ladder, and carried round in that dignified position to pay his respects to the dean and the canons who may be in residence.

Sometimes, under the old system, the severity of the trial had this bad effect, that after the strain was over and the places finally awarded, the successful candidates were apt to relapse into idleness. For the places thus gained remained virtually unchanged during the four years of college life, and each moved off to the universities in order of seniority. Under recent regulations, however, boys who are persistently idle are formally degraded. The expenditure of time which the contest involves, both on the part of master and scholars, is still an admitted drawback. On the other hand, the system has its advantages. The connection between the seniors and those to whom they act as "helps" is good for both: a greater amount of work seems to be got out of the younger boys than could be secured by any other system of "private tuition," for the young tutors are very strict indeed, and do not spare a practical stimulus if required; while they themselves are at the same time benefited by having to keep up their knowledge of grammar. But perhaps the greatest advantage of all is that it gives a boy in some measure the training so valuable in after-life, and in which most public schools, and even the universities themselves, have grown lamentably deficient—the habit of bringing out acquired knowledge aptly and readily on the spur of the moment, of putting questions and expressing answers with ease and clearness, not upon paper, but to a living and speaking opponent. The "challenge" is so popular with all Westminster men, young and old, that even the most ardent school reformers shrink from suggesting its abolition.

The King's scholars remain in the school four years, their place in college being now subject to change every year by examination. At the end of this time they become, if they please, *majores candidati*, and are elected by competitive examination to the two universities. There are now three studentships to Christ-Church of the annual value of £120 each,* and three exhibitions (they are no longer "scholarships") to Trinity Cambridge of the value of £40; the holders of these latter, however, have generally a second exhibition of £40 or £50 awarded in addition. The boys who stand first at this examination have now their choice between Oxford and Cambridge.

There are many other customs which must have continued unchanged from a very early date, and which have a pleasant old-world formalism about them. There are still three monitors besides the "captain" (*monitor monitorum*), each having special duties, which, however, they interchange week by week. There is, 1. The monitor "of school," whose duties are connected entirely with the school work. 2. "Of chamber," whose chief business is to sit during the evening in the large room where the juniors now prepare the lessons for the next day, to see that all are busy (or at least decently quiet), and that they have their lights out and go to bed at ten. 3. "Of station"—*i.e.*, virtually of play-hours—

---

* A munificent benefaction from Dr Carey, in the award of the Christ-Church authorities, raises these studentships in many cases to as much as £200 per annum.

the juniors being expected to remain "on station," in college for the short intervals after breakfast and after dinner, and at other times in the playgrounds (the "Green" in Dean's Yard or Vincent Square, according to the time of year or the game that happens to be in season); except on decidedly wet days, when "station" is always in college. These officers are formally appointed by the head-master in school, who publicly instals them by giving a rod into their hand, with a few words of charge; and this rod is always carried by them when on duty in school as an ensign of office. Whenever a monitor has occasion to address a master officially, the latter always removes his cap and remains uncovered until the communication is over.

Besides the regular weekly half-holidays, there are others specially granted, known as "Early" and "Late Plays." The latter, given by the head-master at his discretion, consist in the remission of all school work after eleven A.M. But an "early play"—when school is "up" at nine—is a much more formal indulgence, accorded by very ancient custom only to the personal request of some visitor of distinction. St David's Day (March 1st) and St Patrick's (March 17th) have always been holidays of this class: for the former, the late and the present Sir Watkin Wynn have always come down to Westminster; and for the latter, the late Marquess of Lansdowne (as an Irish peer) and Sir Everard Home. The custom, even now observed on some occasions, was for the visitor's arrival at the gate to be formally announced to the head-master by *Monos*, who received a "tip" for his services. The master at once "came down school," and reappeared through the great door, accompanied by the hero of the day, who was received by the boys with great demonstrations of welcome, expressed by the vigorous rapping of books upon the desks. Both knelt down side by side, while the "monitor of school," kneeling immediately in front of them, proceeded with the usual school prayers. The visitor then "begged a play," which was granted. The applause was renewed, and acknowledged by a bow; after which the whole of the boys rushed joyously down school, the masters following in more grave and stately fashion. The visits of the "King of North Wales" were doubly popular, since he presented every Welsh boy with a sovereign—a custom which the present baronet liberally continues.

The highest form in the school was originally called the "Seventh," as was also the case at Eton; and in both schools it consisted, with rare exceptions, exclusively of the senior King's scholars. This arrangement was altered about 1840, and the forms are now numbered thus: Sixth, Remove, two "Shells," three Fifths, two Fourths, and two Thirds—these two last forming the "Under School," of which the under-master has the distinct charge. There are, besides, four assistant-masters.

When a boy is first placed in the school, he is attached to another boy in the same form something in the relation of an apprentice. The new boy is called the "Shadow," the other the "Substance." For the first week the Shadow follows the Substance everywhere, takes his place next to him in class, accompanies him as he rises or falls, and is exempt from any responsibility for his own mistakes in or out of school. During this interval of indulgence, his patron is expected to initiate him in all the work of the school, to see that he is provided with the necessary books and other appliances, and, in short, to teach him by degrees to enter upon a substantial and responsible existence of his own.

The "silver pence"—the small money rewards recognised in the old "customary" which has been already given at length, and which were the pride of Westminsters in Cowper's day*—are still continued. The coins are furnished to the school by the Queen's almoner in their unmilled state, prior to their issue as currency. Some are given by the head-master every week, and are valued quite as much as more substantial prizes. Silver money is also furnished by the college steward to the guests at the Election dinners, that they may be prepared to reward the epigrams; but this is ordinary coin of the realm.†

The King's scholars have a very ancient privilege (said to have been granted by Queen Elizabeth) of attending the debates in the House of Commons, where they are admitted, as of right, to the seats at the back of the peers' benches. This privilege seems to have been more valued by them in past days than it is now—the late hours of modern parliaments effectually preventing their being present at many of the most interesting debates—but they are still to be seen there from time to time. The late Sir James Graham, in one of his best speeches

---

* "Where Discipline helps opening buds of sense,
And makes his pupils proud with silver pence."
—Cowper's Table Talk.

For the "Customary," see p. 91.

† A former steward was a well-known coroner for Middlesex. One of the epigrams celebrated him as being rather the "*semi*-coronator"—"the *half*-CROWNER."

in the House, declared that his first ambition to become an orator was roused by listening, as a Westminster boy, to the great speeches of Pitt and Fox. They have also a customary right to a place at the royal coronations, which they appear to hold by the tenure of a Latin salutation at the close of the entry of the procession into the Abbey. Many who were present on the last occasion remember the hearty and prolonged shout then raised of—" *Vivat Victoria Regina!*"

As was said before, the question of the removal of the old school is not one to be discussed in these pages; but it will be a subject of deep regret with all to whom an English public school is something more than a mere collection of boys under instruction—who look upon it rather as a great ancestral family whose individual members pass away, but which itself, like the sovereign, never dies—if any considerations, sanitary or social, should make it necessary to break the links of historical association which, for above three hundred years, have bound the school to the shelter of the Abbey.

SHREWSBURY SCHOOL

The chief printed authorities are—

Owen and Blakeway's History of Shrewsbury.
Rudclyeff's Memorials of Shrewsbury School.

SHREWSBURY SCHOOL.

CHAPTER I.

FOUNDATION AND EARLY HISTORY.

STANDING on the border-land of England and Wales, few places have been of more account in British history than the "pleasant" town of Shrewsbury—*Amwythig*, as the Welshmen call it to this day. As the modern stranger wanders up and down, admiring those picturesque timbered mansions in which once the knights and merchants of Powys-land kept their state, and reads the quaint names written up in modern characters upon its thoroughfares—Mardol, and Wyle Cop, and Dogpole, and the like—he feels that every yard of the old town has a story to tell him, if he could only catechise it.

Shrewsbury was the rallying ground of English civilisation in the Marches of Wales. The advisers of Edward VI. would have been wise in their generation if, when in 1548 they issued in his name their grand commission for public education, they had fixed at once upon the capital of the Welsh border as the natural centre for one of their new foundations. But it is to the credit of the Shrewsbury citizens that the movement came from within. Hugh Edwards, a London mercer, but unquestionably a Shrewsbury man, and then living in the town, and Richard Whitaker, one of the then bailiffs, presented to the young King a humble petition, in the name not only of the burgesses and inhabitants of the town and county of Salop, but of the whole neighbouring country, that a grammar school might be there established. There were two collegiate churches, they said, which had recently been dissolved—St Mary's and St Chad's—and no better disposition could be made of some part of their revenues. The King granted the prayer, and letters-patent (bearing date February 10, 1551) conveyed a charter for the school and a grant of certain prebendal tithes, amounting in the whole to £20 per annum, which had belonged to the collegiate bodies aforesaid. It was provided that there should be the usual head-master and usher, to be chosen by the bailiffs and burgesses with the advice of the Bishop of Lichfield and Coventry.

The school is called in the charter "*Libera Schola Grammaticalis Regis Edvardi Sexti;*" words which any small Shrewsbury boy would translate off-hand, for non-intelligent readers, as "The Free Grammar School of King Edward the Sixth"—and there, it might have been thought, would be an end of it. Not at all. *Libera* means "free," no doubt; but "free" in what sense? as implying a "gratuitous" education, or as "exempt from control"? The translation of this single Latin word has given occasion to a pamphlet by one of the ablest scholars of the day, has roused the ire of a very respectable Recorder, and has exercised the critical powers of her Majesty's Commissioners, who, with a modest reticence which may be variously appreciated, decline to give their own decision. It would be very presumptuous, and perhaps not very entertaining, to pronounce judgment on such a vexed question here. It may be enough to say that all argument from the use of the word in classical and medieval Latin is in favour of the interpretation maintained by Dr Kennedy—"free from the jurisdiction of a superior corporation."[*] Public educational foundations had been hitherto more or less dependent upon ecclesiastical bodies—chapters, or colleges, or conventual houses; and from such dependence and control it was a main object with Edward and his Council that their schools should be "free."

The charter was obtained; but there were many obstacles in the way of the school's taking actual shape. The sweating-sickness—a visitation hitherto unknown, "that most terrible of all English diseases"—had just broken out in the town, and the bailiffs must have had enough to do. The corporation could not as yet get possession of the tithes (which were under lease to individuals), but only of the reserved rents, which were but a poor provision. And in the midst of all this King Edward died, and it may be guessed how far his "free" school was likely to be encouraged by Queen Mary. The burgesses did something, however. They had hired a master, and got up a school somewhere.

[*] Libera Schola: A Letter to Lord Westbury, &c. By B. H. Kennedy, D.D. 1862.

There appears in their accounts about this time a payment of twelve pence " to the master of the free school, Sir Morys." Sir Morys disappears, and then we have an entry of 6s. 8d. paid "on account to John Eyton, hired to keep the free grammar school." Mr Eyton was even less satisfactory to his employers than Sir Morys might have been; for very soon, under date October ult. 1556, occurs the following:—

"Agreed, that yf Mr Bayliffs can heare of an honest and able person which will serve the office of head-scholemaster of the Free Schole of the towne, and that shall be thought meete—that then Mr Bayliffs shall avoide the said John Eyton, now scholemaster, giving him one half-year's warning. And the said John Eyton to have for his wages from St Michs. last past £14 by year and not above." *

Whether John Eyton was "avoided," whether he was content with his wages, or what became of him, no known records inform us. With Elizabeth came the time and the man for Shrewsbury School, when Thomas Ashton, M.A. of St John's, Cambridge, was appointed head-master in 1562. He must have possessed remarkable ability, not only as a teacher, but as a man of business. It was agreed by the burgesses that he should have a patent for life of all the tithes which formed the school endowment, on condition of his maintaining a third master. He begins his school register in December of this year, with Thomas Wylton and Richard Atkys as his under-masters, and it would appear that he entered at once 256 boys; but this number probably includes those whom he found already under some

* Blakeway's MS. Collections (Bodleian Library).

instruction. In the seven years of his mastership he admitted no less than 875 scholars. Of these only 238 lived in the town (*oppidani*); the rest were strangers (*alieni*) from the best families in Shropshire and the neighbouring counties. Salusburys, Mackworths, Whitakers, Corbets, Myttons, Egertons, Montgomerys, Devereux, Hoptons, Eytons, Mainwarings, Herberts, Wrottesleys, Oatleys, Wycherleys—there is scarcely a family of any note in the north-west of England that had not at least a cadet of the house under Ashton and his immediate successors. No school ever started at once into such vigorous life. It needs only a glance at the names in the original register (which, or rather an early transcript of it, has been happily preserved) to understand the ground upon which Camden calls it "the best filled in all England"—a testimony the more emphatic, as coming from one who had himself been head-master of Westminster. On the most moderate computation, there could not have been less than four hundred scholars, on the average, in these earlier years—a number which neither Eton nor Westminster reached until some generations afterwards.

A house and land had been already bought for twenty pounds, of John Proude; a timber building, to which some additions were probably made to provide accommodation for the three masters. Here Ashton taught for seven years, with undiminished reputation; "a right good man," as Camden justly calls him, in favour alike with the courtiers of Elizabeth and with his humbler fellow-townsmen. Among the many scholars of ancient families whom he had under his charge, two who came to school together on the same day, in the third year of his mastership, and continued fast friends through life, bore names never surpassed in honour by any gentlemen of England. Sir Henry Sidney of Penshurst (the bosom friend of King Edward, who had died in his arms) was at this time Lord President of the Welsh Marches, and residing officially in the Castle at Ludlow. The near neighbourhood of the school, his connection with the founder, and Mr Ashton's high reputation, were sufficient reasons for his placing there his eldest son, Philip, a boy of eight years old, and may explain why his young cousin, Fulke Gryvell (or Greville), heir of Sir Fulke Gryvell of Beauchamp's Court in Warwickshire, should have come to the same school on the same day. The son of a wise and excellent father, Philip Sidney profited well by Ashton's teaching. Two letters from the boy, written in Latin and in French in his twelfth year, drew from Sir Henry that remarkable letter, too often reprinted (would one could hope too well known!) for insertion here, but which, even to this day, continues a model for an English father's advice to his son. What public-school boy would not be the better for bearing in mind some of his noble words? There is no need to retain the antique spelling—the thoughts and language are not limited to any date:—

". . . Let your first action be the lifting up of your mind to Almighty God by hearty prayer; and feelingly digest the words you speak, with continual meditation and thinking of Him to whom you pray. . . . Be humble and obedient to your master; for unless you frame yourself to obey others, yea, and feel in yourself what obedience is, you shall never be able to teach others to obey you. Be courteous of gesture, and affable to all men, with diversity of reverence according to the dignity of the person. There is nothing that winneth so much with so little cost. . . . Give yourself to be merry, but let your mirth be ever void of all scurrility and biting words to any man. . . . Be you rather a hearer and bearer away of other men's talk, than a beginner or procurer of speech. . . . Let never oath be heard to come out of your mouth, nor word of ribaldry; detest it in others, so shall custom make to yourself a law against it in your own self. . . . Above all things tell no untruth, no, not in trifles; for there cannot be a greater reproach to a gentleman than to be accounted a liar. . . ."

No wonder that his mother, in the fond postscript to her "lyttel Philip," which she wrote "in the skirts of my Lord President's letter," felt she could add nothing to that complete and perfect manual for the English schoolboy. Philip Sidney grew up the worthy son of such a father; ending a short but stainless life by the death which he would perhaps have most desired,—"treading," says one of his many eulogists, "from his cradle to his grave amidst incense and flowers, and dying in a dream of glory." He was the "prince of gentlemen," says Lord Brooke; that same Fulke Greville who had entered with him at Shrewsbury School, had gone with him to Cambridge, had loved him, boy and man, with an unchanging affection, and who, after surviving him forty years, had it recorded on his tomb as the climax of his honours, that he was—" Friend to Sir Philip Sidney."

Another cousin of the Sidneys was entered in the same year under Ashton—James Harrington, the author of 'Oceana,' son of Sir James Harrington of Exton. The Bishop of Worcester (Sandys, afterwards Archbishop of York) had also a son and a nephew there. Sir John Salusbury of Rûg sent two sons; in fact, the school under Ashton had a more distinctly aristocratic character than under any of his successors.

It is to be regretted that fewer details of its internal life have come down to us. The one great feature in Ashton's school management which seems to have impressed his contemporaries, was his successful exhibition of those sacred and other dramas, which formed at once the exercise and relaxation of nearly every school in England in Elizabeth's days—encouraged, no doubt, by the Queen's well-known taste for such exhibitions—a custom which still survives in all its glory at Westminster. But Ashton's plays at Shrewsbury were on a grander scale than at any other school. They were performed, usually at Whitsuntide, in an open amphitheatre in the picturesque ground known as the "Quarry," and seem to have attracted visitors from all quarters of the kingdom. Elizabeth herself, on one of her progresses in 1565-6, had intended to have been present, and had got as far as Coventry on her way, when she found that she should be too late. Ashton and his scholars presented that year 'Julian the Apostate;' two years later the piece was the 'Passion of Christ.' The authorities of the town considered the spectacle a matter of public interest, and voted liberally for its support.*

---

* The place had been used for dramatic performances a century before Ashton's days. When Henry VII. visited the town, a miracle play was acted before him "in the Quarrell." The citizens of Shrewsbury seem to have had a specialty for exhibitions of this kind: the "Shrewsbury Show," a kind of festival and grand procession of

1569. "Agreed, that there shall be given out of the treasure of the town the sum of £10 towards the maintenance of the play at Whitsuntide, over and above any moneys which shall be levied by all the occupations of the town, and any other that will give any money toward the same; and further, that if Mr Ashton shall declare, by his honesty, that there shall be wanting of any money, rather than the said Mr A. should thereby be a loser, that the said money wanting shall likewise be discharged by the town."

The Drapers' Company, as one of the "occupations," are recorded as having contributed five pounds.

Notwithstanding all this, the head-mastership of Shrewsbury was not a post of such honour or emolument as to induce a man of Ashton's abilities to retain it long. In 1569, he left it for what we should in these days consider a far less eligible position—to be private tutor to the young Robert Devereux, afterwards the unfortunate Earl of Essex. But he always retained the deepest

---

the trades of the town, with some peculiar ceremonies, survives to this day, though much shorn of its ancient honours.

The following notice of Mr Ashton's play in the Quarry occurs in Churchyard's 'Worthiness of Wales.' (He was a Shrewsbury man, but of too early a date to have been one of Ashton's scholars.)

"And somewhat more behind the walls as chiefe,
There is a ground new-made theatre-wise,
Both deep and high, in goodlye ancient guise,
Where well may sit ten thousand men at ease,
And yet the one the other not displease.
A space below to bait both bull and beare,
For players too, great room and place at will,
And in the same a cockpit wondrous faire
Besides, where men may wrestle in their fill;
A ground most apt, and they that sit above
At once in view, all this may see for love;
At Ashton's play who had beheld this then,
Might well have seen there twenty thousand men.

interest in the school which he had in truth created. It would seem that he had been employed by Queen Elizabeth in some business of importance, and had considerable influence at court. In 1571, he obtained from the Queen an increase of the revenues of the school, by the gift of the tithes of Chirbury, contributing at the same time one hundred and twenty pounds from his private resources. No statutes had hitherto been made, though the charter gave powers to do so; but now Ashton, with the consent of the Bishop and of the Corporation, drew up a set of "Ordinances," which have always since borne his name, and continued, until the year 1798, to be virtually the statutes of the school.

By these ordinances, a head-master and three others—the fourth being termed an "Accidence Master," for "young beginners"—were appointed, with yearly salaries of £40, £30, £20, and £10 respectively. "I think," says Ashton in one of his letters, "no school in England hath a salary exceeding this." The election of these masters was transferred from the Corporation to St John's College, Cambridge; that is, the Bailiffs were to nominate and appoint, but the College was to "elect and send" an able, meet, and apt man—the sons of burgesses, and such as had been old scholars, to be preferred—and the Bailiffs were to have a *veto* on the appointment. The terms of this compromise (for such it seems to have been) of the old Corporation rights led to abundant disputes and litigation in the future. The second and third masters were to be promoted to the higher places, if they proved able to discharge the office. The head-master was to be a Master of Arts, "well able to make a Latin verse, and learned in the Greek tongue;" the second-master the same; the third might be a B.A., and in his case no Greek was required. None of them were to preach, or practise physic, or to keep an alehouse or gaming-house. The hour for beginning school was to be six in summer and seven in winter: they were to work till dinner-time—eleven o'clock; to come to school again at a quarter before one, and be finally dismissed at half-past four in winter, and an hour later in summer. As in the old Winchester statutes, no candle was to be used in the school, "for breeding diseases, and for danger and peril otherwise." Thursday was the half-holiday; on which day the highest form were to "declaim and play one act of a comedy before they went to play." Like John Lyon, the founder of Harrow, Ashton made provision for the scholars' practice in the use of the national weapon; their recreations were to be "shooting in the long bow and chess-play, and no other games, unless it be running, wrestling, or leaping:" they might play for "a penny the game, or fourpence for a match;" but there was to be no betting. No scholar was to be admitted to the higher school until he could "read, and write his name, and know his Latin accidence, and make a concord." The entrance fees were graduated on a scale which showed that the admission of boys of all ranks was contemplated: a lord's son was to pay 10s.; a knight's, 6s. 8d.; a gentleman's eldest son, 3s. 4d.; other sons, 2s. 6d.; below that degree, if born within the county, 12d., if without, 2s. A burgess's son was to pay only 4d. Probably no annual payments were demanded from any scholars; but the custom of the times seems to have been for the more wealthy boys to make presents to the master. The books to be used were—for Latin, Cæsar, Cicero, Sallust, Livy, Virgil, Horace, and Terence; for Greek, Demosthenes, Isocrates, and Xenophon's 'Cyropædia.' The holidays were to be eighteen days at Christmas, ten days at Easter, and a week at Whitsuntide; but each master was allowed, besides, thirty days' absence in the course of the year.

Ashton just lived to see these ordinances come into operation; one of his last acts was to revisit the school, and to preach a farewell sermon in St Mary's Church, as knowing that his end was approaching. He took his leave of the town amidst tears and blessings, and retired to Cambridge, where he died within a fortnight.

CHAPTER II.

THE SCHOOL UNDER LAURANCE AND MEIGHEN.

Ashton had been succeeded in his office by his second-master, Thomas Laurance, who carried on the school with almost equal success. But the plague, which visited Shrewsbury during his mastership, was a sad interruption. The school seems to have been broken up. After 1574, there occur no admissions in the register during the two years following; for the next entry stands thus : " 30th June 1577. After the plague these scholars whose names follow were admitted." Provision had been made, in the ordinances just quoted, for a sanatorium in the country, to which the masters and scholars were to "resort and abide in the time of any common plague or other infection," and there to continue to teach; but it is not likely that any such place had as yet been built or provided. The house at Grinshill was not obtained until some years afterwards. It was "furnished" in 1617, for the reception of a portion of the school in case of need; but there is no record of its ever having been so occupied.

Sir Henry Sidney, the Lord President, had visited Shrewsbury, no doubt, during the six years that his son was at school there. In 1573 he came there, and brought young Philip, now a lad of nineteen, to see his old school again, when father and son were received with hearty rejoicings. In 1581 he made the grand state visit to keep the feast of St George, of which some careful chronicler has left a most elaborate account: how he went in solemn procession from St Chad's Church to the council-house, the bailiffs, aldermen, and different companies of the town escorting him, all "drest in their best livereys;" and how they feasted him there for a week in a style befitting the representative of Majesty. On the 1st of May the school took its turn to be his entertainers. The head-master, Laurance, with his three subordinates, John Baker, Richard Atkys, and Roger Kent, "made a brave and costly banckett after supper before the scoole to the number of forty dyshes, and the masters before them, each scoole presenting ten dishes, with a shewer before every scoole," who introduced the several courses with a very indifferent distich from each master.

"1. These are all of Larrance' lore,
   Accompt hys hart above hys store.

2. These ten are all of Baker's bande,
   Good wyll, not welthe, now to be scande.

3. These ten are all in Atkys' chardge,
   Hys giffts are small, hys good wyll lardge.

4. These ten come last, and are the least,
   Yet Kent's good wyll is wyth the beast."

The next day came a show, in which we may see something like a precedent for the Eton Montem:—

"The scholars of the sayd free schoole beinge taught by the foresaid four masters, beinge in number three hundred and sixty, with their masters before every of them, marchynge bravely from the sayd schoole in battle order, with generals, captens, drumms, trumpetts, and ensigns before them through the town towards a large fillde called the Geye, in the abbey suburbs of Shrewsberie, and there devydinge their banndes into four partes, met the sayde Lord President, being upon a lusty courser, who turned him aboute and came to them, the generall openinge to his lordship the purpose and assembly of him and the rest; then he and the other captens made theire orations howe valiently they would feight and defend their country, at whych the sayd lord had greate pleasure and mutch rejoiced, givinge greate prayse to the sayde masters for the eloquence thereof."

Sir Henry left the town a few days after by water, in his barge, under a salute of "fourteen chamber pieces bravely shot off;" and as he passed an eyot in the river, "certain appointed scholars of the free schoole, apparelled all in greene, and greene wyllows on their heads," addressed him in verse with what the unconscious chronicler describes as "lamentable orations." The nymphs of the island, they said, were disconsolate at the President's departure :—

> "Their woe is greate, great moan they make,
>   With doleful tunes they doe lament;
> They howle, they crie, their leave to tacke,
>   Theire garments greene for woe they rent."

And after considerably more of this "doleful tune," they struck into a grand chorus, of which this was the first verse :—

> "And wyll your honour now depart?
>   And must it needs be soe?
> Would God we could like fishes swymme,
>   That we might with thee goe!"

The whole was so "pityfully done," that "truly it made many both in the barge upon the water, as also the people uppon lande, to weepe;" and it was certainly enough to make, as we are told, "my Lord hymself to change countenance."

The next year the Lord President came again, and seems to have stayed some days, his wife, the Lady Mary, having arrived the day before "in her wagon." As Sir Henry passed "by the Condit at the Wyle Cop," orations were addressed to him by two of Laurance's scholars, "which he praysed very well." It was on this occasion, or at least in this year, that a second son, Thomas Sidney, was entered at the school. We hear of him again two years afterwards, when the Earl of Essex (Robert Devereux), the Earl of Leicester, and Lord North came to the town, and paid the school a visit. Young Sidney, as Leicester's nephew, was selected with two companions (Richard Hoorde and Edward Higgons) to welcome the party with congratulatory addresses, in which Leicester, as the reigning favourite, was profusely complimented on his noble birth and lineage, his imaginary virtues, and his favour with "the Prince," as it was the fashion to call Elizabeth. The Earl, in return, "gratified the masters with sundry rewards." Essex passed through the town again the following year, and again had to listen to orations from the scholars—this time at the castle gates, "they standing there in battle array with bows and arrows"—the only mention to be found of their use of the national arm, in which Ashton had directed that they should be trained.

But meanwhile Laurance, whose health was failing, had resigned the mastership. He wrote a noble letter to the Bailiffs, which Mr Blakeway has copied amongst his MSS., and which is well worthy of preservation, though too long for insertion here. He speaks of himself as "soe wearied with the worke, soe tired with the toil, and soe overwhelmed with the care" of the school, that he "neither can nor will any longer space continue in it." He has an honest pride in leaving it in such flourishing case. "The resort of strangers unto it is notable;" he has "in the last twelve years sent above an hundred scholars to Cambridge and Oxford." His friends, indeed, suggest that he shall continue in office, taking "a master of arts for an helper;" but he says—"I thank God I have ever hitherto had a conscience in my calling, and ever looked rather at the good success of my labours and the profit of my scholars, than the greatness of my stipend or the thankfulness of parents." The Bailiffs, in a letter to St John's to announce the vacancy, state that they "have earnestly entreated him to continue his charge," but in vain. He retired to Wem, where he lived for many years afterwards—it is to be feared, in something like poverty, for in 1602 the Corporation ordered that "Master Thomas Laurance be allowed £5 [per annum?], and 50s. in hand, out of the Corporation estate, for his great and painful diligence in procuring good order in the Free Grammar School." A strong public testimony to the reputation of the school, the year before his resignation, is found in a petition to Lord Burleigh from the Chapter of Hereford, that a free school may be founded there, "to serve as commodiously for the training of the youth of South Wales as Shrewsbury doth for the youth of North Wales."

On Laurance's resignation, the succession to the head-mastership was offered to John Baker, the second-master, who had the modesty to decline it. The College then recommended John Meighen, M.A., who was destined to rule over the fortunes of Shrewsbury for above half a century, successfully on the whole, if not altogether peacefully.

It was the age of pageants, and the Shrewsbury headmasters seem to have delighted in them. Here is an extract from the old chronicler dated the same year as Essex's second visit :—

"1585. This yeare, on the 8 day of Octr., beinge Thursday [their half-holiday], the scollerds of the free schoole in Shrewsberie made a triomphe in warlike manner, in a field called Behind the Walls,* against the Pope's army and other rebells, whom they triumphantly vanquished, to the great joy of the beholders, departing from the field through the town towards the castel there being over the town, when they, with sound of trompet, dromme, and shouting, sounded out their victory, with great fires made, and thankful psalms most joyfully sung to God in the comfortable hearing of all the town with joyful and godly thanksgiving."†

It is plain that the school continued to enjoy a very high repute both at home and abroad, and was very popular with the good citizens of Shrewsbury. One of the last acts of Laurance's mastership had been to secure something like a special school chapel for his boys. They had been used to attend the public services at St Mary's Church, occupying the chapel on the south side. This

---

* The "Quarry."

† From an old chronicle in the school library, known as "Dr Taylor's Manuscript."

was "repaired and beautified" in 1582 by the Bailiffs and St John's College out of the school revenues, and was ordered to be used, not only for public worship on Sundays and holidays, but also for religious instruction on the half-holidays, a custom which continued until the present school chapel was built. It seems from this time to have been known as the "scholars' chapel," and to have become the ordinary burial-place for masters and scholars. A very few years later, we find in the school register entries of the death and burial of Ashton's original third-master, who had continued to occupy the same desk under both his successors :—

"1587. In this yeare, on the 7th day of July, Richard Atkys, late third-scholemaster of this free schoole, departed this life about 3 o' the clocke in the morning, and was buried in the schollars' chapel in St Marie's Church on the next day, being Palm Sunday, in the morning, all the children of the whole schoole going before the hearse to church by two and two, and the rest of the scholemasters then remaining following next after before the magistrates."

And the next year Roger Kent, the humbler "Accidence master," was buried in the same place with the like public honours.

In 1594, one hundred and eighty-one new boys appear to have been admitted—the greatest number in any one year since the first opening of the school under Ashton. The old buildings had long been insufficient; and in the next year, that portion of the present school which comprises the central tower and the range containing the chapel and the library was built—or at least begun, for the chapel was not consecrated until 1617. But neither at this time, nor for many generations subsequently, was any kind of accommodation provided for boarders. There is no doubt but that (with the exception of some few who may have lived with the head-master) those boys who came from a distance were lodged with such of the citizens as might choose to receive them.* This arrangement—which appears to have been common in the earlier days at many public schools †—has prevailed more or less at Shrewsbury up to the present time; some few boys still lodging in the town with respectable tradesmen, known or recommended in some way to their parents, and attending the school lessons, just as they might have done in Ashton's and Meighen's day.

Mr Head-master Meighen still ruled on for half a century, and more than one second-master meanwhile died or resigned, hopeless of any vacancy for promotion. Towards the end of his reign he outlived his popularity. He got into disputes with the Bailiffs and Corporation; apparently from having appointed, or procured the appointment as second-master of one Mr Gittens against their wishes. The real cause of the dispute turned on the religious question. Gittens was "a dangerous suspected Papist," had been arraigned as such before Archbishop Bancroft, and imprisoned in the gate-house at Westminster; the Protestant feeling of the Corporation revolted at him. But there was a counter party, and a very influential one. The women of Shrewsbury were

---

* A melancholy entry in Taylor's MS. is corroborative of this: "1590. A young scholar, who boarded at Master Hamon's, hanged himself."

† For instance, Sir Peter Carew, in 1526, being sent to Exeter Grammar School, was lodged with "one Thomas Hunt, a draper and alderman of that city;" and gave the worthy citizen no little trouble.

for Mr Gittens. The more active among them took forcible possession of the school-house, and held it against all comers " for four days and three nights "—so accurate is the chronicler of the campaign—and nearly killed one of the bailiffs who attempted to force an entrance; Mr Gittens (who was in actual occupation) meanwhile encouraging his friends from an open window, and crying out to the burgesses that he stood there for their rights, —meaning, it is to be supposed, as against the nomination of masters by the College. Altogether it was a very pretty quarrel, and lasted some twenty years. The Bailiffs sent to the Cambridge authorities to complain; and they took the money for their delegates' expenses out of the school chest. Meighen filed a bill in Chancery against them for malversation. The Lord Chancellor issued a commission to Sir Edward Bromley, one of the Barons of Exchequer, and others, who sat at Shrewsbury to examine witnesses. They reported that they found " the school much decayed " (which seems very questionable) " by the froward and ill carriage of the head-master, being a very contentious person, and of a turbulent and mutinous character and disposition." The final result was that the Chancellor dismissed Mr Meighen's bill, and ruled that the under-masters should be elected by St John's College. Mr Gittens was ousted, and James Brooke, M.A. of Caius, and David Evans, B.A. of Jesus College, were appointed second and third masters, November 17, 1627. Gittens was reinstated, however, by some means, four years afterwards, and it was not until 1638 that he was finally got rid of.

In 1630, whatever still remained of the old buildings was taken down, and the present school front, at right angles to the tower and the block containing the chapel and library, was built of Grinshill stone. Over the main entrance, with the date, was placed the following inscription from Isocrates—"Φιλομαθης εαν ης, εση πολυμαθης."—"If thou love learning, thou shalt be well learned."* Above the first word, on a stone pillar, stands the figure of a schoolboy, indicating the lover of learning; and over the concluding word, that of a university graduate—both in those "hyperbolical barbarous breeches," as old Fox calls them, which were the fashionable gentlemen's crinoline of the day. The setting up of this inscription gave Mr Meighen the opportunity of a sly joke against his old opponents the town authorities. The bailiffs of the year wished to have their own names placed over the gateway rather than a Greek inscription—probably as more interesting and intelligible to themselves and their fellow-townsmen. To this Mr Meighen would by no means consent; but he pointed out to them a small neighbouring edifice attached to the school, newly dedicated, not to the Muses, but to Cloacina, and suggested a stone over the door as admirably adapted for such a record. The story goes that the bailiffs fell into the trap, and that their names were to be read there by admiring schoolboys so late as 1798, when the building was taken down.

If such were Mr Meighen's little pleasantries, it was perhaps quite as much his unpopularity as his advancing years which made the good people of Shrewsbury so

* The idea of the inscription was probably taken from the following passage in Erasmus's Colloquies—a book better known in Meighen's days than ours—"*Dictum Isocratis, aureis literis in frontispicio codicis tui pingendum,* φιλομαθης," &c.

anxious to get rid of him. They now kept pressing him to resign, which, after a head-mastership of fifty years, it was perhaps time for him to think of. But he was very unwilling to listen to any such proposal. He certainly had his heart in his work. Through his influence and exertions the school library was gradually filled, chiefly by gifts from old pupils and gentlemen of the county, with so good a collection of books that Dr Parr, on one of his visits there in after years, declared that, with the single exception of Eton, he had "seen in no public school a library equal to that of Shrewsbury." Meighen had a brother a "citizen and stationer of London;" and it was probably through this connection that several London merchants are recorded as having at this time given either presents of books or of money for their purchase. The head-master himself was evidently a lover of books, keeping a careful record of all these donations, and fitting up the presses in the library with iron rods and chains for their better security. That the accusations brought against him of causing the decline of the school by his contentious temper were not altogether true, may fairly be gathered from the note made in one of these books by the donor, Thomas Prichard, Archdeacon of Llandaff, in 1627 (at the very time when these complaints were most rife), in which he styles his old school as even now "the most numerous in all England."* During Meighen's mastership, Welsh names appear on the register in larger numbers than before; the national prefix of Ap—Ap Thomas, Ap Richard, Ap

---

* "Dulcissimæ Nutrici suæ (totius Angliæ numerosissimæ) Scholæ Salopiensi hoc OPEHTHPION d: d: Tho: Prichard Archidiac: Llandaven: et Coll. Jesu Oxon. Vice-princ."

Evan, &c. &c.—recurring continually. But the old Shropshire and Cheshire names are there too, still in good proportion. The eulogy left on record, apparently by a contemporary, cannot have been wholly undeserved —"That famous schoolmaster who to his perpetual memory hath with great industry, since he was the chief schoolmaster, wholly endeavoured the flourishing condition of the same, not seeking to advance himself or his by diminishing anything, having left a good pattern to them that succeed, making it his great care and chief work to perfect that structure and building in a glorious manner." At last, in 1636, he accepted £100 from the school funds as the price of his resignation, and died the following year. It must be remembered, in his defence, that the head-mastership of Shrewsbury in those days was not a lucrative office, and gave little opportunity to make any provision for old age.

CHAPTER III.

THOMAS CHALONER.

BEFORE poor Mr Meighen was got rid of, there was a partisan war going on about his successor. The Bailiffs and Corporation were strongly in favour of John Harding, who had been the *pro tempore* second-master, who had been publicly chosen "in a general and great assembly," and whom they preferred, as "a master of arts of twelve years' standing," to some "young man" whom St John's College had selected for the appointment. Harding seems really to have had strong claims; the Bishop of Lichfield wrote to the College in his favour, as one who had been highly recommended to him "for learning, judgment, method, government, and honesty;" urging his election for the benefit of the school, and "to avoid contention." But the Cambridge men stood on their rights, and maintained their own nomination—not, however, of the "young man," whoever he was, whom the burgesses were so unwilling to receive, but of Thomas Chaloner, M.A., of Jesus College, who was at least Mr Harding's equal in point of standing. The Shrewsbury Corporation must have been a good-humoured body: for though they had spent

£300 in law in the attempt to place their own candidate, they laid out an additional pound on a "banquet" to Mr Chaloner on his admission. Not an extravagant sum, certainly; but it must be remembered that twenty shillings would go further in those days than in our own.

The life and fortunes of this Thomas Chaloner would form one of the most curious of English biographies, if they could be told at length; and there exists a good deal of material for such a history. He entered upon his office in the year when Hampden made his first stand against ship-money; was expelled—stanch Royalist that he was—under Cromwell, and lived a storm-tossed life—the very Ulysses of schoolmasters—till he came to his own again with the second Charles. He was born at Llansilin near Oswestry, and had been himself trained at Shrewsbury under Meighen. He did his teacher credit. He had the reputation of being "an excellent Greek scholar;" it must be confessed that, in his day, a little Greek passed for a good deal, for proficiency in that tongue was a very rare accomplishment; but of his Latin scholarship there can be no question, for he has left us specimens of Latin verses of which even modern Salopians might be proud. He very soon raised the school from the low estate into which it had fallen, owing to Mr Meighen's failing energies and Mr Gitten's inefficiency, and the warfare between the school and town authorities. In the second year of his head-mastership (1637) he admitted no less than 128 new boys; and in each of the three following years, the entrances were 121, 107, and 120 respectively. Not even under the glorious rule of Ashton had Shrewsbury stood higher in numbers or in reputation. The old Shropshire family names still appear on the school register, mixed with a fair sprinkling, here and there, of others from neighbouring counties. The second-master throughout Chaloner's reign, his brother Welshman and most intimate friend, was David Evans—David Ddû (Black David) as he was called—who had been his fellow-collegian at Jesus in Cambridge. The black Welshman was an excellent grammar-teacher, and sent the boys up from the second school well grounded to receive Chaloner's finishing. More fortunate in one respect than his friend, he retained his office under the Puritan headmaster who succeeded; and, as the rules of grammar are of no party, religious or political, he seems to have earned the good opinion of his new chief as well as of his old one. For the epitaph on his monument in St Mary's, where he was buried after thirty years' service, is of the date of Mr Head-master Pigot, and if not of his composition, as seems probable, must at least have expressed his estimate of the man :—

> "Caveto sis puer; prope est David Niger,
> Notandus olim literis rubris senex;
> Is Priscianus temporis sui inclytus:
> Nescis adhuc!—abito! nescis literas."

Excellent and painstaking schoolmaster though he was, Chaloner had a decidedly social turn. He was wont after the labours of the day to refresh himself with a select circle of congenial spirits at a tavern in "the Sextry,"*

---

* Now "King's Head Shutt," leading from High Street to Kiln Lane. It formerly communicated with St Chad's Churchyard by a covered passage over the street, and the sacristy ("sextry") of that church probably stood there. The old house still standing in this narrow "shutt" is probably the tavern of Chaloner's day.

as it was then called, whither his friend and assistant, Black David, accompanied him. Let no Shrewsbury master of modern days imagine for a moment that there was in this anything derogatory to the dignity of the office or the man. The great officials of the town—the bailiffs, recorder, and the like—were wont to settle public matters of the gravest import at a social congress held at the Gullet, a tavern of popular repute; the gentlemen of the county transacted their business at the same place, and on one occasion we find the "high sheriff's daughter" honouring a party with her presence, and "drinking there." And this "knot of company-keepers at the Sextry," to whose pleasant companionship Chaloner looked back regretfully in his after days of loneliness and exile, were no ordinary set of tavern-boosers. Many of them, no doubt, were not above the rank of honest citizens and burgesses. But among them were Sir Francis Oatley of Pitchford and his brother, Sir William Vaughan, Sir Richard Lee of Lee Hall, Sir Richard Earnly, Sir Thomas Lyster of Rowton, with Irelands and Kynastons, and other aristocracy of the town. A genial and kindly fellowship, no doubt, they were—many of them old scholars of the free school; and Master Richard Chaloner, with his well-stored mind and somewhat satirical humour—patent enough even to us now, as we shall see from his curious personal records—must have been a choice companion with whom to hear the chimes at midnight.

But the flourishing school and the pleasant company at the Sextry were soon to be broken up. The record in the old school register (kept in Mr Chaloner's hand) which follows next upon the four successful years which have been mentioned, shows a falling-off in the admissions, such as might be expected in those terrible days of anarchy; in 1641 and 1642 they were only 78 and 79 respectively. "Let my successor blame civill war," is the note made hereupon by the sorrowful head-master; "academies mourne and are desolate, colonyes of the Muses are desolate, and the number of Shrewsbury scholars in these two yeares is small." Yet in the next year, the most troublous of all for Shrewsbury, there was entered on this list (together with his brother William) no less a name than George, son of Sir William Savill— the future Marquess of Halifax; the great Trimmer, as he has been styled, but perhaps the most sagacious and honest politician of his times. In September 1642, King Charles came in person to Shrewsbury, invited by the loyal Corporation in common council assembled, and was welcomed by none more cordially than by the head-master of the Royal School. The King's "Commission for Artillery" held their sittings in the noble library: Lord Capel the Lord-Lieutenant, Henry Bromley the high sheriff, Sir Francis Oatley (one of the Sextry club, and now governor of the town), met there in council with other gentlemen of note almost daily.* Chaloner and his friend David Evans placed their own chambers at the disposal of the King's friends. "When the King kept his court here, successively these lords lodged in the schooles—viz., Lord-Keeper Littleton, Lord Viscount

---

* Their followers left some traces of their visits there which were not altogether to the head-master's liking: in the "Register of Benefactions," 'Andrewes' Sermons' has a note in Chaloner's handwriting— "basely torne by the sacrilegious fingers of a Scotch camp chaplin;" and 'Heinsius on the New Testament' is marked as having been "stolen away while the King's Commis: for Artillery sat dayly in the library."

Grandison, Lord Archbishop Williams, Lord Cholmeley, and Sir Richard Dyott, at my house; at Mr Evans his house, Lord Grey of Ruthin and Lord North his brother. —*Deus pacis pacem indulgeat!*" This pious wish was in vain. Charles, after a second visit, chiefly for the purpose of raising money, finally left the town, first "borrowing" six hundred pounds out of the school chest; and after a long and gallant resistance (stout Sir Richard Earnley, another of Chaloner's " company-keepers," being slain in its defence), the Parliamentary forces became masters of it by treachery in February 1644 (5).

So notable a malignant as the head-master was not likely to escape. He was plundered of all his property, and summarily ejected, to find shelter where he could.* Black David seems to have been thought not of sufficient importance to be meddled with; at any rate he was left in peace to keep the diminished school together until the appointment to be head-master over him of one Richard Pigot, whom the Parliamentarians brought from a school in Newport—not a bad man or master by any means; but the reader will not object to follow for a while the varying fortunes of poor Mr Chaloner.

The ejected master carried away with him the school registers, if nothing else; and in their pages he has jotted down in very fair Latin, quaintly interspersed with Greek phrases, all sorts of personal memoranda: notes of his own movements, anathemas against his enemies, school-boys' accounts, heads of sermons, and private confessions which he certainly never intended for our curious eyes; but which, taken altogether, give us a very interesting pic-

---

* " Bonis omnibus exutis ἀπεσκορακισθην "—" I was stripped of all I had and cast out to the crows," writes the unfortunate master.

ture of the writer—a man one would have liked much to have known, none the less for some peculiarities and weaknesses which these memoranda disclose. He met adversity boldly; made no claim—as no doubt he might have done for a while at least—on the bounty of generous friends, but set up at once an independent school at Ryton, near Baschurch, in the county. After staying there for a few months, molested probably by the Puritan authorities, he went up to London, paid a sum of sixty pounds as a "composition" for his malignancy, and perhaps (some of his expressions may bear such an interpretation) swallowed the Covenant, as many other loyalists did with such stomach as they might. Fortified with this safeguard, he hired a larger house near Shrewsbury. It either bore most appropriately, or he bestowed upon it, the name of *Birch* Hall, or, as he loved to Latinise it, "*Ædes Betulianæ.*" The ominous sound was not enough to deter forty-four of his old Ryton pupils from following him; indeed, the strongest testimony to his character lies in the fact that, go where he would, under whatever unfavourable circumstances, a colony of grateful scholars followed his steps, and wherever he pitched his tent, a school with all the prestige of an old establishment sprang up as it were out of the wilderness. The Birch Hall school soon numbered nearly a hundred. And here he seems to have been tolerably contented; comparing himself to Dionysius, who, driven from the sovereignty of Syracuse, was content to wield the rod at Corinth,—" *Syracusis exulans, Corinthi tyrannidem molior.*" But in that same year a Shropshire friend of some influence, and a member of Cromwell's Parliament—John Corbett of Adderley—procured for him the appointment to the grammar school at Market-Drayton, for which, however, he had to pay ten pounds as a kind of retiring fee to his predecessor. Again most of his boys accompanied him, and again he commanded success. But he was hunted out from this resting-place, on the old ground of malignancy, by the "Committee for Scandalous and Plundered Ministers;" a body whom, in the old school register which received all his confidences, he curses in his queer mixture of Greek and Latin, no doubt in the full persuasion that it would be an unknown tongue to them, even if they had the chance to read it.* He moved off out of their way to Hawarden in Flintshire, a little band of twelve scholars dragging their weary way after him through those Welsh roads in the month of March— "*per nives, per brumam, longum iter,*" as he pathetically words it. The rough Welsh children whom he found there were no doubt, as he complains, a far less satisfactory material to work upon than the well-bred boys of Shropshire. He had to teach them, he says, the very rudiments of English; yet in a few months the name of the great Shrewsbury master had filled the little provincial school with "above a hundred gentlemen's sons." He writes as if he were happy there. He speaks with delight of their docility in learning, and their personal attachment to himself. He tells us how they represented (after the old Shrewsbury fashion) to the great wonder and edification no doubt of the Welsh squires, Plautus's comedy of the 'Captives,' and how they maintained a running fight of satirical verses with the boys of the neighbouring school of Chester. But, in a very few months, his asylum was again invaded; this time by a more

* "Mandato tyrannico τοῦ καταρωτάτου Delegatorum synedrii."

terrible enemy than even a Parliamentary Commission. The plague came to Hawarden. One at least of his most promising scholars, a young actor in the play,* died of it; and in June 1647 the whole school, boys and masters,† migrated to Overton to escape from the infection. Besides these troubles from without, he had also some domestic vexations. His under-master was one David Pierce, who apparently was a member of his household, and between whom and Mrs Chaloner there was a perpetual civil war. The head-master sided with his subordinate in his heart against the lady; but domestic comfort required that David should take his departure; and Chaloner, with the generous unselfishness which was part of his nature, maintained the young man for some time at Cambridge.‡ Mr Pierce's future perhaps justified Mrs Chaloner's dislike; for some time afterwards he is spoken of as likely to lose the mastership of a school which had been obtained for him, "unless Providence interfered,"—which it probably did not. Chaloner's retreat to Overton with his scholars was most likely a mere temporary arrangement; at least he does not remain there many months, and the next three years of his life seem to have been spent at Emrall, as domestic tutor in the family of Sir John Puleston, where he found his pupils more than ordinarily dull—"*pueros pessimæ indolis.*" Somewhere about this date he obtained

---

* "Inter quos incomparabili indole emicuit Gulielmus Barlow, quem pestis paulo post eripuit."

† "Hawarden, 1647, June 20.—*Discesserunt præ timore pestis quæ invasit oppidum*" [here follow a few of the names] "*et circiter* 130. *Væ nobis! Domine miserere nostri!*"—School Register.

‡ "Quem nimium iniquiter ab uxore meâ tractatum misi Cantabrigiam, ibique pro tempore meis sumptibus alo, sperans amicas αμοιβας."

the mastership of the school at Stone, in Staffordshire, where he collected a hundred and twenty-two scholars; and next we find him holding the same office at Ruthin, whence he was once more ejected by Cromwell's Major-General for North Wales; the ill-advised rising of the Royalists in the west having irritated the Protector into fresh measures against "delinquents." He was, however, allowed to return through the intercession of some friends. But either he was naturally of a restless turn, or his wandering life had made him so; for he seems to have contemplated another move. He was a candidate for Wrexham school; but "the cobblers of Wrexham," he says, rejected him. And he admits that his enemies called him—not without some reason—" a rolling stone that would gather no moss." His social and convivial tastes still remained with him, and no doubt he was an acceptable guest at the hospitable boards of the Denbighshire gentry. Some of his private entries about this date betray that a good deal of hard drinking went on at these entertainments, and that the Ruthin schoolmaster took his fair share.* He was always very penitent in the morning; but the penitence did not insure that the next invitation would be declined. He found a friend at last amongst the dominant party. Thomas Gilbert, one of Cromwell's chaplains, and from his influence in such matters known as "the Bishop of Shropshire," recommended him to William Adams, citizen and haberdasher of London, who had just founded his Free Grammar School at

---

* "1653. Jan. 3.—Repetita potatio, renovata pœnitentia.
      ,, 4.—Plâs y Ward convivabar, etsi sobrius, tamen ægriusculé.
      ,, 5.—Nonnihil legi, oravi, meditatusque sum."

Newport; and there, with his son as under-master, Chaloner once more, with that remarkable success which is the witness of his unparalleled ability as a master, created what might have been a rival Shrewsbury. By the end of his second year there he had two hundred and forty-four scholars, "many of them the sons of the first gentlemen in that and the neighbouring counties."

But meanwhile events were preparing his return to the scene of his early triumphs. Mr Pigot, the intruded master, had carried on the work at Shrewsbury with considerable ability and moderation; interrupted only, like Chaloner, by the plague, which caused the school to be closed for some months by an order of the Protector's council.* So well had he satisfied the authorities of St John's, that at the Restoration they gave him a formal nomination with the view of confirming his title to the head-mastership. The popular reaction, however, was too strong. In July 1662, he was ejected (probably by the operation of the Bartholomew Act), and was committed prisoner to the castle in company with Michael Betton, "canoneer" to the garrison, and Mr Tallents, the Puritan minister of St Mary's. They were released in a few days, and Mr Pigot died in the year following. But though his old place was vacant, Chaloner seems to have been not over-anxious to return. His school at Newport was flourishing, and his Shrewsbury associations had been broken up. For six months the head-mastership remained unfilled; Cotton, the second-master, meanwhile discharg-

---

* " You are also forthwith to dissolve both the schools in your towne, and see that they continue soe till it shall please God the infection shall cease.   Jo. Bradshawe, *P.*

" White Hall, *9th Aug.* 1650."

ing the duties. At the end of that time we find the following entry,—rather ungracious, as though the genial temper had been somewhat soured, more by the smaller vexations of a schoolmaster's life than by his heavier trials :—

"I., T. C., after an exile of nineteen years, return to my ancient province. For the under-master of Newport [this surely could not be his own son?] behaved so imperiously and deceitfully to me that I could not bear to associate with him any more, and so removed hither with my second wife and some young gentlemen whom I placed in their several classes on the 4th of March."

So the wanderer found rest. But Shrewsbury was at least as much changed as he was. Whether he frequented as before his old haunt in the sextry, when afternoon school was over, we do not know; but he would have found there very few of the old familiar faces. Time had untied that social "knot of company-keepers." The schoolmaster had made, from time to time, little mournful notes against his old friends' names on the list which he kept during his nineteen years' exile. Black David the grammarian was gone where concords are never broken. Sir Richard Earnley, as we have seen, had died gallantly in the King's cause—"slain at the taking of the town." Sir William Vaughan, too, had met the same fate—"slain at Tredagh." Sir Thomas Lyster was dead also. Lee of Lee Hall had "papisted," which was even worse. How the remaining friends met and welcomed each other after so many years, no one knows now, or will know.

Chaloner lived little more than two years after his restoration. The kindly reader will hope that his second wife did not quarrel with the under-masters like his first, and that the Shrewsbury boys teased him as little as possible in his declining years. He was buried in St Mary's Church, in the "scholars' chapel," on the very day twelvemonth after his late supplanter, Pigot, had been laid to rest in the same place. *Requiescant in pace.*

CHAPTER IV.

DECLINE OF THE SCHOOL.

THERE were heartburnings again about the election of a successor. Poor Mr Cotton, the second-master, who had quietly admitted Chaloner's superior rights, as merely resuming what was his own, now put in his modest claims for promotion to the chief desk, as by statute provided. But the statute appears to have become virtually obsolete. He was thrust aside without ceremony; and the contest lay between a Mr Bull, supported by the strong local influence of Lord Newport, and by Bishop Hacket as Visitor, and Andrew Taylor, Fellow of King's College, who had received his early education in the school before he was admitted on the foundation at Eton. The latter was elected, and Shrewsbury for the first and last time came under an Etonian head-master. But the infusion of the Eton element which, unless school traditions are false, woke into new life the country grammar schools of Harrow and Rugby, had no perceptible effect upon the fortunes of Shrewsbury. The school had been created by Ashton, and re-created by Chaloner; and, after his death, it gradually fell almost as rapidly as it had risen. The school registers of these days have unfortunately disappeared, and the causes and progress of this decay can only be guessed at. One brief notice, left by a chance traveller at the beginning of Taylor's mastership, might indeed, if taken alone, lead to the conclusion that the numbers were then, or had lately been, higher than ever; for this speaks of "a faire free schoole in which are four masters, and there are sometimes 600 scholars, and a handsome library thereto belonging."* But most probably the writer only recorded what he had heard at Shrewsbury. Taylor held his office for three-and-twenty years—probably too long for the welfare of the school, for it is recorded that during the latter part of the time his health had failed him. King James II. was now steadily pursuing the course, so fatal to himself, of forcing Romanists into the headships of colleges and schools by royal mandamus. He made a progress through Shrewsbury in 1687; and though the conduits at Wyle Cop and Mardol ran with wine on the occasion, the Protestant burgesses were by no means glad to see him. The Papistical party in the town were watching like vultures for Taylor's death, having "one Sebrand, a Jesuit," ready to force at once, by royal order, into the vacant place. Taylor disappointed their object by a secret resignation; not much too soon, for he died that year. It was done so quietly that St John's College had time to appoint a master, and the burgesses and bailiffs to induct him, before any mandamus could issue. There was no time for disputes, and probably the choice was a hurried one. Richard Lloyd, M.A., one of their own fellows, whom the college selected, reigned as head-master for thirty-six years; with what success may be partly

* Marmaduke Rawdon's Journal, 1665, p. 167 (Camd. Soc.).

gathered from the fact that on his retirement he left exactly sixteen boys in the school. He seems to have been a man fortunate beyond his deserts; for he held stalls both at Brecon and at Hereford, and a living or two besides; so that at last he was either shamed or compelled into a resignation on the ground of plurality.

Then followed a struggle once more, longer and more determined than ever, between the Cambridge authorities and the burgesses for the right of election. The College nominated another of their own fellows, William Clarke; the Corporation put in, and maintained in actual possession, a burgess of the town and a master of arts of Jesus College in Oxford, Hugh Owen; and he remained *de facto* head-master for nearly four years. But not *de jure*, as it was decided; for the College filed a bill against the Corporation, and won their cause, after much expenditure on both sides. Mr Clarke, their original nominee, had in the meanwhile found more peaceful preferment, and gone off to a living; and they now appointed Dr Robert Phillips, a burgess, who had been an official of St Mary's Church. Whatever might have been his qualifications, he was fifty-seven years old when he first began work as a schoolmaster—not a very likely man to retrieve the fallen fortunes of Shrewsbury. Nor were these constant disputes between College and Corporation likely to conduce to that end. It is said that "the school decreased" under both these last masters; though how it could fall much lower in numbers than sixteen—the point at which Lloyd had left it—is not so clear to an arithmetical critic. But it certainly did not rise, as we shall presently see.

Dr Phillips continued in office eight years, when he

was succeeded by Leonard Hotchkis, the second-master. Mr Hotchkis deserves the more special notice here, because to some of his manifold memoranda these pages are very much indebted. He must have been an indefatigable collector and transcriber, whatever his merits as a teacher may have been: "four folio manuscripts of curious and important collections, bequeathed by him to the library, now unfortunately missing"* (but from which partial extracts have been made), and a wonderful folio volume—a sort of commonplace-book—which is still in existence, and is said to contain 100,000 references upon the most miscellaneous subjects, attest at least a very diligent pen. Leonard Hotchkis had made his first appearance in public life in rather conspicuous fashion. In 1710, the famous Dr Henry Sacheverell, fresh from the trial and conviction which stamped him as a martyr in popular estimation, made a sort of triumphal entry into Shrewsbury on his way to take possession of a Shropshire living. "Near a thousand horsemen," zealous for Church and Queen, went out to escort him; and one young man, a student of Cambridge, claimed the honour of leading his horse by the bridle. This was the future head-master of Shrewsbury. There was some gallantry in the act, because such opinions were not popular with the town authorities. Bennet and Dawes, the two ministers of St Chads, showed their principles in a rather different way. They too wished to sympathise with the popular hero; but, "not choosing to make a public declaration," asked leave to pay their visit to the Doctor *by night*. Sacheverell, with a haughty bitterness which they at least deserved,

* Blakeway's Shrewsbury.

returned for answer that "he would have no *Nicodemuses*." Hotchkis began his work at Shrewsbury as third-master, and rose thence to the head-mastership. His stanch political partisanship brought him into continual collision with the Whig corporation; and though he was undoubtedly a good scholar, he was not a successful schoolmaster. Perhaps his antiquarian tastes may have stood in his way, and he was making entries in his commonplace-book when he ought to have been correcting exercises. It is to his credit, at all events, that he was vexed at the low condition of the school. But for the persuasions of friends he would have retired earlier than he did. He writes thus, August 1, 1750:—

"I have had but two or three boys a-year from Mr Parry [the second-master] for some years past; and I do not see more than seven or eight in his school now, except four who ought to be in mine. It is a melancholy state to be in, and I wish to get out of it."

Four years later he resigned. He was getting an old man, and during the latter period of his rule many boys were removed from Shrewsbury to the neighbouring school of Wem, owing to his failing energies. But he continued to live in the town, near enough to his old quarters to look out into the school garden, dying at the age of eighty, and probably busy to the last about his collections. One of the last glimpses we have of him (if it be him) is a passage in a letter from the Rev. George Ashby to Nichols, in which he speaks of the company he had met at the hospitable table of Dr Taylor (Hotchkis's intimate friend); some of whom, he says, were "the dullest companions possible; one of them, who, I think, had been a schoolmaster, was of all men I ever met with the stupidest."* There is a painful suspicion that this must have been the late head-master of Shrewsbury; perhaps those interminable manuscripts had muddled his faculties.

Yet under such masters, in these darker ages of King Edward's school, were trained perhaps the two greatest scholars in their respective lines of whom Shrewsbury can boast. One was the Dr John Taylor just mentioned, commonly known as "Demosthenes Taylor," a Shrewsbury barber's son, who rose to be a canon of St Paul's, and whose knowledge of Attic Greek surpassed perhaps all his contemporaries. The other, a pupil of Hotchkis, was Edward Waring, of an old Shropshire family, who was senior wrangler of his year, and was chosen Lucasian professor of Mathematics at the early age of twenty-four. So brilliant was his degree considered by his own contemporaries, that the whole body of his fellow-wranglers waited upon him in his rooms to offer him their public congratulations. Waring invited them all to tea, and this extempore entertainment laid the foundation of the society afterwards known at Cambridge as the "Hyson Club."

Upon Hotchkis's retirement, Charles Newling, fellow of St John's, was appointed by the College without opposition. He seems to have done something towards filling the waste places of Shrewsbury School. At least we are told that he had sixty boarders at one time in his own house; and, if a nearly contemporary chronicler is to be trusted, they were "among the most respectable characters in that and the neighbouring counties."†

So much could hardly be said for the school under

* Nichols's Lit. Anecd., iv. 515.   † Owen's Shrewsbury.

Newling's immediate successor, Thomas Atcherley, M.A., of Magdalen College, Cambridge, who was promoted from the second to the head mastership in 1770, and remained in that office for twenty-eight years. The traditions of his rule are not highly to his credit. He was no great scholar, and the school was left very much to take its chance. The upper boys are said to have had the free run of the library, of which they took advantage chiefly to tear out the fly-leaves of the books for their exercises. A letter of Dr Parr (an authority, however, by no means to be implicitly trusted) speaks of Mr Atchérley allowing a copy of Hephæstion, still in the library, and curious from its containing Hotchkis's marginal notes, "to be taken out and used by his servants when they were combing the hair of the boys. On many of the leaves," continues the writer, "were the dry *pedicular* skeletons, which Dr Butler caused to be cleared away before he sent the book to Mr Gaisford."

CHAPTER V.

THE DAYS OF BUTLER.

THE state of the school became such a serious question, that the Corporation consented, in 1798, to the extinction of the burgesses' claim to the exclusive appointment to the head and second masterships. An act was passed by which the election was left entirely to the Master and Fellows of St John's; while at the same time the present right of all sons of burgesses to be educated gratuitously was established. Atcherley and the other masters resigned upon annuities, and the College appointed to the head-mastership Samuel Butler, M.A., one of their own fellows, and perhaps the first classical scholar of his day.

His advent was a new era for the school. He had been educated at Rugby under Dr James, and had carried off at Cambridge nearly every classical honour that was open to him. Under his able rule, the numbers of the school rose gradually, though at first not rapidly. He had been head-master more than five-and-twenty years, when the brilliant success of Shrewsbury at both Universities in 1824 and 1825 swelled the admission-list from an average of 25 to 80 or 100 in the year; and in 1832 there were above 300 boys in the school—the highest number reached since the days of Chaloner. But the mere increase in numbers was no fair criterion of his success. From the time that his teaching came to show its full results, the University distinctions gained by his scholars threw into the shade all other public schools in the kingdom. Rugby must have sighed over the laurels that might have been her own, won year after year by the nursling whom she had rejected from her head-mastership in favour of a stranger. The only approach to rivalry was found in the provincial school of Bury St Edmund's, under Becher and Malkin; and this pressed Shrewsbury close.

The impression left upon his pupils by Dr Butler's personal character differs considerably, as in the case of most energetic masters. It was said by some that he taught them "scholarship, but nothing else"—that he kept even the elder boys a good deal at a distance, and was somewhat overbearing and despotic. It must be remembered that in his day the kindly and familiar intercourse between teacher and pupil which now so happily marks such relations, both in our colleges and public schools, would have been a very exceptional state of things indeed if it had existed at Shrewsbury. But there are many who remember lovingly that most intelligent and benevolent countenance which, no less than the careful neatness of costume, marked the accomplished gentleman as well as the scholar, not too grave, with all his learning, to enjoy a joke with all the heartiness of a schoolboy. He was, in his earlier years, a severe disciplinarian, at least so far as actual school-work went; and the floggings which he administered (with his left hand) are by no means forgotten. Yet he could forgive very readily—the more so if a joke might lend an excuse for it. There is a story told of his coming upon a small boy in some locality which was strictly out of bounds, and the culprit taking refuge in an empty hogshead which stood before a grocer's shop. The Doctor walked up to the shop door, and, after tapping the hogshead all round with his cane, remarked to the grocer that he had been looking out for an empty cask about that size, and desired it to be sent down to him "just as it was"—the fright of the delinquent inside during the negotiation being his only punishment. Stern indeed were his threatenings in the lectures delivered, somewhat incongruously, in lieu of sermons, after evening prayers in the school chapel (when the offences of the week were sometimes reviewed), against unconvicted delinquents who had been stealing ducks, breaking the farmers' fences, or riding their horses bare-backed in an impromptu steeple-chase; but his anger took a much milder form when his own apples and pears had proved too tempting for some of the smaller boys. It was more serious in the case of anything like a personal insult to either of his familiars—Dinah, the boys' housekeeper, or John "Bandy," his factotum, who had to maintain the minor discipline of the hall in such matters as calling in the morning and taking away lights at night. On one particular occasion Dinah made formal complaint—a very unusual circumstance—against the sixth form as a body. Both in their common room and in their studies, they had (according to her account) been coupling her name loudly, during the whole afternoon, with very bad language—"very bad indeed," though happily she did not understand the words. The offenders were summoned before the Doctor in his study, where he sat brimful of very natural indignation. It turned out that the bad language was Greek; the subject of the next repetition lesson was the chorus in ' Œdipus Rex '—

"ΔΕΙΝΑ* μὲν οὖν, ΔΕΙΝΑ' ταράσσει σοφὸς οἰωνοθέτας"—

which the boys had been shouting out, all the more vociferously when they understood Dinah's delusion. It was the kind of joke which Butler could not resist, and he broke out into a paroxysm of laughter.

Butler's senior assistant-master for many years was I——, a sound scholar and able teacher, strong in Tacitus and Thucydides, and with whom Matthiæ's Greek Grammar (the great authority in its day) was a text-book in constant use. Though by no means Butler's equal in elegant scholarship, he was not inclined to give way to him on questions of grammatical criticism. He taught his form (the upper fifth) in "Bromfield's Hall," in the School Lane. Sometimes, in the course of a lesson, some point would arise upon which he was aware that he and his chief differed in their view, when he would conclude his own interpretation with the significant remark, "You may perhaps be told differently lower down the Lane, *but*——;" and there he would stop, with considerable emphasis.

There was a punishment peculiar to the school in those days which is now disused. In the corner of the

---

* It must be explained, for the sake of any gentle reader who may be in the housekeeper's predicament, that the first word is pronounced "*Dinah*."

old "Fourth-form School," now occupied by the boards containing the list of honours, there used to be a small four-square apartment, not much larger than a Punch-and-Judy box, lighted by a single narrow loophole—a receptacle for the flogging-block and other like apparatus. This was known as the Black Hole, or sometimes more familiarly as "Rowe's Hole," from a traditionary culprit who had been a very regular occupant. Here younger offenders were occasionally locked up for some hours. It was patronised chiefly by I——, in whose hall, somehow or other, there were usually a large proportion of those irregular characters who preferred the excitement of a poaching expedition to the due preparation of lessons and exercises. When the original prison was pulled down, a small closet in the upper school was occasionally used for the same purpose. It was a point of honour with a prisoner's friends to supply him, while under confinement, with small luxuries from the pastry-cook's; not always an unnecessary provision, for on one occasion two boys were forgotten, and might have remained there all night, had not one of them made his escape by breaking the lock and climbing down by a water-pipe into the school court below.

There were in Dr Butler's time the usual "speeches" at midsummer, in the preparation of which he took considerable pains, having the boys into his private library to practise. On more than one speech-day Dr Parr, for whom Butler had an intense respect, was present, sitting in the seat of honour next to the head-master, with his pipe in his mouth and his spittoon before him; an arrangement which, together with his buzz-wig (probably the last surviving specimen), attracted considerable attention from the boys. He was good enough to signify a gracious approval of some of the speakers by the quiet tapping of two forefingers of one hand on the palm of the other; an amount of applause which, as Butler assured the young performers, meant a great deal from so great a man. But the great school festival in those days was the annual play at Christmas, in which Butler took almost as much interest as Ashton had done in the more elaborate spectacles which attracted Queen Elizabeth. In the week before breaking up, the large school was fitted up as a temporary theatre, and some time beforehand was spent in careful preparation. The season for the town theatricals was then generally drawing to a close, and some half-dozen scenes, wings, &c., were readily lent by the manager, who liberally supplied all other properties required, even to the thunder, lightning, and rain for 'King Lear.' The performance was public; that is, the trustees, the neighbouring gentry, and as many of the more respectable townspeople as the school could accommodate, received invitations. A play of Shakespeare, with a farce to conclude, was the usual programme. There was a supper for the actors afterwards, not the least important part of the festival, to which old pupils were wont to contribute presents of wine. Some amusing scenes were occasionally enacted, which were not set down in the bill. There was usually an epilogue, written by one of the masters, and spoken in character. On one occasion, Garrick's farce of 'The Lying Valet' had been performed with great applause, and the young actor who had sustained Mrs Clive's part of "Kitty Pry" came again before the curtain to deliver the epilogue. By a not uncommon theatrical licence, one of the audience was to take part in the dialogue. Accordingly, immediately upon Kitty's entrance, a boy who was seated close behind Butler got up and saluted her with—

"What! Kitty Pry again upon her legs!"

Scandalised at what he thought an audacious interruption, the Doctor rose and turned round in boiling wrath upon the speaker; and was hardly appeased, amidst the intense amusement of the house, when Kitty, not in the least disconcerted, replied in her pertest tone—

"None of your *himperance*, young man, I begs!"

No one laughed more heartily at the mistake than the Doctor himself.

Dr Butler resigned in 1836, on his appointment to the bishopric of Lichfield. The numbers of the school had fallen off in his later years, and the discipline had become somewhat lax. But his name will always be held in grateful remembrance at Shrewsbury. A service of plate, of the value of £1000, was presented to him on his retirement; perhaps it is to be regretted that the sum was not rather employed, as suggested by a minority of the committee, in the establishment of some honour at Cambridge which should have borne his name. However, the "Butler" exhibition, founded by the Trustees of the School, supplies that kind of memorial in some degree.

St John's College was at no loss to find amongst its own members a fitting successor to Dr Butler in one of his most distinguished pupils,—Benjamin Hall Kennedy, who retired in 1866, after presiding over the school for nearly thirty years. If, during that time, the numbers have never again risen to what they once were, it only makes the fact the more remarkable, that the Shrewsbury honours have suffered little diminution, and that a school, often consisting of not above a hundred boys, has more than held its own against rivals who have outnumbered it fivefold. Those who have read the Commissioners' Report* on the results of Shrewsbury teaching under Dr Kennedy will be at no loss to account for the fact that, since its publication, the school list rose from 131 to very nearly 200: there have been some fluctuations since, but the numbers are again slowly rising.

* Public Schools Report, i. 314.

CHAPTER VI.

MISCELLANEOUS.

The Elizabethan schools at Shrewsbury are commodious enough, and their antiquity gives them a charm which no modern buildings, with all their other advantages, can ever possess. The library, which might, perhaps, without detriment to its main purpose, be more utilised for the work of the school, is a noble room, much improved by some alterations in 1815. The large school-room in the upper storey, running the whole length of the front, in which the sixth and fifth forms are now taught, is also a fine room, 78 feet long; it has at some time been divided into three by partitions and folding doors. The chapel, though large enough for the present numbers of the school, is little more than a large room on the ground-floor fitted up for the purpose; but it is now in contemplation to build a new one as a testimonial to the late head-master. There is a short morning service in chapel daily before first lesson; full evening service is held there on Sundays, and within the last few years an excellent choir has been formed by the boys, and the service is rendered very heartily and effectively. On Sunday mornings the school still attend St Mary's Church.

But Shrewsbury labours under some disadvantages, as compared with other large schools, in the way of domestic arrangements. The boarders reside chiefly either in the head-master's house, or "Senior Hall," as it is called, or in a house adjoining rented by him, and called the "Junior Hall." The second-master also has a "Hall," which will accommodate about twenty. But the buildings are old, in many cases badly adapted for their present use, and have been either purchased, built, or rented from time to time by the head-master as the numbers of the school required. Even now, he has to rent a third house for the purpose of supplying studies for the senior boys, who are distributed four in each. No suitable buildings for the accommodation of the large number of boys which the school has contained, both under Dr Butler and Dr Kennedy, have ever been erected, though the funds of the school (about £3000 per annum) are certainly large enough to justify a judicious liberality in this respect. Every visitor to Shrewsbury must, however unwillingly, endorse the recorded judgment of the Royal Commissioners, that "the condition of the boarding-houses is undeniably defective, and that to a degree which must seriously affect the wellbeing of the school." A generation or two back, things were very much in the rough at Shrewsbury— almost more so than amongst the collegers of Eton and Winchester. A single bed, although most boys had it, was charged as an "extra"—a luxury which must be paid for. In each hall there was but one common washing-room for all the boys, and no accommodation at all of that kind was provided in the bedrooms. Attempts to establish anything in the way of a private "tub" were rather jeered at as an effeminate affectation. A basin of skim milk and a supply of thick dry toast formed the breakfast; there was no tea; and the supper was bread and cheese. At dinner, pudding was served before meat. The dinners themselves were fairly good, with the exception of the "boiled beef" days, which were highly unpopular. The beef was probably good enough; but it was cured with saltpetre, and the consequent redness was, in the boys' eyes, objectionable. Remonstrances had been made in vain; and the result was something like a school rebellion, well remembered as the "Beef Row." By concerted arrangement, on one day the boys in every hall quietly rose from the table in a body, and left the masters and the boiled beef in sole occupation. Butler was indignant; he came into each of the halls after locking-up, and demanded from the heads of the school a public apology for the insult, giving them an hour for consideration, and placing before them the alternative of immediate dismissal. The boys held together; and, early the next morning, the whole of the sixth form—comprising no less than three who were to be future heads of colleges—were started by chaise or coach for their respective homes. The rest of the boys declared themselves *en revolte*. They would not go into school; and the masters walked about the court, alternately threatening and persuading. At last a gentleman in the town—an old Shrewsbury boy, much respected—harangued the rebels, and persuaded them to surrender. Some sort of concession seems also to have been made by a portion of the absent sixth form, under home influence; and the affair ended in the return of all the exiles. This appears to have been the only occasion on which the discipline of the school was seriously disturbed.

The Shrewsbury games are the universal ones of all public schools—cricket, fives, and football. The latter has of late years been played vigorously enough; but it is singular that Butler, himself brought up at Rugby, the natural home of the game, should have forbidden it in the earlier days of his reign at Shrewsbury, denouncing it as "only fit for butcher-boys." The matches of the school cricket eleven have hitherto been played only against the neighbouring clubs in the county, but the increasing facilities of railway communication will open the way to a meeting with other schools. Boating, at one time forbidden, has gradually crept up through several stages of toleration to be a recognised institution, sanctioned by the masters, and under the regular superintendence of a "captain;" and no boy is now allowed to go into the boats until he can swim. The old tub-like craft, in which Salopians of past days were content to take the water, have long given way to modern outriggers, and the school crew have pulled three well-contested matches with Cheltenham College, losing a time race in 1864 only by a few seconds, winning the following year (at Tewkesbury), after a most exciting struggle, by some two or three feet, and more easily in 1866, at Worcester. The boating season concludes with a "regatta," which affords a good deal of amusement to the townspeople as well as the school. The "R.S.S.H." (Royal Salopian School Hunt) is the old "Hare and Hounds" developed into rather an elaborate system, under which each boy finds his place, either as huntsman, whip, "gentleman," or hound—the latter character, as may be imagined, implying some compulsory liabilities. The sport used to have an additional excitement from being followed against the school regulations, and involving a state of perpetual feud with the neighbouring farmers: but even its legalisation within the last few years has not much diminished its attractions.

In each of the halls, at the beginning of the school half-year, there takes place a ceremony known as the "Election." Certain officers of the hall are elected by universal suffrage; amongst others a "Lord High Constable," charged with the general maintenance of order, and whose powers and duties assume all the more importance from being very undefined; and two "Hall-criers" (or latterly one), whose chief business was to read out at breakfast-time lists of the fags on duty for cricket or football, descriptions of lost articles, &c. &c. This office, in former days, had commonly to be performed under a fire of such missiles as came handiest —amongst them often the regulation iron spoons supplied for the bread-and-milk breakfast which was the fare in the rougher days of Shrewsbury. Each proclamation began in due form with "Oh yes! oh yes!" and ended with "God save the King (or Queen)! and d—— the Radicals!"—an addition highly suggestive of the conservative sentiments of Shrewsbury. The excitement at these elections in past days was very great; a polling-booth was erected with the tables and benches at one end of the hall, where the votes were taken by the returning officer. Canvassers and voters stripped to their shirt-sleeves, and a general "scrimmage" began to bring supporters up to the poll, and to keep opponents in durance till the election was over; the object of each party being to secure the least burdensome offices for their own friends. The successful candidates stood on a table to return thanks, receiving the popular compliments in the shape of pinches from behind, and a shower of books, bread-crusts, &c., in front. They were finally inaugurated by being tossed in a blanket—not an agreeable operation in itself, and the less so because Shrewsbury ceilings are low, and the blankets were sometimes thin. In these days of good behaviour, election reform has extended itself to the halls at Shrewsbury; and a half-holiday is now given on the express understanding that at least the pelting and blanket-tossing shall be omitted.

The authority of the upper boys at Shrewsbury, although fully recognised as a principle of school government (Dr Kennedy, indeed, considers it "the very bone and sinew of English public education"), has always been strictly limited. The first twelve boys in the sixth form, which is unusually large, rank as "præpostors," and have certain distinctive privileges, such as wearing a hat instead of the regulation cap, going out of bounds, and carrying a stick,—which, however, they are not allowed to use in the way of personal correction, though they have the power of setting "punishments" in the form of lines to be written out. Fagging, as an individual service, is forbidden, and has never been regularly established in the school. But four boys are "put on" by rotation every week as general fags for the head common-room, whose duties in modern days consist chiefly in fetching and carrying. These fags are called "*douls*" (δουλος) in the classical Shrewsbury vernacular. But very much has always depended, as to the nature of these services, on the tyranny or the moderation of the upper boys. It used to be common for a younger boy on coming to the school to be attached to one of the seniors in the relation of client to patron—receiving help in his lessons and protection out of school, and in return performing for him little personal services, even to the cleaning his boots. A good deal of unlicensed service used also to be exacted from the day-boys, or *Skytes* (Σκυθαι), as they were termed; who, sooth to say, had formerly rather a hard time of it, being usually stoned out of School Lane at twelve o'clock, unless they were put upon some duty. In one form, at every repetition lesson, it was the recognised duty of the *skyte* in office to tear out of his own book the leaf containing the lesson, and stick it on the front of the master's desk, where it was safe from his eyes, and very useful to the form in general. On one occasion the boy had left his book at home, and had to copy the passage out on paper. Either carelessly, or of malice prepense, he had left out two lines; and the master was considerably puzzled and irritated by the strange coincidence of every boy in succession, as he stood up to recite, omitting the very same two lines, though in every other respect the lesson was said perfectly. It may be imagined that he was not a very lynx-eyed disciplinarian. It was remembered of him that during the Shrewsbury races he was left to superintend an extra composition lesson to be done in school by one of the upper forms—the chief object of which was to secure their presence there, and so keep them out of harm's way. Very soon after they had sat down, one boy after another brought up to his desk a few lines hastily scribbled, and, saying that he "could not do any more," left the room; and it was long before the master, whose dreamy studies took no account of races, discovered that he was left alone with one solitary and conscientious pupil.

But such stories are mere spots in the sun of Shrewsbury teaching. In that respect, at least, it has borne, and may bear, comparison with any school in England. Its catalogue of University honours, both under Dr Butler and Dr Kennedy, may fairly be said to be unrivalled in proportion to the numbers of its scholars. In the somewhat dingy room on the ground-floor, known as the "Fourth-form School," there runs round the walls an inscription, put up by Dr Butler in 1806, surmounting a series of wooden tablets, which record the triumphs of half a century:—

> ' Tu facito, mox cum matura adoleverit ætas,
> Sis memor, atque animo repetas exempla tuorum,
> Et tua te virtus magna inter præmia tollat." *

There stand in goodly rows, extending still every year, the names and dates of those who have won for the school any University distinction. The outside world smiled indeed a little, when Dr Butler, in the pride of his heart, inserted the name of one pupil in gilt letters as having won the "Ireland" at Oxford, while yet a schoolboy at Shrewsbury. But it was a pardonable vanity; and that great teacher's enthusiasm at such triumphs reacted on his boys. It is indeed, as one of the Royal Commissioners termed it, "a magnificent list." The Porson Prize at Cambridge (for Greek verse) has of late years, as the same Report says, been "almost

---

* An adaptation from Virgil, Æn. xii. 438.

monopolised" by the school; Shrewsbury scholars having gained it fifteen times in the last eighteen years.* And nowhere will the scholar find more elegant modern Latin poetry, than in the pages of 'Sabrinæ Corolla,' or the Shrewsbury contributions to the 'Arundines Cami.'† If the new head-master (the Rev. H. W. Moss),

* This Prize has now been founded fifty years; in that time it has been gained by Shrewsbury men no less than twenty-eight times.

† It is almost invidious to quote special instances amongst compositions, many of which are equally excellent, and in any such selection tastes will differ. Yet any one who wishes to know what Shrewsbury men have done in the way of translation, can hardly do better than turn to Dr Kennedy's versions of Surrey's 'Sonnet to Spring,' and of Wordsworth's Sonnet to Milton, '*Sabrinæ Corolla*,' p. 85, 183; or Shilleto's clever translation from Shakespeare (Christopher Sly), in the '*Arundines Cami;*' or James Hildyard's rendering of Swift's 'City Shower' (*Arund. Cami*, 136), which gained an "extra" holiday as a school exercise, and of the 'Burial of Sir John Moore,' written during the examination for the Chancellor's Medal at Cambridge. The version of the difficult passage, "But half of our heavy task was done," &c., will give a sample of its character:—

> "Nec media ingrati pars est exacta laboris,
> Cum sonus, horarum nuntius, ire jubet;
> Quin prouludentem ad pugnas audivimus hostem,
> Et pigra fulmineas fert temere aura minas."

So again, Marmaduke Lawson's translation of Sheridan's graceful verses, which begin thus—

> "I ne'er could any lustre see
> In eyes that would not look on me;
> I ne'er saw nectar on a lip,
> But where mine own did hope to sip."

> "Phillidis effugiunt nos lumina: dulcia sunto;
> Pulchra licet, nobis haud ea pulchra nitent.
> Nectar erat labiis, dum spes erat ista bibendi:
> Spes perit; isque simul, qui fuit ante, decor."
> *Arund. Cami.*

Not less worthy of note are the many beautiful versions, both in Latin and Greek, by Professor T. S. Evans of Durham, and Mr Munro, the learned editor of Lucretius.

himself one of Shrewsbury's most distinguished sons, carries out as a teacher the brilliant promise of his academic career,* the school only needs a judicious liberality of outlay on the part of its trustees, to be what it has been in numbers under Ashton, Laurance, and Chaloner, and in scholarship under Butler and Kennedy.

* Craven Scholar, Brown's Medallist, three times Porson's Prizeman, and Senior Classic.

HARROW SCHOOL

The chief printed authorities are—

Ackerman's Public Schools.
Radclyffe's Memorials of Harrow School.

HARROW SCHOOL.

CHAPTER I.

FOUNDATION AND STATUTES.

THE traveller who runs into London either by the Great Western or North-Western Railway can hardly fail to notice a church spire crowning a hill, not very lofty in itself, but appearing so from its commanding elevation above the champaign country round it. That is Harrow-on-the-Hill — Charles II.'s practical realisation of the idea of a "church visible," as he told the divines who were disputing on that point in his royal and irreverent presence. Upon that hill his unhappy father lingered, escaping in disguise from Oxford, and took his last look on his capital before he returned to it as a prisoner; hesitating for some hours whether he should not yet throw himself upon the loyalty of his citizens of London. The tall brick buildings forming part of the group, which, with the church, occupy the height, are the school and its dependencies; and some of them have stood there nearly three hundred years.

The antiquarian will not give you any very satisfactory history of the little village itself, which, however, was not without its share of local celebrity long before it became the seat of a great public school. It appears in Domesday as Herges—said to mean "church"—has been Latinised into *Herga*, and in later English records is called "Harewe atte Hulle." The Welshman, who holds his own to be the one primeval language, and would have laughed Zadkiel's crystal spirits to scorn when he found they did not speak Welsh, tells you that the word is a mere corruption of the Saesneg from *Ar rhiw*—"on the ridge." The place seems always to have borne a high reputation for healthiness. In 1524, William Bolton, prior of St Bartholomew the Great in Smithfield, hearing that astronomers foretold the speedy coming of a second deluge, built himself a house of refuge on the highest ground at Harrow, and victualled it for two months—rather a short allowance under the circumstances; whereupon it is recorded that many of all ranks followed his example. Its ancient manor-house was long a favourite residence of the archbishops of Canterbury. There young Thomas Beckett arrived one evening, to enter the household of Archbishop Theobald, as an aspirant to holy orders. He put up at a hostelry in the village, where the old hostess was struck with his personal appearance, and dreamed a dream of him, in which it seemed that he covered the church with his vestments; which her husband interpreted to show that he should some time be lord of that church and place. He was; and spent some of his last days there in great hospitality, a fortnight before his murder.

If a somewhat vague tradition is to be trusted, the

reputed virtues of certain springs in the neighbourhood were the remote cause of the foundation of the great school; for it is said that John Lyon, yeoman, of the hamlet of Preston in the parish of Harrow found the first source of his prosperous fortunes in the small pieces of money thrown by grateful pilgrims into a healing well on his little estate. Be this as it may, the historical fact is that the said John Lyon, in the reign of Elizabeth, when grammar-schools became a favourite form of alms-deed, determined to set one up in his native parish. He procured his charter from the Queen in 1571; by which the trustees of his property were constituted a body corporate, and he was empowered to draw up statutes for the government of his proposed foundation. But these statutes, for some reason or other, were not drawn up, nor any school established, for more than twenty years afterwards. In 1592, two years before his death, Lyon drew up a " will and intent," in which he embodied, in very minute detail, the " orders, statutes, and rules " for his free grammar-school. His lands in Harrow, Alperton, Preston, Kilburn, and Paddington were conveyed, after the decease of himself and his wife Joan, to six trustees, gentlemen of position in the neighbourhood, for the building of a schoolhouse and payment of a master and usher, and certain other local charities, especially the repair of the highroads from Harrow and Edgware to London. The master was to be a M.A., and to have for his yearly stipend forty marks (£26, 13s. 4d.), with an additional five marks for coal; the usher, who was to be not under the degree of a Bachelor, was to have half the amount of stipend, with the same allowance for fuel. Both were to be unmarried men, and both were to have apartments in the school building; for which the sum of £300 (or more if needed, and if the estate would bear it) was set apart, in case it should not have been erected in the founder's own lifetime.

Whatever doubt there may be as to the intentions of other founders of village grammar-schools, it is plain from Lyon's own regulations that he contemplated for his scholars a liberal education. Even the Lord's Prayer and the Church Catechism, which all in the school were especially taught, were to be learnt in Latin as soon as might be; and Latin only was to be spoken, even in play-hours, by every boy above the lowest form. If Harrow boys have claimed from old times to be rather specially "gentlemen," there is something in the spirit of the old founder's rules which almost excuses the assumption. Not only does he provide that no original Harrovian is to come to school "uncombed, unwashed, ragged, or slovenly;" but the following, amongst the "articles to be recited to them that bring any scholars to be received into the school," show plainly that his foundation was not intended for the benefit of the lower classes of his fellow-parishioners:—

"You shall find your child sufficient paper, ink, pens, books, candles for winter, and all other things at any time requisite and necessary for the maintenance of his study.

"You shall allow your child at all times bow-shaft, bow-strings, and a bracer, to exercise shooting.

"You shall be content to receive your child and put him to some profitable occupation, if, after one year's experience, he shall be found unapt to the learning of grammar."*

---

* These articles are copied, nearly word for word, from those drawn up in 1570 by Sir Nicholas Bacon, Lord Keeper to Queen Elizabeth, for the

There can also be no question but that the founder of Harrow School had in view the possibility of the extension of its privileges beyond the boundaries of his native parish. His most sanguine hopes could hardly have foreshadowed the day when it should be thronged by the young aristocracy of all England; but, unlike most local benefactors, he inserted in his deed of foundation a special clause, which stood the school in good stead in a subsequent litigation. He provided that his schoolmaster might receive, "over and above the youth of the parish, so many foreigners as the whole number may be well taught and applied, and the place can conveniently contain by the judgment and discretion of the governors; and of the foreigners he may take such stipends and wages as he may get, so that he take pains with all indifferently." When, therefore, the Master of the Rolls, in 1810, gave his judgment in favour of the governors, maintaining the present constitution of the school, he was acting in strict accordance with the spirit of the founder's bequest. An appeal had been made to the Court of Chancery by certain inhabitants of Harrow, setting forth that "the gratuitous instruction of the poor was neglected in the commodious education of the rich," and that there were but few parish scholars, because there were "but few parishioners who wish to give their children a classical education." But nothing can be plainer than that the education which John Lyon meant to provide could hardly be called instruction for

---

Grammar-School of St Albans. The practice of archery is enjoined by statute upon many schools which were either founded or remodelled under Elizabeth; as, for instance, at Shrewsbury, Wilton, and Dedham.

the poor in any sense; and that if a boy were not "apt to the learning of grammar," he would have desired that his parents should remove him from the school, and put him to the loom or the plough, or some such "profitable occupation," as soon as might be. But what Lyon did intend, as the founders of other local grammar-schools intended, and what Sir William Grant quietly ignores in his judgment, was, that by the help of his bequest the means of a liberal education should be provided, at a moderate cost, for such "poor" as are not paupers or hand-labourers, but too often men of liberal breeding and liberal professions themselves. Such, surely, was the intent both of John Lyon of Harrow, and of Laurence Sheriff of Rugby, and such would be their desire now, if they could see the enormous increase in value of the estates which they devoted to education.

The founder's regulations for his school go into very minute detail as to the hours of work and the books to be read. From six in the morning ("or as soon as they may conveniently, having respect unto the distance of the place from whence they come, and the season of the year") until eleven, and again from one to six, gives something like ten hours of daily work for the original Harrovians. He is careful to provide that during this time "they shall not be allowed to play, except on Thursdays only, sometimes, when the weather is fair, and on Saturday, or half-holidays, after evening prayer." The school is to be divided into six classes; the "Petties," "which have not learned their accidence, or entered into the English rules of grammar"—the first, second, third, fourth, and fifth classes, for each of which he prescribes a list of books. In the fifth, the highest, they were to read Virgil, Cæsar, Cicero 'De Natura,' Livy, Demosthenes, Isocrates, and Hesiod. It is singular that the last is the only Greek poet named, and that even Homer finds no place in the curriculum. As the books of the school are all specified, so are the games, which were to be " to drive a top, toss a handball, to run or shoot, and none other." Correction was to be of no other kind " save only with the rod moderately," or with " a very light ferule on the hand for a light negligence ;" and it was specially provided—one would have thought unnecessarily—that the master should " receive no girls to be taught in the same school." The monitorial system, of the use and abuse of which so much has been said in late years, was a part of the original constitution of Harrow: two monitors were appointed, who were to report weekly on irregularities out of school hours ; and a third, who was to act as a check upon the other two.

CHAPTER II.

THE SCHOOL BUILDINGS.

It does not appear that Lyon lived to see his school in actual operation. For some years he had been used to pay the sum of twenty marks "for the teaching of thirty poor children" of the parish; and this payment he desires in his will to be continued until his new school should be built, for which he allows three years after his decease, if not completed before, which does not seem to have been the case. Probably it was not until 1593 that the original schoolhouse was built. It stands now very much as it stood then, a substantial but not very elegant structure of brick, forming the western portion of the present block of school-buildings. It still contains the "large and convenient schoolhouse, with a chimney in it," as ordered in the founder's will, wainscoted with oak, and lighted by heavy square windows with wooden transoms; in the basement below is the cellar for wood and coals, "divided into three several rooms, the one for the master, the second for the usher, and the third for the scholars," according to his most minute and equitable directions; and above, five rooms, which were probably the private apartments of the masters; over which, again, is a large attic. But the head-master, at any rate, did not long remain content with this very confined accommodation. As early as 1670 there is record of grants made by the governors for the rent of a private house, and for fitting it up to receive boarders; as indeed must have been very necessary, if the master was to avail himself at all of the founder's permission to "take wages of foreigners." Two years afterwards, a house which formed part of the estate in trust was formally made over to the head-master and his successors free of rent. This house was very much enlarged and improved by Dr Heath, and subsequently refronted by Dr Butler, soon after his appointment: the governors made a grant of £1200 for the purpose, but Butler himself expended on it £5000. It was burnt down October 22d, 1838, by a fire which broke out in one of the boys' studies, and destroyed at the same time the boarding-house occupied by Mr (now Bishop) Colenso. The present head-master's house was built at a considerable cost by Dr Wordsworth, partly by the subscriptions of Harrovians, and partly by a sum of money raised on mortgage by Act of Parliament.

The school-buildings themselves had in the mean time been found quite insufficient for their purpose, notwithstanding the conversion of what had once been the masters' apartments into class-rooms. In 1819 the more modern half of the present school was added by a general subscription of the governors, masters, and old and young Harrovians. Dr Butler was at that time headmaster; and it is a remarkable evidence of the very different notions of liberality entertained by his generation, as compared with our own, that he was accused of "ostentation," because his own name was put down for £500.

It contains the "speech-room"—used on ordinary occasions for the general gathering of the school, called in the Harrow tongue "a speecher"—with other rooms above; and was built so as to correspond in style, as far as might be, with the original structure. The old school was then assigned to some of the lower forms, and is now known as the "Fourth-form Room;" the upper and second Fourth at present occupying it. But it still remains the great object of interest in the place, all unadorned as it is, with its gloomy old windows and oaken wainscot and plastered walls, covered with rude inscriptions which no "restorer's" hands have been allowed to touch; of little interest to the professional archæologist, but to Harrovian eyes more precious than the arrowheads of Nineveh. For here, cut by their own hands in boyhood with more or less skill, may be read the names of some of the foremost men in England's modern history; the schoolfellows "Byron" and "R. Peel"—the latter in bold deep capitals, as determined to leave his mark legibly amongst the boys or men of his time; and not far off, his successor in the Premiership, but his senior at Harrow by five years—a whole school generation—"H. Temple," Viscount Palmerston, with the date 1800. There, too, may be read an older name, which carries with it even now a deep and pathetic interest, from the sad fate which struck it so early from the rolls of the living—"Spencer Perceval." It is the story of a past generation, yet well remembered—the better, perhaps, because his fate was so nearly repeated in the case of Peel; and even the modern visitor can scarcely help being affected by the brief note appended to the "speech-bill" of 1812, in which the younger Perceval is set down to recite Gray's 'Bard'—"Not spoken, in consequence of the assassination of his father." Many other such memorials of the boyhood of remarkable men may be traced on those old school-walls; many have disappeared under the vigorous knife of some modern Smith or Thompson, too eager to record that he too had dwelt in this Arcadia. It is to prevent this desecration of old memories by modern ambition that all carving on the walls themselves is now strictly forbidden, and long boards have been set up upon which the modern Harrovian may hand down his name to posterity, if so disposed, in legible capitals executed by the school *custos* for the moderate consideration of half-a-crown.

But even the new additions to the main building have of late years proved quite insufficient for the increasing numbers at Harrow. Six new schoolrooms have been built on some of the land belonging to Lyon's trust, and three more have just been added under the new library; so that every form, with the exception of those who are still in joint occupation of the old school, has now its separate room as well as separate master.

Lyon's most sanguine expectations never contemplated the possibility of his scholars overcrowding the parish church. An excellent Churchman himself, he not only made it an especial direction that they should be taught the Articles and the Catechism in school, but also that they should "come to church and hear Divine service and Scripture read and interpreted with attention and reverence," on pain of summary correction. It was probably for their especial benefit that in his will he left £10 for the preaching of thirty "good, learned, and godly sermons" yearly; for he directs that if his schoolmaster or usher "can well, and will do the same, without any hindrance to his teaching," one of them is to have "before any other," the preaching and the preacher's fee. But when the school rose into a public one, the parishioners of Harrow were fairly swamped in their sittings by John Lyon's scholars; they overflowed even the supplemental galleries built for their special accommodation, which galleries were not very favourable to the "attention and reverence" desired by the founder. A great step was gained in this respect when, in 1839, they moved into a chapel of their own. It was under the mastership of Dr Wordsworth, and to him much of the credit is due, both for his energy in raising subscriptions and for his own liberal contribution. But the chapel thus erected proved too small for the increasing numbers of Harrow; the chancel was first taken down, and subsequently the nave, to make way for the present building. The chancel was Dr Vaughan's gift to the school, and the Crimean Aisle on the south was the tribute of old schoolfellows and friends to the memory of those who fell in the Russian war. The six stained windows in this aisle bear underneath the names and rank of twenty-two Harrow men who fought their last fight there; Anstruther, who won the first of these red laurels at the Alma, at eighteen; Dawson, Allix, Sir Robert Newman, Greville, and Clutterbuck, who fell at Inkerman; Lockwood and Montgomery, in the death-ride of Balaclava; Patullo, Clayton, Ryder, and Holden—the last yet a mere schoolboy—who died at the fatal Redan; with others who either met a soldier's death in the trenches, or sank under fever or cholera. Of them it was well said in Dr Vaughan's address, when the first stone was laid by Fenwick Williams of Kars—"Their bodies are buried in a far land; but their names live amongst us for evermore."

CHAPTER III.

EARLY HEAD-MASTERS.

So much for the mere outward Harrow of bricks and mortar; it is time to say something of the men who have made it what it is. So far as it can be traced, it remained a mere country grammar-school of decent repute for many generations after the founder's death. It had no royal foundation, like Eton and Westminster; no collegiate establishment, with rich fellowships and scholarships, like Winchester; nor did its revenues swell year after year from the spreading wealth of London, like Sheriff's very similar foundation at Rugby. Harrow may boast, if any school can, of having risen by merit. Probably, when once it had gained a certain amount of reputation under an able master, its neighbourhood to London, in days when locomotion was a very different thing from what it is now, contributed to its success; and no doubt, when any cause had once made it a fashionable school, fashion kept up its numbers without much reference to the quality of its teaching. But Harrow was and is a poor foundation compared with any other school of its rank. The head-master receives from the trustees of John Lyon but £30 a-year, with an allowance of £20 for coal, and a house, with accommodation for his boarders,—upon which house, however, successive masters have laid out considerable sums to make it what it is. Until some alterations were made at the last appointment, the under-master (or "usher" of Lyon's foundation) drew from the estates only £24, 8s. 4d.; a sum, at the present value of money, much less than the twenty marks which Lyon assigned him. He also has an allowance of £20 for fuel, and £25 in lieu of the rooms in the old schoolhouse which he was originally to occupy. There is no statutable provision for any of the other masters at all; they are paid out of the annual proceeds of the school. Each of them even had, until a recent date, to pay for the necessary repairs of their own schoolroom.* Yet John Lyon's estates, as may be supposed in the case of property so near London, have risen in value five-and-twenty fold. But it must be borne in mind that part of his rents were to go to the repairs of the roads between Harrow and London; pretty nearly as much a work of charity, in those days of painful travel, as the founding of a grammar-school. His intention, as is plain from his will, was that something like two-thirds of the whole rents were to go to his school, and the remaining third to the highways. But unfortunately he specified *which* rents—those from his lands at Kilburn and Mary-le-bone—were to be applied to this latter purpose; and these have, of course, increased much more than the others; so that, according to the present interpretation of his will, the proportions are pretty nearly reversed, the roads getting something like £3500 per annum, while the school trust receives,

---

* A scheme for the remodelling of the distribution of the school funds is now being carried out.

for all purposes, not more than £1100. The proceeds of the road estates are now applied, under the provisions of successive Acts of Parliament, partly to the paving of Oxford Street, and partly to the repairing, watching, and lighting of the other metropolitan roads.*

The earliest recorded masters are Thomas Johnson, M.A. of Oxford, and Thomas Martin, M.A. of Christ-Church in that university.† But the first who raised Harrow to anything like a public school‡ was an Etonian, William Horne, M.A., Fellow of King's College, Cambridge, who next succeeded in or about 1660; though little is now known of him beyond what can be gathered from his epitaph in the chancel of Harrow Church—that he was "*preceptor strenuus*." He had at least one very extraordinary pupil. There came to Harrow in 1668, from an obscure village in Shropshire, one William Baxter, then eighteen years old, and knowing (if his own words are to be trusted) "not one letter in a book, nor understanding one word of any language except Welsh." It must have taxed the energies of even that strenuous master to teach him under such difficulties. But teach him he did; so that he afterwards taught others successfully as master of the Mercers' School in London, and his well-

* Public Schools Report, i. 208.
† Wood's MSS. (Bodl. Libr.)
‡ Perhaps the earliest notice of the school may be traced in Ben Jonson's comedy of 'Bartholomew Fair' (A.D. 1614), in which one of the characters, Bartholomew Cokes, "a tall young squire of Harrow-o'-the-Hill," among sundry other foolish doings at the fair, "falls scrambling for the pears" from a stall which has been upset, and exclaims—"Ods so! a muss, a *muss*, a *muss*, a *muss*" (which may be old Harrovian for a "squash"); upon which one of the lookers-on remarks—"A delicate great boy! methinks he outscrambles them all. I cannot persuade myself but that he *goes to grammar-school* yet, and plays the truant to-day."—Act iv. sc. 1.

known edition of Horace drew a compliment even from Bentley. Upon Horne's death in 1685, another Fellow of King's succeeded—Thomas Brian, M.A., who continued in the mastership no less than thirty-nine years, and resigned probably five years before his death. On this supposition, it was in 1725 that James Cox, M.A. of Merton College, Oxford, the usher or lower-master, was elected to the vacancy. He had married his predecessor's daughter, "a woman of very remarkable beauty;" but he seems to have had family troubles, and others of his own making: he was finally removed by the governors for misconduct in 1745. He was followed by the first of the many great names amongst the rulers of Harrow. Thomas Thackeray, "a great scholar in the Eton way, and a good one in every way," says a contemporary, had been an assistant-master at Eton, a Fellow of King's, and a very nearly successful candidate for the provostship of his college against the Eton head-master, Dr George.* His orthodoxy seems to have been questioned at Eton, owing to his having taken the side of Bishop Hoadly in what is known as the Bangorian controversy; and he resigned his situation there in consequence. It must be presumed that the Harrow governors were more latitudinarian in their opinions, for they elected him to their head-mastership without scruple. Hoadly did not forget him. When translated to Winchester, he sent for his stanch supporter, and offered him the archdeaconry of Surrey. Thackeray was so overwhelmed by the unexpected offer, that (according to Dr Pyle, before quoted) "he nearly fainted." The Bishop "had never seen this

* For a highly amusing account of this election, see Nichols's Lit. Illustrations, i. 95.

man in his life, but had heard much good of him." Evidently Dr Pyle was far from knowing the whole story.* Thackeray was a man of striking personal appearance and polished manners, and he added to his classical accomplishments the much rarer one, in his days, of a good knowledge of modern languages. Those who were educated under him always spoke of him with affection and gratitude. "I loved and revered him as a father," writes Dr Parr. He acted upon the somewhat peculiar principle of never applauding his pupils' exercises, for fear of making them vain. He is said to have remodelled the school system upon the Eton pattern. After a mastership of fifteen years, during which the number on the school-list rose at one time to a hundred and thirty—considerably more than at any previous date —he resigned from ill health in 1760, and died in the year following. Another Eton scholar, also a Fellow of King's, succeeded—Robert Sumner, grandfather of the late Archbishop. If half the eulogies of his contemporaries be true—and they have all the air of truth—he was, both in character and ability, such a master as few schools have seen. The eloquent tributes paid to him by perhaps his two most distinguished pupils, Sir William Jones† and Dr Parr, are too long for quotation here, and the latter (inscribed on his monument in Harrow Church) might be thought to speak too much the usual language of epitaphs; but there are less formal and equally warm testimonies both from them and from others. "One of the six or seven persons whose taste I am accustomed to consider perfect," writes Parr, in a

---

* Richards's History of Lynn.
† Preface to Treatise on Asiatic Poetry.

private letter; and again, to another correspondent, "One of the best-tempered men in the world." He seems, indeed, to have possessed every qualification for his office in a very remarkable degree. Under him the numbers of the school rose rapidly, until from eighty (at which point he found them) they reached two hundred and fifty.

CHAPTER IV.

THE SCHOOL UNDER DR SUMNER.

It is now that we meet with the first printed bills of the school, a number of which were collected and privately printed by Dr Butler; and it may be interesting to note from them the staff and working arrangements of Harrow a hundred years ago, as contrasted with the present.

In 1770 (the first year in these printed lists) the under-master was the Rev. Richard Wadeson, and there were three assistant-masters—Samuel Parr, David Roderick, and Joseph Drury, the future head-master. The three "monitors" of Lyon's regulations had been increased to four; next year there were six, subsequently seven, then ten—reduced, as the numbers of the school gradually fell off in later years, to five; and again increased by Dr Vaughan in 1854 to their present number, fifteen. Next in rank to the monitors came the fifth form, according to Lyon's original scheme, and these two forms were taught by the head-master; there was no sixth until many years afterwards. Then followed the shell, fourth, and third forms; all these ranking as the "upper school." The "under school" was divided in a very peculiar fashion; there was first the "Scan and

Prove" class, then the "Ovid," the "Phædrus," the "Upper Selectæ," "Under Selectæ," "Nomenclature," "Grammar," and "Accidence." It is impossible not to wish, as we read, that these latter classes were to be found existing in fact, if not in name, in our public schools at present; and we readily understand that Dr Sumner was indeed the able teacher he is recorded to have been. At the end of the bill come a few names "unplaced." The following year a "Prayer-book" class appears, next below the Grammar; a few years later, "Terence" comes in place of "Scan and Prove," and in 1796 gives the name to the lowest form in the school; "grammar," it is to be feared, beginning even thus early to go out of fashion; though in 1803 the Ovid Class (with a duke in it) and the Phædrus reappear. At present there are, besides the monitors, an upper and lower Sixth, four separate divisions of the Fifth, two "Removes," four "Shells," and three Fourths; there is usually a very small Third, but a First and Second are practically ignored at Harrow, as at most public schools. There are now fifteen assistant classical masters, besides four mathematical, two for modern languages, and one for natural science. The number of boys in any one form is restricted as nearly as possible to thirty-five as the *maximum;* in former days, when the school was full, and the masters much fewer in number, there were in some forms as many as seventy; plainly quite too many for anything like individual attention on the part of the teacher; only a very small percentage could be "put on" at any one lesson, and an idle boy, with the gambling spirit more or less common to all boys and men, took his chance of not being called upon. No defect of arrangement has fostered idleness in the mass of boys so much as the overgrown numbers too often assigned, in our larger schools, to each individual master.

Sumner's most celebrated pupil was Samuel Parr. The son of a Harrow apothecary, he entered the school in 1758, when he was six years old. Before he was fourteen he was at the head of it; when, to his great mortification, his father, who was little able to afford him a university education, took him to assist in his business. But the young scholar is said to have carried on his school studies in some sort, by working over at night, with one of his old schoolfellows, the monitors' lessons for the day, with Sumner's criticisms and corrections. He also took upon himself to criticise now and then the physicians' Latin which came before him in the form of prescriptions; which is recorded to have drawn very little encouragement from the more practical father: "Sam," said he, "d—— the language—make the mixture." After three years' trial, however, his tastes and abilities showed themselves so decidedly, that Sumner persuaded his father to allow Sam to leave the mixtures, and enter at Emmanuel College, Cambridge. But after hard struggles and hard study, want of means compelled him to leave before he took his degree; and Sumner, who continued always his steady friend, took him as an under-master in his twentieth year. A Harrow mastership in those days was not quite so good a thing as now; all Sumner could offer was £50 per annum, with the chance of another £40 or £50 from pupils. Of Parr's life there for the next five years little is known, though many traditional stories of his eccentricities used to be current. He is said to have been, as a boy, so quaint and prematurely old-looking, that his schoolfellow Jones (Sir William), after looking hard at him one day during a walk, said, "If you have the luck to live forty years, Parr, you will stand a chance of overtaking your face." He had the luck, at all events—if luck it was—while still a very young master at Harrow, to win the affections of a well-to-do widow in the neighbourhood. The lady's fancy became known to the boys, and many were their jokes about Parr and his fair admirer. One day the following was found lying on his desk:—

> "When Madam Eyre prefers her prayer,
> Safe from the eyes of men,
> 'Tis this alone her lips make known,
> '*Parr*—donnez-moi! Amen!'"

From what subsequently happened, it is clear that he was not only an able teacher, but very popular amongst the boys. His secret, according to his own account, was one which has seldom been unsuccessful. "I tried to treat the boys," says he, "as young gentlemen." One of his pupils has recorded how, in the Virgil lesson, he poured out from his remarkable memory illustration upon illustration, tracing the Roman poet back to his Greek sources with a merciless ability which might have satisfied even Professor Conington. He complained of the little attention paid to Latin prose composition, and highly applauded the Winchester practice of committing large portions of Greek and Latin to memory. Upon Sumner's death, which occurred in 1771 from apoplexy, when he was only forty-one, Parr was encouraged by his friends to become a candidate for the head-mastership. He had in his favour the highest reputation for scholarship, and the hearty good wishes of most of the under-masters and scholars. According to his own statement, Sumner was known to have marked him out as his successor; against him was his youth, and his want of a university degree. If the impression which prevailed in the school at the time is to be trusted, there was another objection, not so openly avowed. The governors had been in the habit of frequently requesting holidays for the boys, against which Dr Sumner had strongly remonstrated, as interfering with the school-work: Parr had also warmly backed his chief in this resistance; and it was not forgotten at the election. His own belief was, that a vote which he had given for Wilkes at Brentford stood most in his way. To meet the most valid of these objections, his friends succeeded in obtaining for him, previous to the election, the degree of Master of Arts, by royal mandate. To give additional gravity to his appearance, Parr now for the first time adopted the wig which became afterwards almost as well known as himself. A petition was sent in to the governors, signed by the boys, but evidently drawn up by a more experienced hand, praying them to take into consideration "the unanimous wishes of the whole school, which are universally declared in favour of Mr Parr;" and (in anticipation of the election of Mr Heath), "that a school of such reputation ought not to be considered as a mere appendix to Eton;" the two last head-masters having been assistants there. When the day of election came on, and it was understood that Heath was chosen, an actual rebellion broke out; an attack was made upon the house where the governors met, and the carriage of one of their body, Mr Bucknall, was dragged out of the inn-yard and broken to pieces. Mr Roderick indeed, one of the assistant-masters, trusting to his popularity as a known partisan of Parr, interfered to rescue it, and rendered the owner the ironical service of saving "one entire side of the vehicle." One of the most conspicuous of the rioters, though only eleven years old, was the late Marquess Wellesley. He was immediately sent for by his guardian, Archbishop Cornwallis; but far from showing any penitence, he came into the room waving one of the tassels from the wrecked carriage, and shouting "Victory!" Within a few hours he was entered at Eton, and Harrow lost one of the most elegant of modern scholars. Parr and Roderick at once resigned their offices, and in consequence the governors adjourned the school for a fortnight. Order was not restored until three weeks after Heath had entered upon his new duties. The accusations brought against Parr, as having instigated the rebellion, seem to have been quite unfounded; but when he retired from Harrow, and set up a private school at Stanmore, about four miles off, he was accompanied there by some forty or fifty of the upper boys in the school (amongst whom were two sons of Lord Dartmouth), and by his faithful ally, Mr Roderick. Mr Joseph Drury, another of his fellow-assistants, also proposed to follow his fortunes; but, happily for himself, was persuaded to remain at Harrow, where he subsequently became head-master on Dr Heath's resignation. Many of the other boys were withdrawn from the school at the same time. But Harrow suffered little from what might have seemed the formidable rivalship of Stanmore. Sumner appears to have left two hundred and thirty-two boys in the school; and a list of 1774, the third year of Heath's rule, gives the numbers at two hundred and five.

Parr left Stanmore in a few years for the mastership of the grammar-school at Colchester, from which he afterwards removed to that at Norwich. It was well, perhaps, for his Harrow popularity that, as assistant-master, he had not the power of flogging there as he did at Norwich; although sharp corporal discipline is not a master's worst fault in the eyes of schoolboys. He seems to have not spared the rod in his last school. "I'll flog you all!" he thundered to his form on one occasion; the "praepostor of the week" having only Ulysses' privilege of being the last victim, after assisting in due official form at the previous executions. The Doctor had a commendable horror of geniuses amongst his pupils. One of his under-masters told him one day that "S—— appeared to him to show signs of genius." "Say you so?" said Parr, with a grin—"then begin to flog to-morrow morning." The execution-block at Norwich must have inspired more than the usual horrors; for Parr's lictor there was a man who had been sentenced to be hanged, but had been cut down, and resuscitated by the surgeons, and from whose hand, according to the account of one of his pupils, Parr "used to receive the birches with a complacent expression of countenance." One of his Stanmore pupils, Beloe, speaks, as if feelingly, of "the lightning of his eye, the thunder of his voice, and the weight of his arm." Yet the stern disciplinarian must have been naturally tender-hearted; for in his Harrow school-days he fought young Lord Mountstewart in defence of a worried cat. He took great interest in the athletic sports of the boys, and even enjoyed greatly the sight of a fair stand-up fight; issuing an edict that all such encounters should take place on a piece of ground opposite his study window, where, with his blind half-drawn, he could see without being seen. His many eccentricities of character make it very doubtful whether, in spite of his great scholarship, Harrow suffered any loss in his non-election. He was again brought forward as a candidate on Heath's resignation in 1785, but took no active steps in the contest.

Parr's schoolfellow and bosom friend at Harrow was Sir William Jones, the favourite pupil of both Thackeray and Sumner; whom Dr Johnson called—not without some truth, allowing for Johnsonian diction—"the most accomplished of the sons of men." Whether he really knew twenty-eight languages or not, he at least knew a great deal more about them than any man before him, or possibly since. He was very popular with his schoolfellows because of the many holidays given for his exercises; and Sumner is said to have remarked of him, that he knew more Greek than himself. The proceedings of the three boy-friends—Jones, Parr, and Bennet (afterwards Bishop of Cloyne)—were very unlike the usual doings of schoolboys. They disputed together in Latin logic, and parcelled out the neighbouring country into separate dominions,—Arcadia, of which Jones was king, under the name of *Euryalus;* Argos, under *Nisus* (Bennet); and Sestos and Abydos, where Parr reigned as *Leander.* Of their wars and politics we have no record. Jones, after distinguishing himself at Oxford, returned to Harrow for a short time as private tutor to the young Lord Althorp. His subsequent career as a judge in India, where the Brahmins held him in almost as great esteem for his learning as any of his English friends, can be only alluded to here; but it is worth recording that, had he lived to return to England, it was his favourite dream to end his days at Harrow. Another constant companion of Parr and Bennet was Richard Warburton (who took the name of Lytton), of whom Parr spoke in after life as the first Latin scholar of his time.*

Amongst Sumner's pupils was Richard Brinsley Sheridan, whose brilliant and irregular genius plagued and delighted his masters at Harrow, as it did the political world afterwards. He entered as a foundationer, his parents at that time residing at Harrow. Parr, who was in office as a master when he entered the school, soon noticed his remarkable powers, and did what he could to coax him into exertion. He was not very successful: Sheridan left school early, "a shrewd, artful, supercilious boy" (says his tutor, Mr Roderick), never reaching the sixth form. Amongst the boys he was, in some measure, a butt for his oddities; but in one not very creditable form of enterprise he seems to have taken the lead. Orchard-robbing was at that time not beneath the dignity of Harrow boys; and Sheridan had somewhere or other a regular apple-loft, for the supply of which all the orchards and gardens in the neighbourhood were laid under contribution, and younger boys were employed as collectors under more or less compulsion. Parr was aware of it, and tried, unsuccessfully, to convict Sheridan of the leadership of the gang.

There were at least three boarding-houses at this time besides the head-master's. One was kept by a Dr Glasse, and was almost a separate establishment. His pupils were chiefly boys of rank, and during Thackeray's

* His grandson Sir Henry Bulwer, and great-grandson Robert Bulwer-Lytton (son of Lord Lytton), were both Harrovians.

time had been exempted from appearing at "bills."*
Sumner stopped this privilege, to the great disgust of Dr
Glasse and some of his aristocratic friends. Earl Radnor
even threatened to "ruin the school" if Sumner refused
to give way; but the new head-master was firm. Lord
Dartmouth, on the other hand, supported him, and
removed his sons into his house from Glasse's, who was
beaten in the struggle, and left Harrow. Mr Reeves,
the writing-master, had also a few boarders; but the
largest house was Hawkins's, between the occupants of
which and Thackeray's a great fight (in the matter of
some fireworks) took place in December 1757, which
Bennet commemorated in a clever poem in English
heroic verse, entitled 'Pugna Maxima.'†

* Calling over the names on half-holidays, &c., usually at intervals of two or three hours, to keep the boys within reasonable bounds.

† Portions of it are quoted in the Memoirs prefixed to Parr's Works, vol. i. p. 22.

CHAPTER V.

DRS HEATH, DRURY, AND BUTLER.

Dr Parr's successful rival for the head-mastership of Harrow was, as has been said, the Rev. Benjamin Heath, again an Etonian and Fellow of King's. He was the son of Benjamin Heath, well known as a commentator on the Greek tragic poets; and it is remarkable that his brother, Dr George Heath, was some years afterwards elected head-master of Eton. He carried on the school for fourteen years, with no diminution in its numbers or reputation; and resigned in 1785, on being elected Fellow of Eton College. He retired to his rectory of Walkerne in Hertfordshire, where the magnificent library which he had collected at Harrow was arranged in a gallery built (in imitation of Sir Thomas Bodley's at Oxford) in the form of a T, in which Dr Dibdin luxuriated with his usual raptures; as he appears to have done also in the excellent "larder and cellar," which he tells us his host maintained. The collection of books was subsequently sold in London for £9000. "Never," says Dibdin, "did the bibliomaniac's eye alight upon sweeter copies; and never did the bibliographical barometer rise higher than at this sale."

Mr Joseph Drury, one of the assistant-masters, whose family name has since become one of the household words of Harrow, succeeded. The rapid rise of the school in numbers and importance is the best evidence of his efficiency as a master; and many of his old pupils—Lord Byron among the number—were strongly attached to him. At one time during his mastership there were above 350 names on the school-list, and amongst these very many belonging to the highest families in England. The bill of 1803 shows perhaps the largest proportion of nobility that could at any time have been counted in any school of the size. Out of 345 names there are those of one present and three prospective dukes—Dorset, Sutherland, Devonshire, and Grafton; one future marquis; two actual and five future earls and viscounts; and besides these, four others who bear the title of "Lord," twenty-one "Honourables," and four baronets. Two sons of Rufus King,* then American Minister in London, appear in this list: he professes to have sent them to Harrow because it was the only school in which no special honour was attached to rank. If the old Eton story about the three extra kicks "for the Duke" be true, there was just as much and as little respect of persons in one school as the other; but at any rate the republican contrived to send his boys into aristocratic company.

Dr Drury, after working in the school for the long term of thirty-six years—the last twenty as head-master—resigned, and retired to an estate of his own in Devonshire, where he died. A very close competition ensued

* One of them was present at the speeches of 1866.

for the vacancy. There was a strong party in favour of Dr Drury's son, Mr Mark Drury, then under-master; Mr Benjamin Evans, one of the assistant-masters, was also in the field; and high testimonials were sent in to the governors in favour of the Rev. George Butler, Fellow of Sidney College, Cambridge, and senior wrangler. The votes of the six electors were divided between these three, and reference had to be made to the Visitor, the Archbishop of Canterbury, who decided in favour of Butler. A letter of recommendation from Dr Parr had (according to the writer's statement) some influence in the choice. It was not a popular appointment with the majority of the boys, or with the inhabitants of Harrow, and the new head-master met with some annoyances during the first four months of his government. Dr Drury, much to his credit, wrote a letter to the school, in which he remonstrated strongly against this spirit of partisanship. At the first speech-day at which the new master presided the excitement was very great, and some disturbances were apprehended, but the affair seems to have passed over quietly. Dr Butler was a man of very high abilities; somewhat more feared than loved, perhaps, by those under his rule, but "he was a gentleman," says one of them emphatically—no light word of praise. One of the failings attributed to him as a disciplinarian is in itself a gentleman's characteristic—that he took the boys' word rather too much. He showed very great interest in the speeches, and took some pains to insure good action and elocution in the speakers; but the ordeal of rehearsal before him was rather dreaded, for he was merciless in his criticisms, taking off the tone and manner of an awkward speaker, to the victim's great disgust, and the amusement of the others present.

Lord Byron's school life is already pretty well known. Drury spoke of him as "a wild mountain colt, who might be led with a silken string rather than with a cable." The silken string at least secured Byron's attachment; "the best, the kindest (yet strict, too) friend I had, and I look upon him still as a father," was his record long after he had left school. He was at Harrow from his 13th to his 17th year,—"cricketing, rebelling, *rowing*, and in all manner of mischief;" and occasionally writing his "thirty or forty Greek hexameters, with such prosody as pleased God." He was one of the monitors at the time of Dr Drury's resignation, and resented bitterly the non-election of his son, and the accession of Butler. In conjunction with his friend Tom Wildman, he headed with all his influence the opposition to the new government; it is said that he even carried a loaded pistol, with some vague idea of shooting the new head-master. He kept up his animosity for some time, and Butler must have shown great patience with him. Once he tore down the gratings in the windows, and condescended to make no other excuse but that "they darkened the hall." He refused the usual invitation (regarded by the boys as a "command") to dine with the head-master at the end of the half-year; explaining, that he should "never think of asking Dr Butler to dine with *him* at Newstead." Some of the earliest efforts of his muse were satires, bitter, if not very poetical, against his new preceptor.* One of

* See 'Lines on a recent Change of Head-Masters in a Public School.'

these he has preserved; but there were many others current in the school which are probably just as well forgotten. Byron seems himself to have been conscious of an unjust prejudice. "I have retained," he says in his diary, "many of my school friendships and all my dislikes, except to Dr Butler, whom I treated rebelliously, and have been sorry ever since." He sought an interview with his old master before he embarked for Greece; and they parted good friends. An actual rebellion broke out at one time, which is said to have lasted three days, when, amongst other hostilities on the part of the boys, a train of gunpowder was laid along a passage through which Dr Butler was in the habit of passing at a certain hour every night to see that all lights were extinguished. The train was fired, happily without injury to the Doctor; the perpetrators were never discovered, and the secret had been confided to very few. It was probably to this outbreak that Byron referred, when he told Captain Medwin that he "saved the schoolroom from being burnt, by pointing out to the boys the names of their fathers and grandfathers on the walls."

Very different in character was Byron's schoolfellow, Robert Peel; but we know most of his school-days from Byron's record; "as a scholar he was greatly my superior; as a schoolboy out of school, I was always in scrapes, and he never; and in school he always knew his lesson, and I rarely; but when I knew it, I knew it nearly as well." Peel's room at Harrow is still shown, and every trace of him carefully preserved. The story of Byron's offering to "take half" of a licking which some bigger boy was giving the future premier, is interesting, but of doubtful authenticity. They "spoke" together in 1803, Peel as *Turnus*, and Byron as *Latinus*, with Leeke as *Drances*, from the 'Æneid;' Byron originally intended to have spoken *Drances*, but, ever sensitive on the subject of his lame foot, shrank from the too pointed allusion in the words—"*pedibusque fugacibus istis.*"

CHAPTER VI.

MODERN CONSTITUTION.

The numbers in the school, after some fluctuation, declined rapidly in the later years of Dr Butler's rule. His highest number was 295 (in 1816); on his promotion to the deanery of Peterborough and consequent retirement in 1829, he left only 115 names in the bill. There were some reasons for this decline for which he was not responsible; some of the under-masters had become unfortunately involved in debt, and the reputation of the school suffered in consequence. He was succeeded by Dr Longley, a Westminster student of Christ-Church, Oxford, who was nominated by the governors though not a candidate for the appointment; and under whom the school rose again, and again declined. After remaining seven years at Harrow, he became Bishop of Ripon—his first step to Canterbury. His successor was a Wintonian—Christopher Wordsworth, Fellow of Trinity, Cambridge—a highly distinguished scholar, but certainly not a successful schoolmaster. He found 165 boys at Harrow; the number rose in his second year to 190; and after eight years of office he left there only 78—the lowest point which the numbers have reached since any record has been kept. It is not our intention here to enter into any criticism of the acts, merits, or policy of living head-masters (of whom Harrow has an unusual number); but it is fair to Dr Wordsworth to say that he had many noble qualities which attached his better pupils to him strongly, and that the decline of the school is partly attributed, by those who are in a condition to judge impartially, to causes which existed before his appointment. The discipline had been previously sapped, and it needed a very able and judicious hand to restore it. The vice of drinking, which at different times has infected all our public schools, had crept into Harrow to a serious extent, and cost subsequent masters much trouble and anxiety to suppress. But under Dr Wordsworth's successor, Charles John Vaughan, Fellow of Trinity, Cambridge, one of Arnold's most brilliant and favourite pupils at Rugby, Harrow rose again in numbers and repute far more rapidly than it had fallen. In three years the increase was from 78 to 321; and this shortly rose to 485, a number which Harrow had never reached before. Dr Vaughan's wish had been to limit it to 400; and this alone prevented even a larger influx, the admission-list being always full for some years in advance. In strength of numbers, and in University distinctions, Harrow has more than resumed its rank amongst public schools; but it has never regained that almost exclusively aristocratic character which it had under Dr Drury; and possibly neither its discipline nor its scholarship may be the worse for a more general mixture of ranks amongst the boys. It long maintained, however, the questionable distinction of being the most expensive school in England. Dr Vaughan, upon his accession, reduced the charges considerably. Yet the school-fees for tuition are only £17; and foundationers (those resident within the parish of Harrow) pay in all only 17 guineas, which includes the *private* tuition.

Dr Vaughan retired from Harrow, somewhat to the public surprise, after fifteen years of uninterrupted success, and whilst still in the vigour of life; declaring that in his own mind he had from the first fixed upon that period as the fitting limit to so laborious and responsible an office. The surprise was hardly less when he soon after declined the offer of the bishopric of Rochester— a well-deserved tribute from a Harrovian Premier. He has been succeeded in the head-mastership by Henry Montague Butler, son of the former head-master, and himself the "head" of the school only nine years before—the first Harrovian on record who has been elected to the office. At the time of his appointment he was only twenty-six, but his reputation as a scholar stood very high. It is enough to say that under his rule Harrow has increased in numbers, and certainly not lost in reputation. The last "bill-book" contains 492 names.

It need hardly be explained that so large a number are not lodged in any one building. Besides the head-master's house, which, although the largest, accommodates little more than sixty boys, there are sixteen other boarding-houses, in which the numbers range from fifty to as few as six or seven. All these are kept by assistant-masters, and form one considerable source of their income. No "dames'" boarding-houses are now sanctioned; and for the good order of his own establishment each master is responsible.

There is one peculiar feature of Harrow which deserves notice, as combining to some extent the advantage of private with public education. This is the establishment of "small" boarding-houses (strictly limited to seven or eight boys in each) kept by some of the junior assistant-masters with the head-master's sanction. It is quite a modern arrangement, having been in operation not more than twelve or fifteen years. The inmates of these smaller houses enjoy almost of necessity considerably more personal and home-like supervision than would be either possible or desirable in houses containing forty or fifty boys. It is usual for them to take all their meals with the master and his family, of which, in fact, they may be said to form a part. Not only does this exempt a boy from many of the hardships of public-school life, but his moral character and general habits are thus brought more under observation and control. In fact, as it seems very fairly put by a Harrow witness before the late Commission, they "extend the advantages of a public-school education to many boys who, from delicacy of organisation, physical or intellectual, would not otherwise have enjoyed them." * For these advantages, parents who can afford it, and who think that their sons, for any reason, require such exceptional treatment, are not unwilling to pay; and the average yearly expenses of a boy at one of these small houses are stated at £210—some £50 above the average of the larger houses. There is, of course, another side to the question. There may be some loss to set against the gain. Dr Butler says—and few public-school men will gainsay him—" I have a strong conviction that if a boy

* See Harrow Evidence, 1180-1236.

is thoroughly qualified by temperament and by health to gain the full amount of benefit which the public-school system is capable of affording, he will gain that benefit and that bracing influence most thoroughly as a member of a large house."

And he has occasionally found it advantageous for a boy to be transferred from a small house to a large one: "It not unfrequently happens that boys who have begun their course in a small house, and may be supposed to have been there fairly habituated to the public-school system, are, by the advice of the small-house master, removed, during the latter part of their career, to the freer system of a large house."

Plainly there are disadvantages in too much of the master's supervision, and the hardier and more independent elements of a boy's character may lose in development. "Roughing it" amongst large numbers is a valuable element of public-school education. The Commissioners are unquestionably right when they say in their Report that, "were the number of these houses permitted to increase beyond what is required for the particular class for whom they are supposed to be adapted, it would become a serious evil, by increasing the expensiveness and diminishing the usefulness of the school." Still there seems to be, in this "small-house" system, something which may be very well adapted for special cases. It appears to provide for boys who are somewhat below the mark in physical health or strength of character, a share, if not in all, yet in many, of the benefits of public-school education, without the risk of breaking down in the training.

There exists also at Harrow, as elsewhere, that anomaly

in our public-school system, private tuition. Each boy has some one of the masters appointed as his private tutor, to whom he pays £15 a-year. Under the present arrangement each master has his fair proportion of pupils; but there were days in which a popular tutor had as many as 100 out of the whole 250. The office was probably introduced, with other Eton elements, by Dr Thackeray. In former days every lesson and exercise had to be taken to the private tutor in the first place, before it was considered ready for the regular master of the form. This system, absurd in principle, proved even worse in practice. The whole preparation of the lesson consisted too often of a hasty construe in the pupil-room; while the written exercises were submitted to the master of the form, after receiving the tutors' corrections; and, since even among masters there is not always an entire unwillingness to catch each other tripping, it was not uncommon for the former (if either ill-natured or over-fastidious) to slash away mercilessly at his colleague's emendations, ostensibly for the instruction, and certainly very much to the amusement, of the boy.

At present, all the lower forms prepare some of their lessons and exercises in the pupil-room, under the tutor's eye, and with his discretionary help; both the original copies of the exercises, and the corrected ones, being sent in usually to the form-master. Each tutor also reads with his pupils, one or two hours in the week, some book or subject not included in the regular school-work. He also prepares for confirmation; is supposed to take pains to know his pupils' characters, and to be ready to give advice; and in case of any serious complaint against a boy, the tutor would be consulted by the head-master as to his view of his pupil's general character before any severe punishment was inflicted. In these points the connection is found to be useful. Indeed, most of the Harrow authorities, like those of Eton, speak confidently of the general good results of a system which, to the uninitiated, seems at best a needless complication.

The system of promotion at Harrow is now almost entirely a matter of competitive merit. The removes from form to form depend upon a regular system of marks, of which part are given for the work done during the quarter, and part for the examination at the end. A certain proportion of the removes are, however, assigned to boys who have remained in the form below for three successive school quarters. The intention of these "charity removes" (as they are called) is to prevent boys of dull abilities being continually outstripped in the race of promotion by boys younger than themselves; but practically the cases are very few of boys who would be left in the same form for above three quarters; and even then the promotion is refused if the boy has been "notoriously and ostentatiously idle." By a rule lately adopted, no boy can remain in the school after he is sixteen, unless he has reached at least the "Shell;" nor after seventeen, unless he has reached the Fifth. An entrance examination has also been established, which insures a certain amount of the rudiments of Greek, Latin, and arithmetic, as the qualification for admission.

The hours of Harrow are not so early as at most public schools. The work of the day begins at 7.30, when the whole of the boys assemble for prayers. The lesson lasts until 8.30 nominally; but a boy seldom gets away much before nine. At nine, at all events, comes breakfast; of which the simpler materials only—tea or coffee, bread, milk, and butter—are supplied by the boarding-house; whatever accessories a modern schoolboy requires in the way of relishes being a matter of private account at the pastrycook's. Second "school," after an hour's preparation in pupil-room for the lower boys, begins at eleven and ends at twelve. Dinner comes at one, on a very liberal scale as to quality; indeed, it may be questioned whether the present tendency, in some masters' houses, is not to rather too much indulgence on this head. Some years ago the system was more homely, and occasional complaints were made, but without much foundation. If the day be a whole-school day (Monday, Wednesday, or Friday), third school begins at 3 or 3.30, and lasts an hour. Fourth and last school follows after the interval of an hour, usually spent in preparation (for the lower boys, in pupil-room), and lasts until 6 or 6.30. On the alternate three days, which are half-holidays, there is no regular third or fourth lesson; but there is more work in the forenoon, and a part of the afternoon is employed in the correction of exercises. Thus the lower forms have on the average rather more than five hours' work *per diem* in school, and the time required for preparation out of school would occupy nearly three more—making the average day's work above seven hours. On Wednesdays and Fridays, which appear to be the *dies carbone notandi* with Harrovians, they have very nearly ten hours in the whole. This is plainly too much, and in most cases is corrected practically by the boys themselves, who almost necessarily shirk what they can of it. The higher forms, of course, are less tied to actual work in school, but not less is expected from them; and those who have any regard for school honours and position give even a larger proportion of their time than this. The composition alone, in the head form, takes up many hours in the week, if carefully done: a Latin theme or translation (occasionally varied by an English essay, or translation into Greek); a copy of Latin verses; and another either of Latin lyrics or of Greek iambics. It is therefore no unwise indulgence, but almost a necessary relaxation, if cricket and football matches are ever to be played, which allows one whole holiday instead of a half about once a-fortnight; these, however, are only given for University honours won by Harrovians, and on a few fixed occasions, the list of which is kept by the head-master. On the mornings of the saints' days there is chapel instead of first "school;" and on Sundays an hour is employed in the study of Old Testament history.

Tea follows as soon as the boys return to their different houses after fourth school, or about six o'clock: the gates of each house are locked at dusk, the hour being altered from time to time according to the season. At half-past eight there is a supper of cold meat, &c.; bed-time is 9.30 or 10; lights are out at 10 or 10.30, and all is soon quiet for the night. The discipline is now too good to allow of the nocturnal escapades which took place in other days; and perhaps the day's work has been too hard to leave much relish for them. But there were sporting nights, within present memory, when a bagged cat was occasionally turned out in the dormitory, and hunted under and over the beds for an hour or so; and many an old Harrovian, now grown into a staid Paterfamilias, whom it would be very hard indeed to move from his chair after dinner farther than his drawing-room, could tell tales of dropping down over the headmaster's yard-wall on moonlight nights, and making forays into Lord Northwick's waters, where fish of fabulous size were reported to lie, and where smaller ones were occasionally caught; or of hiring some wretched horse and trap of Jem Martin, and driving out miles to breakfast in the dawn of a saint's-day morning, which less adventurous spirits devoted to extra sleep, and returning just in time to answer to their names at the nine o'clock bill;—expeditions whose main pleasures must have lain in their unlawfulness. The Martin family were celebrities of Harrow for at least two or three generations, and were purveyors-general to the school of all kinds of sporting apparatus, and other illegitimate or questionable luxuries. There was an old Dick Martin in Dr Heath's days—nearly a hundred years ago—who, amongst other ingenious speculations, sold to the new boys—always eager to invest their pocket-money—painted sparrows, which he called "cocky-olly birds." Dr Heath was quite aware of his character, and used annually to give out as a subject for Latin verses, "*Alpheus vafer*," under which Horatian *alias* Mr Martin was well understood to be proposed for poetical treatment. Latin verse was not then so rare an accomplishment as now; and some of the wits of the school took great pleasure in setting forth, in very graphic style, classical enough even for Heath's critical ear, the queer dealings which went on in their old friend's establishment. Two junior branches of the family, Jem and Jack, were equally well known in later days; they kept two or three wretched quadrupeds for hire, which occasionally figured in tandems, the only possible excitement in driving them consisting in the chance of a "double flogging" as the certain penalty of detection. They also dealt in birds (they are not accused of painting them—perhaps the art died with the father), dogs, ferrets, rats, and all manner of saleable vermin; kept badgers for gentlemen to try their dogs upon, and game-cocks for fighting, though the latter sport was not so popular as in the father's time. They had latterly a formidable rival in a Mrs W——, who had once seen more respectable days, and held a situation of some trust connected with the school, then tried the confectionery line, and finally took up the peculiar sporting business which, till then, the Martins had held exclusively. Her menagerie—so says a recent autobiography—was under her bed, where a badger, game-cocks, rats, &c., formed a more or less happy family: and the proprietress was accustomed to stand at the door, and invite the "young gentlemen" to "walk in and have a little pastime" on half-holidays.

The monitorial system, as it has been called—that is, the internal government of the school, out of school hours, by some of the elder and more responsible boys—has been the subject of so much discussion, that the briefest sketch of the school would be incomplete without some notice of it. This is no place to enter upon a defence of a system which has been so often attacked and defended with great ability and pertinacity on both sides,—which has always been, in a greater or less degree, a vital principle in the constitution of all English public schools,—will certainly always continue to be so as long as such schools exist, and as certainly will always be loudly abused by a good many unruly boys and foolish parents. But at Harrow, especially, it was a part of Lyon's original constitution. He directed, as has been seen, that three monitors should from the first have authority to maintain discipline over their fellows. No doubt their privileges and responsibilities have been modified from time to time, partly by the general habits of the age, partly by the character of successive headmasters; but when an unfortunate occurrence brought the whole system under discussion during Dr Vaughan's mastership, a good many writers and speakers seemed to regard the system as of foreign introduction—an adoption of Arnold's mode of government at Rugby. Nothing seems more unfair than to attribute to Dr Vaughan either the credit or discredit of such an introduction. No doubt, the pupil of a man like Arnold was likely to use this instrument of government in Arnold's spirit; but (as will be more fully noticed hereafter) it was a similar popular mistake which ascribed to Arnold its introduction at Rugby. It had existed both at Rugby and at Winchester before Arnold himself was a schoolboy. As the moral character of public schools rose, this recognised aristocracy of the school came to exercise a more distinct moral influence; and when head-masters began to feel that they had to teach morality as well as Latin and Greek, monitors and præpostors began in their turn to take a higher view of their responsibilities. The monitorial system was the introduction of no particular headmaster into any public school within living memory, though its actual working would necessarily take a colour in every school from the master for the time being.

There is no material difference between the powers and privileges of the monitors of Harrow and the prefects of Winchester or the præpostors of Rugby. They are expected to maintain the domestic discipline, as it may be termed, of the school; they are responsible for the good order and honourable conduct of their juniors, both within the walls of their several boarding-houses and on the playground; they are expected also to put down, as far as possible, bad language, bullying, and ungentlemanly habits of all kinds. To enforce their authority they have the power of setting punishments or impositions, and of personally correcting a delinquent with a cane within certain limits, which are pretty well understood and generally observed. Both as a support to their authority, and as a privilege to make their position the more desirable, they have the right of fagging; which, however, they share with the whole of the sixth form. The "Removes" and all below are fags; but the boys of the third form (the lowest in the school) are by custom exempt, as being too young and too ignorant. By a custom of later date, any fag may claim exemption after three years' service. The fags are expected to stand out at cricket on the sixth-form ground; but in this case there is a very fair arrangement which seems peculiar to Harrow; two fags are appointed as "slave-drivers," who send down as many as are wanted on the ground in regular rotation, keeping a roster of their names. This prevents an undue share of work falling upon a few unpopular boys, as used to be too much the case in some other public schools. And in spite of "slave-drivers" and monitors, a fag's life at Harrow is a tolerably happy one. Like the Southern "nigger," he is not half so much shocked at his condition as the good old ladies who overwhelm him with their sympathy.

CHAPTER VII.

THE GAMES.

It has been seen that Lyon had limited the sports of his scholars to four kinds—tops, handballs, running, and archery. The first have long ceased to be recognised by public-school boys at Harrow or elsewhere; the second, in the improved form of racquets and fives, flourishes still; and foot-races have been lately revived as an important portion of the athletic games which now take place in the school annually. But archery, of which John Lyon made most account as physical training for English youth, after maintaining its ground at Harrow long after it had fallen out of use in other schools, came to an end there some ninety years ago. Lyon's ordinances required of every parent to furnish his son "at all times with bow-shafts, bow-strings, and a bracer, to exercise shooting;" and the practice appears to have been vigorously kept up for nearly two hundred years. From time immemorial, a silver arrow was annually shot for by the best archers in the school, with a certain amount of pomp and ceremony, which latterly drew a good many visitors. The competitors were at first six, then increased to eight, and latterly to twelve. They shot in fancy dresses of satin, usually green and white, embroidered with gold, with green silk sashes and caps. The masters, in full academic costume, attended the contest, which took place at the Butts, a very picturesque spot on the left of the road entering Harrow from London. Steps cut in the grassy slope of a wooded knoll at the back formed the seats for the spectators—"worthy," said Dr Parr, "of a Roman amphitheatre;" but after the suppression of the archery practice, the hill was worked for brick-earth, and the site is now covered by houses. The rules of the contest are not very clearly handed down. The first who shot twelve times nearest the centre is said to have been the winner. Each hit within the inner circle was saluted with a fanfare of French horns—just as, at some modern archery meetings, a flourish of bugles is made to proclaim a gold. The winner was escorted home to the school in procession, and usually gave a ball in the schoolroom to the neighbouring families. It seems probable that the competitors, at least in later times, were only such as could afford the necessary expenses. In 1744, it is recorded that an Indian chief was present, who remarked that the boys shot well, but that he could have beaten them. Some Indian warriors are said also to have been among the spectators in 1755. The arrow won in 1766, by Charles Wager Allix, was presented to the school by his son, and is now in the Vaughan Library. There also may be seen an old print of the contest, in one corner of which is a figure going off the ground with an arrow sticking in his face, to which he applies his hand. Tradition says that it represents one Goding, a barber of Harrow, who was shot on one of these occasions, through his own or one of the archers' carelessness, either in the eye or the mouth—for on this point the authorities differ. It has been said that this unlucky accident led to the suppression of the custom. The expense of the costumes and entertainment is also said to have been the cause; but the real reason was, that the practice which the competitors required was found a serious interruption to the work of the school, and the shooting-day also brought down an influx of very undesirable company from London. For these reasons Dr Heath, immediately on his entrance into office in 1772, abolished the time-honoured festival, to the intense disgust, as might be concluded, of the then Harrovians; for schoolboys are essentially conservative. He had at first only suggested certain curtailments of the practice-days and other archers' privileges; whereupon the boys took huff, and declined to shoot at all. The last prize arrow, in 1771, was won by Lord Althorp, the second Earl Spencer. The only remaining trace of the ancient custom is in the two crossed arrows, the device still stamped upon all the school prize-books.*

The rifle corps, which has been more successful at Harrow than at most schools, might perhaps be accepted by the founder as now supplying, in some degree, his purpose of a national training. In the

---

* The arrows, grouped with a broken bow, first appear on some of the speech-bills, printed after the suppression of the shooting in 1771. They were first placed on the prize-books by Dr Butler, who also substituted the present motto of the school, "*Stet fortuna domus*," for the original one, dating probably from Lyon's days, "*Donorum Dei dispensatio fidelis*." The old red lion (probably the cognisance of Lyon) which held the weathercock on the old school, was taken down when the new speech-room was built, and carelessly destroyed.

Public Schools contest at Wimbledon, Harrow has now five times in succession carried off the Ashburton challenge shield, and also, in 1865 and 1866, Earl Spencer's cup for the best marksman in the school elevens.

As a substitute for the suppressed archery contest, Dr Heath introduced the "speech-days," which still continue to form the annual Harrow festival. Originally there were three; the first Thursdays in May, June, and July. The speakers were the ten monitors, who appeared on each of the three days, and six in rotation from the sixth form, who spoke each on one day only. Dr Longley reduced the speech-days to two, and Dr Wordsworth, in 1844, limited the performance to a single day in June or July, as it remains at present. The old speech-bills (of which a collection, made by Dr Butler, may be seen in the library) contain only selections from Greek and Latin orators or poets, with occasional scenes from Shakespeare; but in 1820, the successful compositions for the governors' prizes for Greek and Latin verse —then first given—were also recited by their authors, to which were added the English Essay and English Poem, given by Dr Vaughan as head-master in 1845, and since continued. But, with the exception of the English verse, which, like the Newdigate at Oxford, is always popular with the ladies, the prize compositions do not interest the audience like the dramatic scenes; and of late years the former have been judiciously curtailed in the recitation. The latter are sometimes admirably performed, and a good deal of pains is taken by such of the school tutors as have histrionic tastes in drilling their pupils; and though there exist dim traditions of wonderful speakers in old times (schoolboys are very much given to refer to earlier heroic ages, when "there were giants in the land"), yet those who had the good fortune to be present in 1862, and heard the well-earned applause which was brought down by the scenes from Sheridan's 'Critic,' from Molière, and from the 'Clouds' of Aristophanes; or again, in the following year, by the impersonations of *Bob Acres*, and *M. Jourdain* and his *Maitre de Philosophie*, in spite of the disadvantage of acting without scenery or costumes, will not think that Harrow speakers have degenerated. Of the advantage to the boys themselves of this annual exhibition there can be no doubt. To be early accustomed to face such an audience as is then gathered together, without nervousness or awkwardness, and to hear the sound of their own voices in public, is a portion of general education which English gentlemen very much require, and which, to judge from their ordinary public performances in the way of speech-making at maturer years, must have been very generally neglected. The future debater, or pleader, or preacher, or even the future country squire, may be thankful for any modicum of school-training which may save him from utter helplessness when he gets upon his legs before or after dinner.

In earlier days, under Thackeray's mastership, regular English plays were acted by the boys on the last three nights before the Christmas holidays, the costumes being lent by Rich, the Covent Garden manager. Thackeray himself wrote some of the prologues, and the families of the town attended the performance. The plays or selections were usually of a serious cast; but when Tate Wilkinson, afterwards actor and manager, was a Harrow boy, boarding with Mr Reeves the writing-master, he delighted the family circle there with his powers as a comic actor, which had already earned some applause amongst his father's friends in London. In consequence, Dr Thackeray was persuaded to allow 'The Provoked Husband,' in which Wilkinson made quite a sensation as *Lady Townly*. He next appeared as *Romeo*, in the garden scene, after some difficulty in finding a *Juliet*; Frederick Thackeray, the head-master's son, who had supported him admirably as *Lord Townly*, declining to represent the fair Capulet, for which part another school-fellow, Sir John Russiate, at last volunteered. But Harrow morality was scandalised, and the plays were from that time stopped.

The great game at Harrow, as at all public schools, is of course that which honest John Lyon had no prevision of, but which has now become an English institution— the noble science of cricket. If he could have seen the Harrow eleven in their glory at Lord's he might almost have forgiven their neglect of archery. If an old plate published in 1802 was taken from life, cricket was then played in the school court, with the *two* stumps and the old bludgeon-like bat; but the school gained a high reputation early in the history of the game. Long before the regular establishment of the public schools matches they had contests of their own with Eton. The first on record of which the score is preserved took place in 1805; but in this they were unfortunate, only scoring 55 and 65, while Eton made in their first innings 122—thus winning in a single innings by two runs. Lord Byron played in this match, but only contributed 7 and 2. No score appears to have been preserved from that date until 1818, when Harrow won, and again in 1822. In the year following a match was played at Oxford, which deserved a more special record than it seems to have obtained. The Harrovian undergraduates felt themselves strong enough to challenge the rest of the university, and the match came off on Bullingdon Common. In the single innings of Harrow, the two first who were sent to the wickets—Clutterbuck of Exeter College and Calvert of Merton—made up the score to 100, in those days a great innings of itself. Clutterbuck's was the first wicket to fall, for forty runs; and Harrow won the match in a single innings. Afterwards the school eleven appear to have fallen off; for in the next year Eton beat them in one innings, and repeated their victory for six years in succession. Then the fortune of the field was various until 1844-5-6, when the Etonians won each year without the trouble of a second innings. These reverses were compensated by a series of Harrow victories from 1851 to 1859. The four following years showed excellent play on both sides, but owing to the length of the innings there was not time (except in 1862, when Eton won) to play the matches out. The three last matches which were played out proved easy victories for the Harrow eleven, who won each time in a single innings. In the present year (1867) a well-contested game was drawn. On the whole, success has been very evenly balanced, Harrow now standing one ahead on the total account of matches.

In 1825 the first match was played between Harrow and Winchester, on the Harrow ground; the two brothers Wordsworth — Charles of Harrow (afterwards second-master at Winchester), and Christopher of Winchester (afterwards head-master of Harrow)—being captains of their respective elevens. The Wykehamists won easily, and for many years afterwards, whenever a match took place, which was only at intervals, seem to have been too strong for their opponents; but, on the whole, the honours have in this case also been pretty evenly divided.

The original cricket-ground was on Roxeth Green, or the Common, as it was called, but several acres of this were enclosed and made over to the school for playground about 1806. To this have lately been added nine acres adjoining, bought by the subscriptions of Harrovians. The great hero of early times seems to have been Godfrey Vigne, whose reputation (especially for wicket-keeping), great in his school-days, was kept up for many years at Harrow by the local matches in which he played there against the school eleven, and was maintained in the following generation by his son. The names of Nicholson, of Currer, and of Broughton (who could cover three places in the field), of Davidson, Hankey, and Digby, are well remembered still, though of a later date. But the play has probably continued steadily to improve at all points; the batting of the last generation could show no such scores as that of Daniel's 112 against Eton in 1860, or Fuller Maitland's 71 in 1862; and even such veteran critics as Mr F. Ponsonby and Mr R. Grimston —well-known and honoured faces amongst the lookers-on at the matches on the school ground—would allow that young bowlers like Lang, Plowden, and Money gave the batsman quite enough to do to hold his own.

Football is played, of course, at Harrow, and played vigorously, though it does not form such a specialty as at Rugby. The actual personal encounters, individual and combined, which are the essence of the game, will always make it a favourite with English schoolboys. Its very dangers form its attraction in great measure; more than any other English sport, it is a mimicry of war: though, after all, if the casualties of recent seasons are considered, cricket seems now the more dangerous of the two. But it is not given to every man to be a cricketer; whereas any fellow with a decent share of pluck can do something at football. As played at Harrow in former generations, it must have been a curious game. It was played on the gravel in the court which surrounded the old schoolhouse on three sides; so that the goals, instead of facing each other, were on a parallel line, with the building between, *round* which the ball had to be kicked. The gravel cut the leather case of the ball occasionally, as well as the hands and faces of those who scrambled over it in a "squash," as that close *mêlée* is called, which Rugby men know as a "scrummage," and Etonians as a "rooge;" and these marks of the combat were esteemed honourable scars, like the sword-cuts on the face of a German student. But when the addition to the school-buildings filled up one side of the court, football was transferred to the cricket-ground, and underwent a considerable change in its character, which, no doubt, the ancient heroes of the gravelled arena pronounced to be for the worse. There is now a spacious piece of ground kept for the especial purpose, where as many as six separate games can be played at once, besides four smaller grounds belonging to different houses. The "big game," in which only the *élite* of the school players take part, is managed by the monitors under very stringent regulations.

Hockey was long a favourite game at Harrow, as at most schools a century ago; it was then played in the street, to the considerable annoyance of the householders;

perhaps for this reason, when the school increased in numbers, as well as from its really dangerous character, it was disused. Lord Byron, spite of his lameness, was an active hockey-player as well as cricketer. A few years back there was an attempt made to revive it, but it never became very popular; and the nature of the turf on which it was played (the street being now out of the question) was not found well adapted to the game, owing to the subsoil being clay.

"Hare and Hounds" is another old school-sport which has gone out of favour of late years in most of our public schools (Rugby excepted), though in some it still survives under the name of a Paperchase; the scent by which the hares are traced being of a substantial kind, formed out of the leaves of dilapidated grammars and dictionaries torn up small by the fags for the purpose. But there was an ancient form of it at Harrow, so especially attractive as being pursued at unlawful hours and under unusual difficulties, that it deserves special mention. It was known also in former days at Eton, and in both schools went by the name of "Jack o' Lantern." About seven o'clock on winter evenings, when it was quite dark, the boys, by sufferance on the part of the authorities, were let out from their several boarding-houses into the fields below the school. A stout and active runner started in advance, carrying a lantern, by the light of which the rest pursued him in full cry. He showed or concealed his light from time to time, and a great point of the sport was to entice the hounds into some pool or muddy ditch (which "Jack" himself had carefully avoided) by showing the light exactly in a line on the other side. The destruction of clothes in consequence may be easily imagined; this, and the sufferings of the younger boys from bush and brier, through which they were "fagged" to follow, drew such energetic and repeated remonstrances from Dr Butler's housekeeper—the worthy Mrs O'Flaherty—that at last the Doctor stopped the custom altogether. This was, of course, bitterly resented by the boys as a breach of privilege, and every window in his house was broken on the following night; but the demonstration had no effect, and Jack o' Lantern was finally abolished.

CHAPTER VIII.

MISCELLANEOUS.

Dr Butler did a good deal during his head-mastership to soften some of the barbarities of which Harrow had its full share in those days. For a short time after his coming he was consequently unpopular with the ruder spirits who led the school; but as more civilised generations succeeded, this prejudice soon passed away. He abolished, amongst other old customs, certain rites and ceremonies which were used in celebrating a boy's remove from one form to the other in the lower part of the school. No such promotion was considered complete, so far as the boys were concerned, until the new member had been duly " pinched in "—remaining a certain fixed time in the play-room, during which all the fraternity exercised a right of pinching him, limited only by the tenderness of their dispositions or the strength of their fingers. There were generally some adepts in this torture, who knew, and taught others, the tenderest places and the most artistic mode of taking hold, and who carried this evil knowledge with them from form to form, to be practised on a succession of victims. The rites of initiation were completed by tossing in a blanket in the dormitory, and a certain number of bumps against the ceiling were required to make the ceremony valid. Both processes of torture were commonly borne with a good deal of heroism; but sometimes the younger boys were very much hurt and frightened by the tossing. Dr Butler, when he put a stop to these traditionary barbarisms, compromised the matter by giving the boys a supper at the "trials;" but for some time the blanket-tossing was still carried on surreptitiously at night. One boy is remembered to have taken refuge from his tormentors in the chimney, from which he was dragged covered with soot, and in such a state of frantic terror that fears were entertained even by the boys that he would lose his senses; and he was rescued from further persecution (not without a hard fight) by some of the more humane spirits amongst them. Another ancient barbarism survived even long after Butler's accession. There were in the head-master's house two public rooms for the use of his boarders—the hall and the play-room. The latter was open to all, but the hall was regarded as a sort of club-room, which no boy was allowed to enter, except at dinner and supper time, until he had become a member by being "rolled-in." Any one who desired the privilege of admission (and none below the upper fifth were eligible) gave in his name to the head-boy some days beforehand, in order that due preparations might be made for the inauguration. Immediately a certain number of rolls (*finds* they were called—etymology unknown) were ordered at the baker's, and were rebaked every morning until they were pretty nearly as hard as pebbles. At nine o'clock on the morning fixed for the rolling-in, the members of the hall ranged themselves on the long table which ran along one side of the room, each with his pile of these rolls before him, and a fag to pick them up. The candidate knelt, facing them, on a form close against the opposite wall, leaning upon a table in front of him, with his head resting upon his hands, so as to guard the face, while they held, as well as they could, a plate on the top of the head by way of helmet. Thus protected, the head itself formed a mark for the very peculiar missiles which were ready to be aimed at it. When all was ready, a time-keeper, watch in hand, gave the word "Now!" when fast and furiously—and very spitefully, if a boy was unpopular—the rolls were showered upon the devoted head for the space of one minute, neither more nor less. Such protection as the plate gave was soon lost by its being broken to pieces. It was, as may be imagined, a very severe ordeal, the bruises being very painful for weeks afterwards. Some boys dreaded it so much as never to claim admission to the hall; but it was very seldom indeed that any one was known to flinch during the shower of rolls, after once taking up his position at the table.

Another practice in the school, of later date, would probably be now condemned as savouring too much of barbarity, though it did not arise from a mere wanton love of tormenting, like those just mentioned, but from a stern popular sense of justice. When a boy was known to have been guilty of any highly disgraceful conduct, reflecting on the character of the school—stealing, for instance—he was subjected to a peculiar form of Lynch law, called "Handing-up." If the monitors had satisfied themselves, after careful inquiry, of the guilt of the accused, he was called out before an assembly of the upper school in Butler's Hall, and there received from each monitor a certain number of blows with a study *toasting-fork*. Severe as the punishment was, it was often a merciful alternative to the criminal, who would, in the worst cases, have been punished by expulsion if the charge had been brought before the head-master; and for that reason this rude democratic justice was winked at by the school authorities, who tacitly accepted it in place of taking any formal cognisance of the case.

It may readily be imagined that in those rude ages the time-honoured institution of Fagging was a very different thing from what it is now. The fags of those days would have laughed at what their modern successors call hardships. In truth, they were very little better than menial servants for some hours in the day. They had not only to prepare their masters' breakfasts, to make coffee, toast bread, go on errands, &c., as at present, but also to clean boots and shoes, and to brush clothes covered with mud from football, Jack-o'-Lantern chases, or even from actual hunting—for some ambitious sportsmen amongst the elder boys did now and then steal a day with the hounds, mounted on a miserable "screw" hired out by Jem Martin, the purveyor of all kinds of forbidden indulgences to the school. An unfortunate fag might often be heard brushing away at five o'clock on a December morning. Poker and tongs were unknown luxuries in the "play-room" at Butler's; and the junior fag, at the call of "*lag poker*," had to rush out in the cold to pull a hedge-stake of substantial dimensions from the nearest fence or faggot-stack. The demand was frequent, and often made in the mere wantonness of authority.

But there were acts of positive tyranny practised, far less justifiable than such service as this. Fags were sent out at night to fetch beer and other materials for surreptitious suppers; to do this, they had to scale the gates of their boarding-house, and the penalty, if caught by any of the masters, was invariably a flogging,—no boy daring to excuse himself by representing that he was a mere compulsory agent. One unlucky fag (a future head of the school) remembers being caught twice in the same night, and receiving two separate floggings the next day. But this pretence of a rigid discipline, which was, in fact, the cruelest injustice, was more discreditable to the authorities of those days than to the boys who thus made others their scapegoats; for even in a well-remembered case, when a monitor voluntarily came forward to exculpate his fag, and offered to bear the punishment, his appeal was disregarded; yet it must have been perfectly within the knowledge of the masters that in very few cases were the victims the real offenders. But it was a system of pseudo-discipline by no means peculiar to Harrow. It was the age when, at most public schools, a false quantity invariably brought down a flogging, while a lie or an act of immorality escaped; when a headmaster (not of Harrow) is said to have replied to a parent who remonstrated, that he had undertaken to teach his son Latin and Greek, but not morality. We need not wonder much that the boys of that day turned out more accurate scholars; but one does feel inclined to marvel that so many of them grew into honourable and upright men. But a public-school boy in those times could hardly fail to learn at least the Spartan virtue of endurance. Harrow fagging had no special reputation for cruelty; yet there are those living who can remember having been called out of their beds at night to have cold water poured down their backs,—for no special reason, but as a part of the hardening process considered good for fags generally; or to start from Leith's boarding-house in the dark, to go round the churchyard by the North Porch—"Bloody Porch," as it was called, from some obscure legend. Once a boy was sent upon this dreaded tour at night, when it so happened that there were a party concealed in the porch, watching the grave of a newly-buried relative—for those were the days of resurrection-men; they mistook the unfortunate fag for a body-snatcher, and fired at him, wounding him slightly, and frightening him almost to death.

It is remarkable that Harrow should have been able to show three of the best private libraries in England,* and yet have so long continued unusually ill-provided with anything like a public library belonging to the school. One of the small rooms over the old school, already mentioned, known formerly as the "monitors' library"—it was only open to them, and a key of it was their badge of office—contained a very limited collection of books, chiefly given by monitors on leaving the school. It had some few interesting relics of another kind; one of the old archery dresses of 1760,† a staff with a Runic

---

* Besides Dr Heath's, there was a very valuable one belonging to the late Rev. Henry Drury, formerly an assistant-master; he is the "Menalcas" of Dibdin's 'Bibliomania.' Mr James Edwards ("Rinaldo"), who lived in the old manor-house, had also a large collection of rare and costly books. He was buried, by his particular desire, in a coffin made out of some of his library shelves.

† Worn by Henry Read, and presented by his relative, John Read Munn, M.A., Vicar of Ashburnham.

inscription brought from Abyssinia by Bruce, Byron's school copy of Æschylus with notes in his handwriting, and other memorials of old Harrovians. But a splendid room has lately been built at an expense of above £4000, raised by subscription, as a testimonial to Dr Vaughan's work as head-master, to bear the name of the "Vaughan Library." The first stone was laid by Lord Palmerston in July 1862, and on the speech-day in the following year it was formally opened. Contributions of books are already flowing in, and Harrow will soon have a school library worthy of its reputation. It has also been enriched by the munificent gift from Sir Gardner Wilkinson, an old Harrovian, of his private collection of antiquities. Portraits of Spencer Perceval (the only one known), of Lords Palmerston and Dalhousie, with busts of Peel and the late Lord Herbert of Lea, form the commencement of a gallery of Harrow worthies. This library is open to the monitors at all times, and to others of the upper boys at stated hours.

Choral music has of late years been taken up very warmly in the school, chiefly owing to the exertions of the present organist and music-master, Mr Farmer. The larger boarding-houses have now each their choral society, who meet every week for practice, and a concert is usually given at the end of each quarter.* From such materials

---

* The following is a specimen of one of the most popular "house-songs:"—

HERGA.

Super campos caput tollis
Quam dilectum, noster collis!
Præstas cæteris Parnassis;
Vix unius valent assis.

Scholam hic Johannes Leo
Fundat olim, fretus Deo;

an excellent volunteer choir has been formed for the chapel services.

Bathing was always, until very lately, practised under difficulties at Harrow. The common bathing-place, known as "Duck-puddle" (and by no means inappropriately so named) was a long piece of muddy water, varying from four to eight feet in depth. There, after it had been stirred up by all possible means into more of a puddle than usual, new boys were formally dipped. Yet in that miserable place, in 1826, the only son of Sir Charles Lemon—sent to Harrow in preference to Eton to avoid this particular danger—was drowned, when

> Felix sit faustumque omen
> Quod tam forte praestat nomen!
>
> Sicut quercus glande parva
> Grandis facta velat arva,
> Ita domus nostra crevit,
> Ita vivax adolevit.
>
> Nos heredes sæculorum
> Æmulemur decus horum
> Quos, adeptos olim laudes,
> Herga, celebrare gaudes.
>
> Quot augusti nobis patres!
> Quot dilecti circum fratres!
> Simus digni! sint minores
> Nobis longe meliores!
>
> Semper sis virtutis ædes,
> Herga, sis musarum sedes:
> Domus sanæ disciplinæ:
> Fons amabilis doctrinæ!
>
> Quin et hic juventus vacet
> Omni mari ludo placet:
> Pede, manu, pilam pellant,
> Cursu, nando, antecellant.
>
> Sanis membris, mente sana,
> Nostra spes non erit vana:
> Patria ipsa nos amabit,
> Et fortuna Domus stabit!

he had been little more than a week at the school, having been seized with a fit while bathing. To avoid mixing in the general wash at Duck-puddle, many boys used to go out to the Brent at Perivale, or even as far as Ellestree reservoir, for bathing; and these were favourite expeditions on the mornings of saints' days. But Dr Vaughan had the old "puddle" lined with brick, and supplied with water by a steam-engine, to the great additional comfort of the bathers.

On the whole, if a boy is not happy at Harrow, it will be pretty sure to be in some way his own fault. Even the stranger, as he sits on "Byron's Tomb" in the churchyard and looks down on that purely English home landscape, and hears the merry voices come up from cricket-field or racket-court, may be excused if he almost wishes himself a schoolboy there. He has probably harder lessons to learn, harder fagging to go through, and less genial companionship, in the great school to which he is going back again, when his little holiday is over, by the next train. Let him whisper to himself as he turns away, even if not himself a Harrovian, the wish of the school motto—"*Stet fortuna domus.*"

RUGBY SCHOOL

The chief printed authorities are—

Nicolas's History of the Town and School of Rugby.
Radclyffe's Memorials of Rugby.
The Rugby Register.
The Book of Rugby School.

RUGBY SCHOOL.

CHAPTER I.

LAURENCE SHERIFF.

> "There is a little town, within short space
> Of England's central point, of various brick
> Irregularly built, nor much adorned
> By architectural craft—save that indeed,
> As you approach it from the south, a pile
> Of questionable Gothic lifts its head
> With somewhat of a grave collegiate air,
> Not unbefitting what in truth it is,—
> A seat of academic discipline
> And classic education. . . .
> . . . But for this
> The place might pass unnoticed—to speak truth,
> As insignificant a market-town
> As may be seen in England."
>
> MOULTRIE'S *Dream of Life*.

FROM almost all parts of England railway lines now converge at Rugby. But middle-aged gentlemen, to whom that "pile of questionable Gothic"—not visible from the station—may have been familiar in their school-days, might as well be landed at Melbourne or New York, for any knowledge of the localities which can serve them in finding their way now to the school-gates. Not Laurence Sheriff himself, the founder of the school, if he could come down again from London on that "grey ambling nag" of his, riding along the old London road, and look at the approach to his native town, could feel more hopelessly bewildered. The last five-and-twenty years have changed this aspect of Rugby almost as much as the two previous centuries. It still remains, indeed, as its own poet has described it in his younger days, "as insignificant a market-town" as well may be; but "architectural craft," if it has not much adorned it, has added to it very considerably. The old Rugbeian who revisits the haunts of his boyhood will find himself terribly bewildered. As he rumbles into the old High Street, and catches at last a glance at something which reminds him of old days, his driver probably asks where he shall set him down. "The Eagle," he replies, joyfully recognising the old familiar sign—"the Eagle, of course." And lo! the Eagle has become a temperance eating-house! Baffled and humiliated, he allows himself to be driven to the George, formerly despised as the resort of mere "commercials;" and there, over his solitary chop, he may meditate on the fortunes of Rugby.

Not all the curious research of an antiquarian friend, who opens for us his stores of local and historical knowledge, can rake up very much that is interesting as to the old town itself. For an old town it is—Rocheberie of Domesday Book; which name might imply that it was founded on a rock, if there had been any possible rock to build it on. A prettier name was Rokeby, which it had afterwards; but the Lords "De Rokeby," whose manor it was, have left little mark behind them for good or evil. We listen reverently to our friend's ingenious theories as to what might have been in those earlier days; but, zealous as he is for the traditional honour of his native town, he feels that the pious fraud which would localise anything heroic there, antecedent to the invention of football, would be too transparent. Our obdurate Tory feelings are unmoved by the remembrance that Lieut.-General Cromwell was quartered here before the battle of Naseby with fifteen hundred horse; or that the Dutch King William, passing through the town on his way to Ireland, and taking a local guide, one Gill Morris, to conduct him over the marshes of Dunsmore, was left in the lurch by that worthy Rugbeian (no doubt a stanch loyalist), whom he therefore cursed lustily in his native gutturals. One great and good name, however, is linked with the little town. Margaret Beaufort Countess of Richmond—the munificent "Lady Margaret," whom Oxford and Cambridge both gratefully acknowledge—" is said to have held this manor in dower, as widow of Sir Henry Stafford, knight, from 1482 to 1484." For the rest, the fame of Rugby must be content to rest on the undoubted fact which Dr Arnold satirically claims for it—it has fourteen cattle-fairs.

But it was the school, not the town, we came to see. Here also early history and even tradition is somewhat curt and scanty. Rugby, it is well known, can boast no royal foundation, or even subsequent benefaction. No wonder that there has always been a jealousy against admitting it into the sacred band of public schools. It had originally no claim whatever to the title. It was a mere local charity, the bequest of a grateful citizen to his native town; of one who wished to impart to the future boys of Rugby something of that liberal training to which he perhaps consciously owed his own rise in life. It has benefited the town, if not exactly in the way in which the founder wished or expected, yet not less directly or decidedly. The class of children at Rugby and Brownsover, for which he intended to provide education—especially those of the latter place—derive little benefit from his pious bequest. Here and there one, of especial promise, may have been enabled to rise from the ranks by its aid; but it has become almost impossible, within present memory, for a "foundationer" of humble parentage and narrow means to maintain his place, without a superhuman indifference or endurance of humiliation, in what has become a school for the sons of "gentlemen." In this respect at least we have made no advance upon the wisdom or liberality of our ancestors, that in modern times the "poor scholar" has become a class almost extinct. Even Christ's Hospital is crowded with scholars who protest against wearing the peculiar dress which the rules enjoin; and with some justice, since it is the badge of a charity to which they have no legitimate claim. But the disgrace lies not in the dress, but in its appropriation. Such malversations of founders' bequests are among the sins for which, if there be any limbo for bodies corporate, our schools and universities have a heavy account to render. Still, Rugby does as yet offer a gratuitous education to the sons of Sheriff's townsmen; but a higher education, and therefore to a higher class, than he could have contemplated. It is too curious a speculation, and not very profitable, to conjecture whether, if he could have foreseen that the third part of his "Conduit Close," which he made over to his trustees for his educational project, and whose cost price was but £106, 13s. 4d., would produce a rental in 1860 of £4500 per annum, he would rejoice to find it employed in maintaining one of those great Public Schools which are the pride of England, or be vexed at having alienated so valuable an inheritance from his own family.

Of the early life and education of this Laurence Sheriff simply nothing is known beyond the fact that he was a native of the town, and that the somewhat superior rank of his parents is proved to some extent by their burial *within* the parish church. In 1551, during the short reign of Edward VI., we find him settled in London as a citizen and grocer (the French *epicier* would perhaps better express his line of trade), living somewhere near Newgate Market, and connected, probably only as a privileged tradesman, with the household of the Princess Elizabeth; supplying her with spices to a considerable amount. That he was a stanch and loyal servant to his royal patroness, is apparent from an anecdote recorded of him in 'Foxe's Martyrs.' As Sheriff, after all, was no martyr, the story is perhaps more to be depended upon in its details than some which are to be found in that not very scrupulous chronicle. He had a friend named Robert Farrer, a haberdasher, who, "being on a certain morning at the Rose Tavern (from whence he was seldom absent), and falling to his common drink," did, in the hearing of Sheriff, call the princess by an uncivil name, and accuse her of complicity in Wyatt's late rebellion. For which disloyal words, "the aforesaid Laurence Sheriffe, grocer, being then servant to the Lady Elizabeth, and sworne unto her Grace," delated him forthwith to the Royal Commissioners, then sitting "at Bonner the Bishop of London's house beside Paul's," and of whom that terrible prelate was the chief. It was "not to be suffered," said the loyal grocer, in his complaint against Farrer, "that such a varlet as he is should call so honourable a princess by the name of a Jill," or should "wish them to hop headless that shall wish her Grace to enjoy the possession of the crown when God shall send it to her." But Bonner contented himself with a pious hope that such a dispensation of Providence might not be looked for just at present—for he and his fellow-commissioners had little more affection for the Protestant princess than the haberdasher had— and Sheriff's complaint was civilly pooh-poohed. In due time, however, the Lady Elizabeth came to the throne, and Sheriff arrived at the dignity of an esquire, and obtained a grant of arms; but he always seems to have retained an honest pride in his status of citizen and grocer, for by that title he prefers to describe himself in his last will and intent. He still continued his connection with the Court; for in 1562 his name is recorded amongst those who, after the fashion of the time, made presents to the Queen upon New-Year's Day; "a sugar-loaf, a box of ginger, a box of nutmegs, and a pound of cynomon," were his offering; still a grocer, and, a few years afterwards, Second Warden of that honourable company.

So much is known of him historically; what follows is gathered from his will and its codicil, and from a document called his "Intent." He had, he says, "intended, by God's grace, to erect and build" a grammar-school in his native town during his lifetime; but sickness and death came upon him, perhaps somewhat suddenly. In July 1567 he made his will, bequeathing to two trustees—George Harrison of London, gent., and Barnard Field of London, grocer—£50 for the building of a school and certain almshouses, the glebe and parsonage of Brownsover (lately purchased by him on the suppression of the Abbey of St Mary at Leicester) for their endowment, and a further sum of £100 to be laid out by his trustees in lands for the same purpose. He also left his family "messuage" or mansion-house as a residence for his schoolmaster. The school was to be "chiefly for the children of Rugby and Brownsover aforesaid, and next for such as be of other places thereunto adjoining." It was to be taught, if it might "conveniently be," by a Master of Arts, and to be "called for ever the Free School of Laurence Sheriffe of London, grocer."

But as the pith of a letter is said to lie so often in the postscript, so in this case the existence of Rugby School in its present form depended entirely not on the will, but on a codicil. Sheriff, having probably recovered from immediate danger, paid a visit to Rugby. Perhaps he saw that his bequest, as it stood, was in danger of proving insufficient for its purpose; for some reason or other, he revoked, by a codicil dated at his native town about a month later, the £100 left for the purchase of lands, and substituted one-third of his property in Middlesex, then known as the "Conduit Close"—twenty-four acres, in the whole, of open pasture-land, lying about half a mile outside the city of London, and at that time little likely to be built upon, since a royal order had been issued prohibiting all persons from erecting new houses within three miles of the city gates. The third part vested in the trustees of the school was at that time let for £8 per annum; it now includes Lamb's Conduit Street, Milman, New and Great Ormond Streets, and produces, as has been said, a rental of about £4500. Sheriff died a fortnight afterwards; and though his wish was to have been buried at Rugby, his remains probably lie in the graveyard of Christ-Church, Newgate, in the register of which parish his burial is recorded.* It is possible that they were afterwards removed to his native town, but there is no record of such removal.

* The entry was lately found by Dean Stanley.

CHAPTER II.

EARLY HEAD-MASTERS.

For some time the founder's bequest seems to have been quietly ignored. The property was probably enjoyed by the relatives; one trustee died soon after Sheriff, and the other was either dishonest or careless. It may be doubted whether there was any school at all actually in operation much before 1600, more than thirty years after the founder's death. A decree of Chancery (44th Eliz., 1602) gives the first intimation of its existence. Twelve gentlemen of the county of Warwick—including one of Rugby and one of Brownsover, to represent those interests—were now appointed trustees; thus setting aside, and no doubt for good and sufficient reasons, the succession to that office which the founder's will had vested in the heirs of Harrison and Field. The vacancies in the trust have been from time to time filled up by noblemen and gentlemen of Warwickshire and the adjoining counties, and the number remains the same. The first Master of whom there is any record whatever is one Richard Seele, who appears to have been in possession, though not legally appointed, in the year 1600. For, two years after that date, we find certain "articles objected before the Lords of her Majesty's Privy Council" against Edward Boughton Esquire of Cawston in the county of Warwick—a person who had some influence with Dudley, Earl of Leicester, and possibly presumed upon it—in which, amongst other charges, he is accused of being "a favourer of notorious Papists, and namely with one Bernard Field," the survivor of Sheriff's trustees. The articles allege that Boughton, with Field and others, "riotously and contrarily to justice, hath made a forcible entry into the scoole of Rugby in the county of Warwick, and from thence hath removed by strong hand and displaced one Richard Seele, being quietly possessed of the same for the space of sixteen months before;" and that he had placed there instead, to be schoolmaster, a "notorious wicked" liver (the original is even stronger), one Nicholas Greenhill. But Field, as trustee, had clearly the right of appointment, and Master Richard Seele must have been the real intruder; and when we find it objected against Mr Boughton, towards the close of this list of articles, that he was " an *obstinate Puritane*, and dispiseth the Book of Common Prayer"—he who was described at starting as a favourer of notorious Papists— we see pretty plainly that the policy of the objectors was at all hazards to throw as much dirt as possible, in the hope that "some of it would stick." So let us trust, for the honour of Rugby, that the first of her masters officially recorded in the school register, Nicholas Greenhill, A.M. of Magdalen College, Oxford, settled in his office under Field's authority and by Mr Boughton's help A.D. 1602, by no means deserved the scandalous accusation brought against him by the disappointed faction. How long he held the office is not known; but he retired, long before his death in 1650, to his rectory at Whitnash, near Leamington, where his epitaph may still be seen on the north wall of the church, with the following quaint verses underneath:—

> "This GreenHill periwig'd with snow
>   Was levil'd in the spring:
> This Hill the Nine and Three did know
>   Was Sacred to his King:
> But he must Downe although so much divine,
>   Before he rise never to set, but shine."

There is no hint whatever of his connection with the grocer's school at Rugby, unless that mysterious reference to "The Nine" be so considered; plainly, in those early days, the Rector of Whitnash was a much greater personage than the Head-master of Rugby.

To him succeeded Augustine Rolfe, and again Wiligent Greene, of whose appointments not even the dates are known; and then came on a second dispute about the mastership. The inhabitants seem to have claimed, as before, the right of election. A memorial presented by several of the most influential of them, headed by the rector of the parish, to Francis (Leigh) Lord Dunsmore, sets forth that they had "chosen and placed as schoolmaster"—speaking of this as their "accustomed right"—one Edward Clerke, Master of Arts, whom they contend to be the fit and proper person; but that the trustees had preferred to him one Raphael Pearce. And again, as before, the memorialists weaken their cause by putting too much upon the record. Not feeling sufficiently confident of their "accustomed right," they proceed to argue (quite in opposition to the great Bumble principle) that the said Raphael Pearce "was poor, and had many children, who might charge the town;" and again, "that he had a benefice with cure of souls far remote," which must needs divide his attentions. At the first hearing before the Lord Keeper, the point was decided in favour of Clerke; but upon appeal, Mr Raphael Pearce—it is comfortable to know, for the sake of the small children—was duly installed, and remained in quiet possession probably until his death in 1651; but, except his claims as a family man, we know nothing of his merits or demerits. Of the three next masters—Peter Whitehead, John Allen, and Knightley Harrison (M.A. of Queen's College, Oxford)—we know even less. In fact, during the whole of these generations the school was still a mere local charity; it is not even mentioned by name in Dugdale's 'Warwickshire,' as first published in 1656. There were obscure disputes and lawsuits about Sheriff's estates between his representatives and the trustees of the school, which had never yet derived from them the full benefit to which it was entitled. At last, by an inquisition held in 1653 before the Commissioners for Charitable Uses, the freehold of the Brownsover property was declared to be not in the heirs of the founder (who claimed it, subject to an annual rentcharge of £16, 13s. 4d.), but in the present trustees of his school; all arrears were ordered to be paid up, and hence came the first increase to the Master's original salary of £12: and when, a few years afterwards, the Conduit Close was let for £20 instead of £8, it seems to have been raised to about £40. This is nearly coincident in point of date with the commencement of that record so dear to all Rugbeians, the 'Rugby Register,' begun by Robert Ashbridge, M.A. of Queen's College, Oxford, who was elected to the mastership in 1674. Still, beyond the mere names, and in some cases the residence and parentage of the boys, we can learn nothing of the school—probably there was but little to be learnt —under his government or that of his successor, Mr Leonard Jeacocks, M.A. of New Inn Hall. They admitted between them 110 boys in thirteen years, and of these three-fifths were "foundationers" of Rugby and Brownsover.

But now came the man who was to make a reputation for Rugby. In the year 1687, Henry Holyoake, M.A. of Magdalen College, Oxford—*Henricus de Sacrâ Quercu*, as he loved rather to designate himself—entered upon the mastership in the full vigour of his powers, being then twenty-nine. For forty-four years he presided there; and, considering the disadvantages under which he worked, the high position to which he raised a small country school entitles him to take rank not below the later and more renowned names of Rugby. Be it remembered that there was no magnificent rental, in his days of rule, which could give to the head-master a stipend bearing some proportion to the work required, could provide him liberally with assistants of high academical distinction, and attract and reward ability amongst his pupils by valuable "exhibitions" to the universities. Holyoake had little more than the humble salary which had satisfied his predecessors; for even twenty years after his death, when the estates had become more valuable, it had only reached £63, 6s. 8d.; and he had to supply himself with assistance in teaching as best he might. One large schoolroom, too, the original building, was all the accommodation as yet provided. It is described as having been "a long and rather lofty room," substantially built in the usual style of the domestic architecture of those days, a timber framework filled in with brick or plaster, standing behind and at right angles with the ancient mansion-house of Laurence Sheriff's family, which he had bequeathed as a residence for the masters, and which, with the almshouses of his foundation, occupied the frontage opposite the parish church. It had an entrance at the north end for the boys, and probably some private communication with the master's house. Such was the common room in which Holyoake taught, for so many years, not only the foundationers of Rugby and Brownsover, but the sons of the best families of Warwickshire and Northamptonshire, who were received as boarders into his own family, and must have been content there with rather scanty accommodation. The fourth Earl of Peterborough, the third and fourth Lords Craven, the fourth Earl of Stamford, and many cadets of other noble families, with half the baronets of the neighbouring counties, were amongst his pupils. No doubt, in some cases, this education may have been only preparatory. Sir Theodosius Boughton, for instance — whose unhappy death has become matter of provincial history—entered Rugby at seven years old, but was afterwards at Eton; and this may have been the case with others. No visions of a "School-close," with its ample cricket-grounds and racket-courts, must delude the fancy of those who would try to picture to themselves these old school-days of Rugby. There was not even a playground at all. In spite of the scandalised remonstrances of some enthusiastic Rugbeians, there is no reasonable doubt that the future Barons Craven and Earls of Peterborough played leap-frog and hide-and-seek amongst the tombstones in the churchyard, which lay so temptingly convenient, whenever, in their out-of-school hours, they were not engaged at ball or marbles in the street. The habits and feelings of past generations must not be measured by our own. It would be held as highly indecorous in a modern public-school boy to "knuckle-down" upon the pavement, or practise hand-fives against any convenient gable-end, as it would be shocking to his feelings of reverence to make a playground of the graveyard; but the æsthetics of the nineteenth century were not those of the seventeenth, and we should be slow to assume irreverence where none was felt or intended. It is at least a certain fact, that in another provincial grammar-school of some repute, the churchyard was the regular cricket-ground within the memory of those now living; and that one of the players broke his arm there over a tombstone. We anticipate the verdict from the lips of scrupulous readers, but we are only responsible for the correctness of the fact; and though we may not be inclined to admit that those particular schoolboys were more naturally sacrilegious than any others, we are far from maintaining that a churchyard forms a desirable cricket-ground, for many reasons. Certainly it must give rise to some puzzling variations in the game. There was a vacant piece of ground, we are told by one who was at the school soon after, "beyond the churchyard, which was sometimes used by the boys;" and one champion of Rugbeian propriety argues that, inasmuch as the houses of respectable inhabitants overlooked the churchyard, such a scandal would in nowise have been permitted; and fondly hopes that it could only be an occasional loiterer on his way thither—"some of the smaller boys"—who thus abused the sacred precincts, and attracted the notice of "some sour and jaundiced passer-by, who out of it trumped up this idle story." Those who understand the nature of schoolboys under all kings that reign, and the especially reverent Church feeling under Dutch William and his good sister Anne, are quite competent to decide on the probabilities.

Of the kindly nature and paternal discipline of Mr Holyoake we have some pleasant glimpses in his will, which makes us long to know more than we are ever likely to recover of his life and labours. His establishment—for he appears to have been a bachelor—was under the domestic management of his cousin, Judith Holyoake, to whom he leaves a legacy on the express ground of her having been "very serviceable and seemingly kind" to the boys. One charitably hopes that the kindness was something better than seeming. At any rate, the good man's evident desire was that his pupils should be well looked after and kindly treated. Another relative, Elizabeth Story, also succeeded or assisted in the same useful capacity, and has her services similarly acknowledged by a legacy. There is a third small cousin —one Tommy Durnford—who also appears in the will, supplying another proof of Mr Holyoake's kindness and liberality. He was entered at the school in 1723, and was boarded and educated in his kinsman's house. His parents seem to have been of that type of affectionate relatives which most families have belonging to them, who disdain to submit the claims of blood to the rules of arithmetic. Nobody ever paid for Master Tommy's schooling; and Mr Holyoake, in his will—partly, perhaps, as a good-natured satire upon those who had promised to do so—"freely gives" to his "cosin Tommy Durnford the board and schooling of six years, and the expenses in that time"—money paid for clothes, books, &c.—"which amount to about ten pounds." Even after making every allowance for the higher value of money, we may imagine how astounded the testator would have been at the sight of a modern Rugbeian bill for "extras." Plainly the head-master of Rugby was a man whose good-nature was found very convenient by the less successful or less industrious members of his family; and there is something amusing in the device by which he *pays himself*, as it were, by means of legacies; not allowing to himself or his heirs that he was weak enough to be cheated; "forgiving" to the Rev. Mr Pinley (one of his assistant-masters) certain notes of hand, which were probably about as marketable as poor Tom's school debentures. Holyoake bequeathed to the school the portraits of his father and grandfather (who had some reputation as lexicographers), and his library. Neither are now to be seen. If the books exist, they are not distinguishable; yet surely a separate niche might have been found, even in the "Arnold" Library, for the bequest of one of his earliest predecessors: such heirlooms have a value above the bookseller's. There is another legacy in his will which is worth notice, as throwing some light upon the *cuisine* of the school-house in those days, even at the risk of shocking the sensibilities of its modern occupants, who are rather luxurious livers, if 'Tom Brown' is to be trusted. The honourable Masters Cecil and Craven and Greville must have dined occasionally upon *tripe*. For, unless that had formed an important article of consumption, on what possible ground could the worthy head-master have bequeathed so large a sum as £30 to the daughter of Widow Harris, "his tripe-woman"? The only consolatory reflection is, that it must evidently have been tripe of a very superior quality.

The first record of any assistant-masters, then, is under Mr Holyoake. One, Mr Pinley, has been already mentioned; another, Mr Joseph Hodgkinson, who had been educated under Holyoake, had the charge of the school during a short interregnum between his death and the appointment of his successor; and a third was that successor himself, John Plomer, M.A. of Wadham College, Oxford, who had also been a Rugbeian. The repute into which the school had now risen, and the increased value of the appointment in consequence of the influx of non-foundationers, may be estimated from the fact that Mr Plomer resigned a valuable rectory— Culworth in Northamptonshire—to enter upon his mastership of Rugby. But under him the school declined; we have no clue to the cause, but the entrances in the register sensibly diminish, and he resigned in 1742.

Then came the second, and perhaps the more remarkable, of those men who formed the steps between Laurence Sheriff and Thomas Arnold, but of whom posterity knows too little. Thomas Crossfield, of Queen's College, Oxford, was the Marcellus of Rugby—scarcely shown to the school before he was taken away.[*] Already he had made his reputation as a scholar, not only at his college, but as master of the small provincial schools of

---

[*] "Ostendent terris hunc tantum fata, neque ultra
Esse sinent."—VIRG. Æn., vi. 870.

Daventry and Preston Capes. The trustees invited him to Rugby, and his appointment was hailed as an era in the school's history. He came there, says his epitaph (the eloquent tribute of his successor, Mr Knail)—

> "Fama praeeunte et commendante,
> Splendidae dux coloniae,
> Summis omnium votis, summâ omnium expectatione,
> Quam morte sola fefellit."

It was indeed a "splendid colony" which he brought with him to fill the waste places of Rugby School. Fifty-three boys—fifty-one of them non-foundationers, implying boys from a distance, whose parents had independent means—were entered on the roll during the first year of his mastership. Many of them were sons of clergymen and gentlemen in Northamptonshire, who had followed him from Daventry or Preston. Fifteen additional scholars—amongst whom was the young Earl of Kincardine (afterwards of Elgin)—were enrolled in the year following, and the whole number on the school-list could not have been under a hundred, which was a much higher point than seems to have been reached before, or for some generations after. At the end of the second year Crossfield died—only thirty-six years old. It is idle to draw a fancy picture; but possibly some minds, to whom these little glimpses of the past are even the more attractive because of the "eternal mist" that we cannot penetrate, will find it irresistible to compare his death with Arnold's, and to believe that if he, too, had found some grateful pupil for his biographer, we might have had an earlier Rugby memoir of scarcely less affecting interest.

William Knail, M.A., succeeded. We know but little

of him, except that he became a fellow of Queen's College, Oxford, and that his Latin scholarship is abundantly proved by the epitaph which has been only partially quoted above. One of his old pupils * has left a very meagre sketch of him, which he would doubtless have made fuller if he had known how much we are interested about his old master. Mr Knail was a bachelor, at least during his Rugby life, and used occasionally to hear some of the boys (probably the higher forms) in his study —"a small room in which he smoked many a pipe, the fragrance of which was abundantly retained in the blue cloth hangings with which it was fitted up." He resigned in 1751, and went back to smoke his pipe more at leisure in the common-room of Queen's, till he was presented to the college living of Carisbrook, in the Isle of Wight, when he proceeded to the Doctor's degree which has been sometimes erroneously bestowed upon him as headmaster of Rugby. Two heroes from amongst his pupils made themselves afterwards a name in history, and still hold their place even in the light of the more recent glories of Balaclava and Lucknow. One was John Mansel, who, as brigadier of cavalry under the Duke of York in 1794, charged and took, at the cost of his life, a French battery of fourteen guns near Cambray; the other was Ralph Abercromby, the hero of Egypt. In this latter instance, if tradition be true, the military taste had not developed itself in the schoolboy; for when the Duke of Cumberland's troops, on their march after quelling the Rebellion in "the '45," passed along the Dunchurch road, scarce two miles from Rugby, all the boys are said to have played truant to see the sight, with the

* This must have been William Bray, the historian of Surrey.

single exception of young Abercromby. Whether it was indifference to the spectacle, or an unusual reverence for school bounds, which kept him from making one of the party—or whether, as is most probable, his national sympathies were with Prince Charlie—tradition does not undertake to certify. But it is a remarkable proof of the isolation of the Warwickshire villages in those days, that the good people of Cosford, which lay only three miles out of the Duke's line of march, not only never heard a word about it, but knew nothing of any rebellion until it was all over.

Knail was the last master who taught in Sheriff's original schoolroom. He had been assisted latterly by the Rev. Joseph Richmond, M.A., "Taberdar" and afterwards Fellow of the same college, and who succeeded him in the head-mastership. Meanwhile, in 1748, the first Act of Parliament was passed relating to the school. The old buildings had fallen out of repair, and it was feared, as the applicants to Parliament represented, "that the Free School, which had for many years been in great repute, and not only a benefit to the neighbourhood, but a public utility, might be lost and become useless." The want of anything like a playground, too, was now beginning to be felt, and was set forth in the application as an additional reason for a change of site. The income of the school estates at this time, taking one year with another, was £116, 17s. 6d., of which £31, 13s. 4d. was paid to the almsmen, and £21, 17s. 6d. expended in clothing them, and in keeping the buildings at Rugby and Brownsover in repair. The Middlesex estate was now let to Sir William Milman on a lease which would expire in 1779, and under which part of Lamb's Conduit Street, Red Lion Street, and Milman Street had already sprung up upon Sheriff's "pasture-close." This promised a valuable revenue to the school within a reasonable period. The trustees were empowered, under the Act, either to sell a portion of the property, or to borrow on mortgage a sum not exceeding £1800 for the purchase of a new site and the erection of suitable buildings. They had first in view a substantial brick-built residence adjoining the original property, and facing the marketplace;* but some obstacle fortunately intervened, and they finally purchased, of a Mrs Pennington, a site which was in every respect much more suitable for their purpose. It was the manor-house of Rugby, built about the time of Charles I., standing clear of the town on all sides but one, where its two wings abutted on the street, and formed, with their connecting palisades and entrance-gate, a square court within. It had four fields attached to it, of which the two upper were at once thrown together, and formed the original "School-close." There a new schoolroom was built adjoining the west side of the mansion-house, which was retained as the residence of the head-master, and thither, in 1755, the school was transplanted under Mr Richmond. The new building, which was of brick, stood as nearly as possible on the site of the present school-house hall, and if the drawings of it which have been preserved are a fair representation of it, was as ugly an erection as might well be: and in spite of its having on the north side "a handsome porch according to the rules of the Doric order," and a wooden cupola with a clock and a vane, did very little credit to its Warwick-

* Now in the occupation of E. Harris, Esq.

shire architect.* The lower storey formed one large room, in which all the classes were taught: it was wainscoted with oak, like the present schools, up to the windows, with fixed seats and desks for the boys; and at the southern end (looking into the school-close), which was built in a semicircular form, was a seat of authority in which the head-master presided. The upper storey was divided: the portion over the semicircular apse forming the main dormitory—distinguished from the smaller ones, and well remembered as "Paradise," from its pleasant look-out, but which nevertheless, we are told, "was not the most peaceable lodging in the house;" while the northern and smaller apartment served as a kind of common sitting-room, called "Over-School,"† where the boys' boxes were kept, and which the elders soon appropriated to themselves for much the same purposes as the present "fifth-form room." In the wings of the manor-house itself was a writing-school, and above some smaller bedrooms for boarders, with two sick-rooms.

* There is a careful drawing of the School as it stood in 1809, made by Mr E. Pretty, then drawing-master. The prints are now scarce. A poor and less accurate sketch may be seen in the 'Gentleman's Magazine' for March 1809.

† In this room it was that, in the latter half of the last century, the punishment of "Ash-planting" used to take place. It was inflicted by order and in the presence of a judicial committee of the præpostors (Sixth form) for some few grave offences against the recognised internal discipline of the school; e.g., a personal assault upon one of their body by a mutinous fag—an offence which would still be severely punished by the masters if not by the Sixth themselves. Three ash-saplings were used; in theory, at least, the two first were to be broken upon the person of the culprit. The punishment was severe—perhaps unjustifiably so; but it had the character of being only inflicted in extreme cases, and with strict justice, and was not regarded as a cruelty in the school.

Such was the second local embodiment of Rugby School. There is considerable doubt whether its progress as a place of education was at all in proportion to these architectural developments. It seems to have become something like an appanage to Queen's College. Mr Knail, as we have seen, handed it over to Mr Richmond. How the school prospered under him, we have even less than the previous data for ascertaining. Either he admitted no new boys at all in his four years of office, which is highly improbable, or he omitted to enter their names in the register, which does not leave an impression favourable to his regularity. He soon grew tired of Rugby, or Rugby grew tired of him, for he retained the appointment only four years, when he also resigned in favour of his fellow-collegian and assistant-master, Mr Stanley Burrough. This gentleman held it for twenty-two years, but there was no great advance made either in numbers or in repute under his government. Yet he left behind him the character of a kindly man and a good master—" blessed with a most happy command of temper."

Few are the glimpses which can now be recovered of the inner life of the school even at his date; but there was one of his pupils whose case occupied the law-courts of England and Scotland for many years, and which gave rise to a scene at Rugby long remembered by those who were present. Archibald Stewart Douglas, who was entered there in 1758, " to be fitted for the army," was the son of Sir John Stewart of Grandtully Castle in Perthshire (the Tully-veolan of 'Waverley'), by Lady Jane Douglas, only sister of the late Duke of Douglas. The lady was forty-seven when she married; and Archibald was born (with a twin-brother who died young) at Paris in the year following. Altogether the circumstances were suspicious; the Hamilton family, who were the Duke's next collateral heirs, and who saw their succession to his vast estates imperilled by these unexpected intruders, endeavoured, and for some time with success, to persuade him that the birth was supposititious. Amongst other steps taken by the Duke to satisfy his scruples, he sent down to Rugby a gentleman named M'Glashan. At his request Mr Burrough assembled the boys in the school, and he was enabled to single out young Archibald Douglas (whom he had never seen) from the rest of his schoolfellows by his remarkable likeness to his mother's family. From this and other inquiries, the Duke became convinced of his nephew's legitimacy, and entailed his estates accordingly; but on his death, in 1761, an action was commenced on behalf of the Duke of Hamilton, then a minor, for their recovery. The "great Douglas cause," after much litigation, was decided by the fifteen Judges of Session, by a single casting vote, in favour of the Hamilton claim. But this judgment was reversed on appeal to the House of Lords in 1769; and so popular was young Douglas's cause in Edinburgh, that the city was illuminated for three nights after the decision was known there. He was afterwards created Baron Douglas of Douglas Castle.

Up to the close of Mr Burrough's administration, the common costume of Rugbeians was cocked-hats and queues, and boys of higher position were conspicuous in scarlet coats. Those who were sent to the school, from whatever distance, came on horseback. It took William Heyrick, coming from Leicester (which the train does now in forty minutes), the whole day, carried on a pillow before a man who was chosen for his knowledge of the quagmires on Dunton Heath, between Leicester and Lutterworth. Great was the excitement when two boys arrived in a post-chaise in 1774: they were sons of an innkeeper at Daventry, to whom such a luxury came cheap. Even at a later date, the Irish and north-country boys, to the number of thirty or forty, remained at Rugby during the winter holidays.

CHAPTER III.

DR JAMES.

It was towards the close of Mr Burrough's mastership, in 1777, that the Act of Parliament was passed which may be called the Second Charter of the School. The lease to Sir William Milman of the London estate was just expiring, and a valuable house-property was coming into the possession of the trustees. By the new Act they were legally constituted as "The Trustees of the Rugby Charity founded by Laurence Sheriff," and empowered to use a common seal. The salary of the head-master was raised to its present amount, £113, 6s. 8d., with the addition of a capitation-fee of £3 for each foundation-boy instructed in Greek and Latin. Provision was for the first time made for an "usher or ushers," at a salary not exceeding £80. A writing-master was appointed, that office having been previously discharged by the master of the Free-school founded at Rugby by Mr Elborow in 1707, who was specially directed to be "serviceable in teaching in the *Latin* school as well as" in his own. The limits of the foundation were extended to five miles round Rugby; and the first exhibitions to the universities, of £40 per annum each for seven years, were founded out of the increased revenues. It was with reference to these, no doubt, that the trustees were directed to meet quarterly and hear the *foundationers* examined; and although an attempt to limit the elections to such boys, in the event of fit candidates presenting themselves, was defeated in the Court of Chancery some years ago, there must remain grave doubts of the justice of extending Laurence Sheriff's "Rugby charity" to the sons of esquires and baronets from all parts of the United Kingdom. But such, in all cases, is the modern liberal interpretation of founders' bequests. Another recommendation in the Act has been distinctly disregarded in the election of the head-master, and, in more than one instance, with very questionable advantage to the school. It was directed that preference should be given "to such as had been educated there," if found duly qualified; but it is somewhat remarkable that, although some of the previous masters had been originally Laurence Sheriff's scholars, no Rugbeian has been elected since the passing of this Act.

These extensive developments were perhaps rather more than good Mr Burrough could keep pace with. They improved his position, but at the same time added to his responsibilities. He had now been master for twenty-two years, and was past seventy. The Act, while making future provision for the removal of inefficient head-masters by declaring the tenure to be only "*durante bene placito,*" had specially maintained his freehold of the office "*quamdiu bene se gesserit.*" But he resigned the next year, before the new regulations could have come into operation, and was presented by a relative to the rectory of Sapcote in Leicestershire, where he died. The improved position of the school now offered attractions to a man of higher mark. Thomas James, Fellow and Tutor of King's College, Cambridge, already twice distinguished there as "Members' Prizeman," was elected to the vacancy. He brought to Rugby Eton scholarship and probably Eton discipline—both the most efficient of that day. Another Etonian Fellow of the same college (James Chartres, M.A.) accompanied him as second-master; other assistant-masters from both universities were added in rapid succession, as the trustees came into possession of their increased rental, and the school rose in numbers and repute. Dr James found there 52 boys: in five years he had raised them to 165.* The one large schoolroom was no longer sufficient: a new building was added on to its west side (communicating with it by the folding-doors of its original entrance) containing two additional rooms, occupying as nearly as possible the site of the present "Fifth-form" and "Twenty" schools. In the first of these were four long tables, at one of which the boarders dined, and the three others were occupied by the First, Second, and Lower Third forms. The upper storey was divided by wooden partitions into "studies" for the boys, leaving a broad passage in the middle. A three-storeyed erection on the north front of the mansion-house was also appropriated to the same purpose. But even the new schools overflowed, for the numbers rose in time to near 300; and the head-master was obliged to migrate into a barn adjoining the Dunchurch road—somewhat lower down than the present chapel—which, with an addition at one end, formed a commodious schoolroom. There, for more than twenty

---

* Dr James appears not to have included in his lists such foundationers as lived in the town.

years, successive head-masters taught the two senior forms; and it was even used as a chapel on Sundays, when the numbers of the boys grew too large for all to be accommodated in their gallery in the parish church. A part of this "Barn-school" (as it was called) was cut off to form a room for the French master and his class; and there was a small lean-to at one end which had very painful memories attached to it, being a sort of execution-dock, so often resorted to by a subsequent head-master of moderate stature for the punishment of delinquents, that a witty Rugbeian suggested as a motto for it, "Great cry and little Wooll." Connecting these buildings with the three schools adjoining the old manor-house, was a line of cow-sheds, which served as a shelter in rainy weather, where the Fifth and Sixth congregated, as now in the cloisters, before lesson-hour, and in which the fags of that day, many of whom are now living to record it—*credite posteri*—played marbles! Such was the Rugby of 1809; for it was not until long afterwards that barn and cow-sheds disappeared, though the present school buildings were begun in that year. Marbles undoubtedly survived longer, for even hoops had their season down to a later date.

We have tolerably accurate descriptions of Dr James's days; for in his time Rugby began to take a public rank, and Rugbeians thought their experiences worth recording. "Good school, Rugby," George III. is reported to have said—"Good scholar, Dr James—very good scholar." His Majesty might not have been the most competent judge, but he had a knack of enunciating facts. "James's school at Rugby is much in vogue," writes Jacob Bryant to a friend; "there is no person under whom I would sooner place a child;" a strong testimony from so thorough an Etonian.* In 1789, one of Dr James's pupils was Charles Apperley, better known as "Nimrod." In his garrulous old age he took to writing some rambling recollections which he called his 'Life and Times;' they were published in 'Fraser's Magazine,' and might have gone on till now (for they never seemed to get any nearer the end) if he had lived, and if the editor had not grown tired of him—which he did. He jots down amongst them notes of his school-days, which are not without interest, and, when corrected and illustrated by contemporary recollections, give a tolerable notion of what those school-days were. There were then six assistant-masters. The head-master taught the Sixth (not numbering more than twelve or fourteen) and the Fifth forms. The Upper Fourth was under Innes, the second-master (afterwards master of Warwick School—"a gentleman," says Nimrod, "in thought, word, and deed;" and, moreover, an admirable player of single-stick, which he much encouraged amongst the boys. The Lower Fourth and Upper Third, under William Sleath † and Philip Homer

---

* Nichols's Illust., viii. 536.

† "William Boultbee Sleath (Broughton, Leicestershire) was appointed assistant-master of Rugby School by Dr James, upon his leaving school in December 1778; so that he was a schoolboy at the close of one half-year, and a schoolmaster at the beginning of the next. From Rugby he was elected head-master of Repton School, June, 1800. Dr Sleath's conversation was always entertaining and instructive, and he did not at any period of his life possess the virtue of taciturnity. In his early days the schoolboy literature at Rugby principally consisted of Smollet's and Fielding's novels, and sixpenny pamphlets, such as 'The Ghost of the Rock,' 'The Peruvian Demon,' 'Adventures of Dick Turpin,' and 'The Life of Thomas Hickathrift,' a work of rather a lower grade than the schoolboy days of Tom Brown. Sleath, however, had read the 'Arabian Nights' Entertainments,' and

respectively, occupied the original "Old School;" while the centre school held the Lower Third, Second, and First, under John Sleath (afterwards High-Master of St Paul's), William Birch, and Richard Rouse Bloxham. There was a terrible amount of flogging; but that was not peculiar to Rugby, being a remedy much in vogue at all schools at that date. William Sleath, who was the executioner of the Lower School, would occasionally reprieve the small boys who were sent up to him, on condition that they would weed a certain time in his garden, thus saving himself the expense of a gardener. There was also the unnecessary addition of canings—always more objectionable, as liable to be inflicted according to the master's temper at the moment—even "double" canings—three blows on each hand.

The boarding-house system was then in full operation. When it was first introduced seems now beyond discovery; but in all probability many boys must have lodged out in Mr Crossfield's time; though it has been stated that Mr Burrough, in his later days, refused many boys for want of room, from which it would appear that the "school-house" (in which he had at one time as many as fifty) was then the only available accommodation. The earliest boarding-house of which there seems to be any certain record is that kept by the Rev. Christopher Moor, at the Rectory: "Elborow's Charity" school-house was also a boarding-house in very early

---

his schoolfellows used to report of him that on one occasion, when they were in bed at night, one of the boys said, 'Now, Sleath, tell us a story.' He began, and after a time the boys dropped asleep one after the other; when they awoke in the morning, Sleath's voice was still heard going on, as he had been all night, with his tales out of the 'Arabian Nights.'"—T. L. B.

times. The recognition of "private tutors"—a great blot in our public-school and university system, amounting to a confession that the *public* teaching, expensive as it is, proves insufficient—was beginning to creep in, probably from Eton. It has been found too convenient a means of increasing the masters' emoluments not to have made good its footing both at Rugby and elsewhere. After long figuring in the list as one of the "optional" items, private tutors and private studies are now charged among "necessaries."* In Apperley's time the tutor was really optional; but this gave the boys who availed themselves of such aid a very unfair advantage; for it was then the custom for the private tutor to "construe" over the lesson to his pupils previous to their going up with it to the master of their form; and young Apperley, whose father considered all necessary instruction fairly included in the regular school fees, took advantage of William Sleath's nearsightedness to slip in, and enjoy a little private tuition unperceived. Fagging—a more venerable but less popular institution—existed then at Rugby in a form which few even of its most zealous defenders would wish to see restored. Instances of great cruelty were rare, but not unknown. The case of half-roasting before the hall-fire, at which readers of 'Tom Brown' may have shuddered, and which is by many supposed to be a myth common to many public schools, certainly took place in Dr Ingles's days at Rugby, and the names

---

* There can be no question but that in all cases good masters should be liberally paid. But "optional" and "private" tuition is an anomaly in a public school: all *necessary* education should surely be included in one single charge.

of the tormentor and his victim (the latter a Waterloo man) are well known to some of their contemporaries now living. But even the common daily life of a fag had its hardships. Warming two or three cold beds by one's own natural caloric was not a pleasant process; neither was running two miles and back, at four o'clock in the morning, to take up the night-lines which the præpostor had set in the Avon, the best preparative for first lesson at seven. Blacking shoes, cleaning knives and forks, and carrying up the water from the pump to the dormitory—even to "Paradise" itself—would be thought hard measure by a school-house fag of the present day; when even "fagging-out" at cricket, that most wholesome practice, is all but superseded by the use of nets. Yet these things do not seem to have broken the hearts of the Rugbeians of the past, or to have interfered with their pleasant reminiscences of "Queen Treen," the popular pastry-cook of those days, or of the great jack that was snared in Caldecott's pond, in face of all perils—perils from Caldecott, perils from præpostors (who always claimed a monopoly of poaching), perils from the masters, and even from jack himself, who snapped his teeth within an inch of Butler's nose, and nearly spoilt a future head-master of Shrewsbury. For a great fisherman was Sam Butler, in all modes, lawful and unlawful—"an idler fellow could scarce be found at Rugby;" solitary and unpopular, always reading novels and plays, and yet knowing the most crabbed bits of Demosthenes, and the toughest Greek chorus, by some sort of intuition, and dictating Latin verses as fast as others could write them down. "Play for Butler," sounded in the school on the "given" half-holidays as commonly as have other well-known names in modern remembrance.* "How do *you* take it, Butler?" was a not uncommon appeal from Dr James, when one of those hopelessly corrupt jumbles of Greek words, whose translation can be only happy guess-work at the best, came on in the course of the Sixth-form lesson; and Butler's solution, if not always certainly correct, was sure to be "*ben trovato*." Very pleasant is this condescension of the elder scholar to the bright young pupil; too really learned to profess infallibility, too generous not to give full scope to vigorous youthful genius, too liberal not to recognise, through the external relations of master and pupil, the equal platform upon which mind meets mind. It will not fail to remind Sixth-form Rugbeians of a later date, how Arnold used in such cases almost to repeat his predecessor's phrase, turning with that smile of his that was always half a frown, to some young student of hardly less promise than Butler—"What do *you* make of it, ——?" when readings and commentators were all at variance, and he was quite conscious that his own limited scholarship made him an unsteady holder of the critical balance. Those were the days, too, in which Walter Savage Landor astonished masters, boys, and neighbouring rustics, by the use and abuse of those remarkable powers which should have made him a pride to Rugbeians; beating Butler himself in Latin versification, and without a rival in boxing, leaping, and all sports allowed or forbidden; now seen on horseback out of bounds, galloping beyond the reach of pedestrian

* One half-holiday in each week is supposed to be given for some specially good exercise in the Sixth.

authorities, and now, after the fashion of a Roman *retiarius*, throwing his casting-net over the head of the miller who had ventured to demand possession of that illegal implement, and reducing his enemy to abject submission under those helpless circumstances; and when good Dr James (on whom he was always writing squibs, Latin and English), with the intention of offering serious remonstrance, knocks for admission at his study-door—that recognised castle of every Rugbeian, which no master dreams of entering without leave—affecting to discredit the reality of the visit or the voice, and devoutly ejaculating from within his bolted fortress—"*Avaunt, Satan!*" Landor carried his licence beyond endurance at last, and was dismissed the school for adding to a copy of Latin lyrics, which he had to write out, *honoris causâ*, in the head-master's book, two clever but very objectionable stanzas.

The epitaph on Dr James in the school chapel probably does him less than justice when it records of him, "*Erat lepore condita gravitas.*" He is said by his old pupils to have been as fond of a joke as he was of flogging; and he certainly seems to have borne with much from really clever boys. The late Lord Lyttelton by turns delighted and provoked him. He—at that time Mr Lyttelton—was the ringleader in a good deal of mischief at the school in his day; but so clever and so amiable that he met with considerable indulgence. He and others tied up a young donkey one morning in the Doctor's desk at school; and Dr James, on proceeding to lesson, found the post of honour already occupied by this strange representative. He must have either been too much amused to preserve his gravity, or have had remarkable forbearance. "Take the young doctor down, but don't hurt him," was all he said; and the culprits seem to have heard no more of it. Lyttelton found the next head-master (Dr Ingles) less indulgent to these practical jokes, and at last received one of those notices to quit which save the pain of expulsion.* He carried himself and his jokes to Christ-Church, where Dean Jackson found him as pleasant and as troublesome as Dr James had. He dressed up the then existing "Mercury" in the basin of Tom Quadrangle in a cast-off wig and gown of the Dean's; to him, at least, the credit of it was given by Jackson himself, on the ground that "no other man in college would have dared to have done it." His insuperable love of fun somewhat interfered, in later years, with the due appreciation of his real abilities in the House of Commons.

* On the Dunchurch road there was a stile long known as " Bags' Stile ;" here a certain set of boys, of whom Lyttelton was one, used to sit and "chaff" the passing "bagsmen"—for the commercial travellers to Rugby then rode with actual saddle-bags ; and this practice led to terrible fights occasionally with the aggrieved riders. When Lyttelton departed he left an elegy, of which the first verses are as follows :—

> " Farewell, ye bagsmen, sons of Grease !
>   Ye men of bags, farewell !
> To Rugby now jog on in peace,
>   In peace at Lambley's † dwell.
>
> " No more the odious cry of ' Bags !'
>   Shall haunt you through the town ;
> In safety mount your lanky nags,
>   For Lyttelton is gone !"

---

† The landlord of the " Eagle.

CHAPTER IV.

DR INGLES.

The annual "Speeches," at which the prize poems and essays are recited, relieved at intervals by dramatic dialogues and orations, ancient and modern, date from a very early period in the history of the school. They used at first to be held at the beginning of the summer holidays, when (in Mr Knail's time) the original school was duly strewed with rushes in honour of the visit of the trustees. For this primitive festal decoration was in after days substituted the dressing the masters' desks, in the school where the speeches were held, with oak-boughs and flowers; and this again was given up, when (in 1815) the time was changed from Midsummer to Easter, when flowers and green boughs were scarce, and when the increasing numbers of the company led to the erection of galleries, and the converting the whole area into an amphitheatre, so that such decorations were no longer practicable. They were then transferred to the "Island," which, with much labour and groaning of fags, was made to assume for the Easter week (and for that week only) the appearance of a highly-kept garden, which the ladies who came to the Speeches were expected to visit, and which sent many an admiring mother home charmed with the Arcadian recreations of her much-maligned schoolboys. That island is, alas! no more an island. Very many have been its vicissitudes: originally (our antiquarian friend thinks) a British tumulus; then possibly the centre of one of the fish-ponds of the monks of Pipewell—they certainly had others close by; then a shady grove in which præpostors of very ancient date sat apart like gods and conned their lessons; then a garden, useful only to keep fags from being idle, or living in unnatural enjoyment (as at present) of half-holidays, where they were fagged to make really pretty flower-beds with the strangest garden-tools —half a pewter-spoon, or a whole dinner-fork; then a gymnastic ground with swings and poles, and the moat drained dry, but only half filled up. A more wretched sight than it now presents is not to be imagined. Who can now believe that in that dry ditch William Heyrick, in 1776, was tempted to *bathe* five times in one day, and caught cold therefrom? It was in Dr James's days that the Bath was built; finished, as says a diary kept by a boy then at the school, September 6, 1779; and amidst all the changes at Rugby, that unpretending structure survives, unchanged in any material feature. From the same source — unfortunately scanty, as most schoolboy records are—we learn that the expenses at this time were sixteen guineas per annum for board, and four guineas for tuition; and that "every boy was expected to bring a knife and fork, six towels, and a drinking-horn." A little further on comes an amusing entry— "No French this day, as Mr Wratislaw is *gone to Warwick races*."

Dr James had done much to make the Speech-day attractive by practising the boys in elocution, with which he took very great pains—a point to which Dr Woull, in his mastership, also paid much attention; but Dr Arnold—himself no orator—rather discouraged any display of the kind, and certainly diminished the interest of this annual festival, by making the recitation of prize compositions, often very badly delivered, and the distribution of the prizes, the sole attractions in the programme. Under the present management, Shakespeare and Sheridan have been very judiciously restored, and portions only of the prize essays are now recited, much to the delight of the ladies, and somewhat to the relief of the boys, by whom the whole proceeding has usually been voted a bore; though those who remember poor Bob Thorpe as *Falstaff* will make exceptions. But even Dr James was unable to train orators at Rugby. Nimrod can only remember one of his schoolfellows who obtained any notice as a speaker in Parliament; and that was a noble lord who rose when he was very tipsy, and had to be pulled down by the skirts of his coat. The vice of Rugby in those days was drinking; it has been its vice from time to time in latter days,—even in the rose-coloured period of 'Tom Brown,' when there was less excuse for it in the general habits of society; but Mr Apperley records that there was " an excellent feeling throughout the school as to what may be called gentlemanlike and honourable conduct."

For sixteen years Dr James continued at the head of the school, which never lost the high position it had gained under his government, though in the last few years the numbers had slightly decreased. He resigned from failing health; and the trustees, as a mark of their appreciation of his services, applied for and obtained his appointment to a prebendal stall at Worcester. He was succeeded by another late Fellow of King's—Dr Henry Ingles, master of Macclesfield School. It is probable that he found the discipline somewhat relaxed; at any rate, he had the credit, as new authorities commonly have even without deserving it, of drawing the reins unpalatably tight. One very honest measure of reform he certainly attempted to carry out. The expenses of Rugby had risen considerably under Dr James. They had amounted, in Mr Burrough's day, to a sum which seems absurdly small to those who have to pay modern school-bills. The little Lord Douglas that was to be only cost his friends for one year's total expenses, "extras" inclusive, the sum of £26, 16s. 2½d. And there were remonstrances from careful fathers, when Dr James raised the charge for board from £12 per annum to £14. Yet at the same time, if Nimrod's recollections are to be trusted, the private personal expenses of some of the boys were very considerable—exceeding, it is to be hoped, any amount that would be possible even in our extravagant times, when London "professionals" are engaged as bowlers, and fags would think it an indignity to roll their own cricket-ground, and the "Eleven" cannot put on their shoes except in a "pavilion," and Volunteer uniforms and football costumes make a severe inroad upon the privy purse; for he speaks of one schoolfellow, a nobleman's son, who spent a hundred pounds a-year in pocket-money. Such abuses probably led to a circular which was issued by the new head-master, on his appointment, announcing his intention to carry out the design of his predecessor in reducing the expenses of the school, "to meet the wants of persons with moderate incomes and large families," and calling upon parents themselves to check unnecessary extravagance.

Dr Ingles appears to have shown a severity of manner, if not of personal disposition, which contrasted unfavourably with the amenity of the late head-master. He was very unpopular at first; and this led to what must be considered the chief event of his reign—the Great Rebellion of 1797. There had, indeed, been an outbreak before this, which Nimrod (whose sensibilities could not have been very easily shocked) characterises as " awful "—a word of more meaning in his schoolboy days than now. But it took place before his time; and as, with unusual reticence, he professes himself unwilling to revive the subject, we may conclude he knew very little about it. A lady's letter,* lately published, places the fact and the date (1786) beyond all doubt, but we are able now to recover nothing of the details. But some actors in the later rebellion survive. It has assumed so many forms in the school traditions, that it may be as well to give the points in which the narratives of eye-witnesses agree. It arose out of the surreptitious purchase of gunpowder for firing a pistol. Dr Ingles required from the culprit the name of the person who had sold the forbidden article; but the cautious tradesman had entered the purchase as *tea*, and the boy was

---

* Mrs Delany's Autobiography, vol. vi. p. 422. Letter from Miss Clayton to Miss Port, Dec. 8, 1786 : " I hope that your brother behaved as you wished him at Rugby, where I was quite sorry to hear there had been a rebellion."

flogged for a falsehood—of course, so far, unjustly. The school, in righteous indignation, broke the cowardly tradesman's windows. The Doctor insisted they should be paid for. The bolder spirits in the Sixth and Fifth —a future Marquess and a Bishop amongst the number —protested in a round-robin that they would do no such thing. Severe measures were threatened by the master. A petard fixed to the door of his school that evening, which blew it off its hinges, was the reply on the part of the boys. On the following morning—the Saturday of the great November horse-fair—the school-bell rang out, after first lesson, violently and irregularly, what was soon known to be the tocsin of war. The benches, desks, and wainscoting, were torn down from the several schools, and piled in one large bonfire in the middle of the Close, to the great enjoyment of the farmers and horse-jockeys, who lined the railings by the Dunchurch road. The schoolroom windows, protected by latticework, were broken with pointed sticks by small boys, hoisted for that purpose on their companions' shoulders. Personal violence was threatened against Ingles himself —the "Black Tiger," as he was irreverently called. He was obliged to shut himself up in his house; and as, unfortunately, most of the other masters seem to have taken advantage of a three-quarters holiday to be out of the way, matters became so alarming, that assistance was claimed from a sergeant's party who happened to be recruiting at the fair. For some time the sergeant was to be seen with his sword drawn, keeping guard at the door of the Doctor's house, but looking very much, as one of the rebels described it, as if he were going to lead him to execution. At last the constitutional party were reinforced by masters, special constables, and volunteer farmers with horsewhips—who probably embraced the opportunity of vengeance for stoned pigeons and poultry—and the confederates retreated to the island; where, however, though they had an embryo general among their leaders,* they seem to have attempted no further defence than fastening the door of the old drawbridge, or, according to some authorities, raising the bridge entirely. In either case, the recruiting sergeant gallantly forced the passage, wading through the moat, sword in hand; his men followed, and the rebels capitulated. They were not allowed any honours of war. Some were expelled, others flogged; some of the Sixth form had their choice; and one of the trustees of the school, whose son had declined the personal punishment, and been sent home in consequence, is said to have brought the recusant back forthwith, and to have himself superintended the infliction with the stern virtue of Brutus. A worthy clergyman who was a fag in those years, and had little personal share in the glories or sufferings of the war, chuckles to this day at the just retribution which then overtook a certain præpostor, who was in the habit of sorely persecuting him. This youthful tyrant was engaged that very evening in making our informant and another small victim jump over a stile, "coaching" them with a four-in-hand whip to stimulate their exertions, when there came a messenger from the school-house—"Mr C——, *the Doctor wants you.*" (C—— had signed the fatal round-robin.) There was no doubt as to the nature of the communication; he tossed his whip to one of the fags to carry home, with a very crest-fallen

* Sir Willoughby Cotton, G.C.B., K.C.H.

air, and repaired to that torture-chamber before alluded to, where he found the Doctor himself prepared to act as "coachman."

Those were the days, it must be remembered, of the Four-in-hand Club; and the passion for handling the ribbons extended itself to the boys, who saw magnificent turn-outs passing continually along the Dunchurch road. A few years later, this taste developed itself considerably. Mr Over, the school carpenter, was appointed coachmaker; and rival chariots, drawn by teams of from four to twelve fags in harness, and *tooled* by a præpostor, raced round the school-close, or took longer drives to the neighbouring villages. Once a return "coach" from Dunchurch overtook an old dame coming to Rugby market with eggs and butter. In spite of all her attempts to decline the honour, she was hoisted into the seat beside the driver, and carried into the town in triumph. "Bucknill's" and "Birch's" were reputed the fastest teams. "I have travelled many a mile in rope harness," says a hero of rather later date. "Long" Parry of Llanrhaiadr, one of the best gentlemen-coachmen as well as one of the best scholars of his day, must have practised at the chariot-races at Rugby.

Ingles's reign had something of a warlike character altogether. About 1804 the Volunteer movement was at its height in England; and the school had its own corps then, as it has now. Our modern riflemen would think it a very quaint uniform—blue lapelled coats, with red cuffs and collars; still more would they smile at the weapons—heavy wooden swords in tin sheaths, with which these ancients practised, with a contempt of practical usefulness which must have come from the War

Office itself, the *cavalry* broadsword exercise. But in warlike spirit they were not a whit behind their modern representatives. Their pugnacity appears to have been such that it would have been hardly safe to trust them with the regulation weapons which the present Rugby corps carry so innocently. They had not only parades, but sham-fights — if a fight could be called *sham* from which the combatants retired with broken heads and bloody noses — attacking and defending the Doctor's farmyard on the "little island" between what were then the two closes; and it was fortunate that the swords were wooden. But there were boys in that corps who handled other weapons almost before they were men: Miller, who led the Enniskillens at Waterloo; Holbeche and Biddulph, who charged in command of troops under their old schoolfellow; and many others of the twenty-five Rugbeians who might have been counted on that glorious field.

Dr Ingles was the first head-master who introduced two regular examiners, one from each university, for the exhibitions. Up to that date there had been one only, casually nominated by the master or trustees—Dr Thomas Clare, an old Rugbeian, holding the office for many years in succession. Yet Ingles is said not to have shone as a scholar, and to have been rebuked for ignorance by one of his own examiners. He was very irregular in attendance at the early first lesson; a remarkable contrast to the punctuality of both Wooll and Arnold.

Upon the whole, the state of affairs under Dr Ingles does not appear to have been flourishing, for the numbers declined considerably as compared with even the later years of Dr James, who left 193 names on the list.

When Dr Ingles resigned, after a ten years' administration, there were only 150. The new head-master was Dr John Wooll, sometime Fellow of New College, who, at the time of his election, was master of Midhurst School. Amongst the unsuccessful competitors was a Rugbeian of high distinction, who had won nearly every classical honour at Cambridge, was then head-master of Shrewsbury School, and seemed to possess every claim to the preference enjoined under the Act of 1777; but the reputation for severity which marked Dr Butler's earlier years at Shrewsbury was possibly the reason of his being set aside. When, subsequently, the Shrewsbury scholars whom he sent up to the universities carried away the highest distinctions, year after year, not only as against Rugby, but against "all England," some of the trustees must have cast jealous eyes towards the rival foundation, and confessed that they had possibly missed their man. Rugby prospered, nevertheless, under its new head-master, and the trustees lost no time in providing him with better accommodation than the old barn-school and cow-shed cloisters, which had been always intended as a temporary arrangement, though, like other makeshifts, it had lasted so long. The school estates were still increasing in value; they were enabled to pay off their mortgage, and in 1808 they obtained a new Act of Parliament, under the provisions of which the old manor-house, schools, and barns, were all pulled down together, and the present buildings took their place at a cost of £35,000. They succeeded, apparently, in solving the very difficult problem of rebuilding on the same site, and yet making use of the old accommodation until the new was ready; for the work of the school was carried on uninterruptedly during the four years which were occupied in the new building. All kinds of temporary shifts were made, and as soon as the workmen were out of one new school the boys were in it, and the room which they had left became a pile of rubbish by the next morning. At last all was cleared away, and the new buildings—certainly very "questionable Gothic"—presented, nevertheless, that substantial and not unpleasing *tout ensemble* which every Rugbeian would protest against seeing disturbed in its main features by the best architect that ever handled pencil. The chapel was not built for some years later—in 1820, under another Act; and although it cost £8000 originally, and it is hard to say how much more in alterations since, even with its modern transepts and stained glass, it fails to be a satisfactory object to an ecclesiological or architectural eye. Its interests are of a higher kind; there lies Arnold, who died "in his harness" (we wish Crossfield lay there too); round him, not a few of those who fought the battle with him, masters and pupils—Grenfell, and Mayor, and Hatch; and others who followed later, not less loved or lamented. There is the Crimean window, "The Good Centurion," commemorating twenty-five Rugbeians, of all ranks and ages—"from the white-headed veteran general * who entered our walls above half a century ago, to the dearly-remembered young boy † from whom we had parted but a few months when he fell so bravely, not in

---

* Major-General H. W. Adams, C.B., mortally wounded at Inkermann.

† J. W. J. Dawson, Lieutenant, Royal Artillery, died of injuries received in removing live shells on the explosion of a French siege-train.

destroying men's lives, but in saving them;"* and the Indian window, the memorial of the not less gallant soldiers who died in that last terrible struggle—foremost amongst whom was Hodson, of Hodson's Horse. We all forget the "Georgian Gothic" when we remember those English hearts.

* The Book of Rugby School, p. 85.

CHAPTER V.

DR. WOOLL.

So much was necessary anticipation; we have to return to Dr Wooll, whose first arrival at Rugby, strange as it may now seem, was in a *tandem*—"Thos.,"* the well-remembered old school-house servitor, being mounted on the leading horse. But the new master and the new schools did exceedingly well for Rugby. Dr Wooll was not a remarkable scholar, but he made the most of what he did know, and scholarship was but moderately prevalent in his day. He succeeded, to a very remarkable degree, in winning the respect and affection of his pupils. In this his monumental inscription does not go beyond the truth: "*Amores omnium singulari quadam suavitate sibi conciliavit.*" "He was a perfect gentleman, and a good disciplinarian," says one who knew him well, both as a pupil and a friend; indeed, the expressions of regard and kindly recollection which may be heard from his old scholars are unanimous. And this is a very high test of worth, and may suffice to cover many shortcomings. Not less pleasant are the reminiscences in "school-house" minds of "*Mother* Wooll;" in that

* Thomas Woolridge.

lady's case no irreverent epithet, for it represented well the maternal interest taken by her (she had no family of her own) in those smaller boys who "had the happiness," as one of them expresses it, "to be under her care." The public dinner in the town, in Dr Wooll's days, on the evening of the Speeches never failed to bring together a body of old schoolfellows, not less enthusiastic and perhaps more jovial (for the "Eagle" had not yet taken to teetotalism) than those who now gather in London. Rugbeians met their old master there, and were met by him, with unfailing cordiality. There John Macaulay of Repton— too early lost—spoke as few could speak; there Sir George Crewe stood up and said, "Show me an 'old Rugby boy' in undeserved distress, and I will instantly relieve him, and do all in my power to restore him to his position;" and there Dr Parr himself complimented the young speakers on their Greek enunciation.

There had been some attempt at private theatricals in Ingles's time, but not with his knowledge. "Bucknill's," then a dame's boarding-house, was the first of these unlicensed theatres. Connected with these performances is one well-known name—Charles William Macready— whom Rugbeians hold in just remembrance as a gentleman, a scholar, and an actor. He was not, however, the originator of the taste; and it was not until he had been more than once a spectator that he made "his first appearance upon any stage" in Bucknill's hall, as *Dame Ashfield*, in 'Speed the Plough.' His next character was *Mrs Brulgruddery*, in 'John Bull.' When Dr Wooll succeeded to power, the company took more courage. They got up 'The Castle Spectre,' which was acted in "Over-School," Oct. 15, 1807, with the following cast:—

Earl Osmond............	T. ROBINSON (Master of the Temple).
Earl Percy...............	G. RICKETTS (Sir G. W. Ricketts, Judge of the Supreme Court at Madras).
Kenrick	HOPKINS.
Father Philip............	WILLIS (Prebendary of Wells).
Reginald............... Motley	} "Doubled" by C. W. MACREADY.
Hassan	WALHOUSE (the late Lord Hatherton).
Saib......................	H. ROBINSON (late Tutor of St John's, Camb.)
Muley....................	W. AYLING.
Allan.....................	Hon. E. FINCH (late British Chaplain at Ceylon).
Evelina	R. TWOPENNY.
Angela	W. DICKENS (Chairman of Quarter Sessions, Warwickshire).
Alice	H. W. WHINFIELD.

"Dr Wooll," writes Mr Macready, "winked at the performance, or rather encouraged it; we being allowed not only to act the play 'after three' to the boys, but to give an evening representation to the people of the town and neighbourhood after locking-up. The last representation was in the 'Doctor's school,' the upper part supplying its benches to the audience, the lower having been converted into a stage, &c.; the French master's schoolroom behind serving us for a dressing-room. Mrs Wooll and her friends, with a numerous assemblage from the neighbourhood and town, with all the masters and their families, except the Doctor and James Moor, were present." On this occasion the play was 'The Revenge,' with Macready as *Zanya*, and Hastings Robinson as *Don Manuel;* the farce of 'Two Strings to your Bow' followed, in which Macready played *Lazarillo*.

Within twenty months of his leaving the Sixth form at Rugby, Charles Macready made his public debut at

Birmingham, June 7th, 1810, as *Romeo;* and it was not long before Dr Wooll, having to pass through that town, made it his special request that Mr Macready, sen., would allow his son to act *Hamlet* on that evening, which he did. Two or three of the other masters came from Rugby to be present, and the whole party dined together before the play. Such a recognition was honourable alike to the young actor and his graver friends. A few years ago, when Mr Macready read 'Hamlet' in the great school for the benefit of the Shakespeare Fund, he inquired with much interest whether any of the old theatrical properties used in his school-days were still in existence.

There was again an attempt at rebellion under Dr Wooll in 1822. This time it was the fags who threatened a sort of servile war. They had been accused of having posted up seditious squibs on the præpostors, for which Wooll had punished their whole body, though the real authors were some boys in the Fifth. They refused to go into school, and set both masters and præpostors at defiance for some time. The disturbance was only quelled by the expulsion of five of the ringleaders. Many boys left the school in consequence, and the decrease of numbers the next half-year was the greatest ever known in the annals of Rugby.

On another occasion the walls were chalked with very terrible manifestoes, calling on the boys to "rise as one man," and demanding "BLOOD!" in large letters. But this time an astute under-master had recourse to stratagem. While all the mutineers were safe in chapel on Sunday, he had the pockets of their week-day clothes searched. In one was found a lump of chalk; the owner was sent for, and, believing that all was discovered, confessed—and disappeared. As he had chalked "*Rebelion*" on Wooll's schoolroom door, his literary promise was no great loss to Rugby.

In the second half-year of 1813, a memorable scene took place, almost rivalling the "Midnight Flogging" at Eton.* It will be best told in the words of one of the culprits :—

"The master of the Lower Fourth form was a worthy, excellent man, a first-rate philological scholar of the old school; but he was not always so wide-awake to the tricks of schoolboys as the other masters, and the boys of his form sometimes took advantage of his good-nature. On one occasion, however, they carried matters too far. The second lesson then began in every form at ten o'clock, and the boys were accustomed to close their books as the clock began to strike eleven ; but one day a notice was passed down the form, that all were to go out when the three-quarters struck, as if they had mistaken the time. All then did rush out, except the boy who was up at lesson by the master's side. Complaint was of course instantly made to Dr Wooll of this conduct, and he immediately sent out a notice that every boy in the form was to be flogged at three o'clock, before third lesson commenced. A few minutes before the hour "Thos." (the well-known lictor) made his appearance in the Gallery Schoolroom, where the Lower Fourth said their lessons, with the necessary paraphernalia for the executions. The folding-doors were then thrown open, where the præpostors all stood. At three o'clock the Doctor came in, demanded the list of the

* Etoniana, p. 104.

form, and, beginning with the head boy, went regularly through the thirty-eight, including the boy who was up at lesson when the school was deserted, and who never dreamed that such a trifling circumstance as his remaining in school when the other boys ran out would be any plea for his exemption from punishment. Etonians boast of Keate's expedition; Wooll began, as was said, at three o'clock, and I well remember that the clock struck the quarter-past as he was finishing the thirty-eighth boy. The Lower Fourth form boys of that day, when they meet their surviving schoolfellows, always talk of this event as the jolliest fun they ever had when at Rugby."

Reform at Rugby, as in larger societies, was gradual. The cruelties of the old fagging system were much modified under Dr Wooll, as they have been since from time to time under his successors. Not that it is fair to attribute the sole credit of these, or other steps in civilisation, entirely to any head-master in whose reign they are adopted; much is due to the improvement in the tone of society, both amongst men and boys. Up to this time, the privilege of fagging belonged not only to the Sixth, but to the "six first" of the Fifth form; and the unfortunate First and Second forms were subject to the whole Fifth indiscriminately. An act of cruelty exercised by one of these led to the confining the privilege in future entirely to the Sixth; and very few have been the instances since in which it has been seriously abused. There were other customs, relics of those barbarous times when they skinned freshmen's noses at Oxford, which Dr Wooll put down. One was called "clodding," and was a ceremony of initiation performed upon those who were promoted into the Fifth. They had to run along the course of a small gutter, which flowed from the cow-sheds before mentioned, through a double line of boys, who pelted them with clods of clay moistened in that not very delicate stream. But fortunate was he for whom the clods *were* moist; for an unpopular victim had them specially hardened for his benefit—it was even said with stones inside. On promotion from the Fourth to the Remove a boy had to run the gauntlet up and down the big school between a double line of his fellows, armed with handkerchiefs tied in "Westminster knots." He was allowed to protect himself with books stuffed inside his trousers; but the punishment was fearful.

Twenty years was Dr Wooll head-master; he had raised the school to the highest point of numbers hitherto reached—381; but it fell off rapidly in subsequent years. He resigned in 1828; and then succeeded Thomas Arnold—a man hitherto comparatively unknown in public life, engaged with private pupils at Laleham, but of whom it was prophesied, not untruly, that, if elected at Rugby, "he would change the face of public education throughout England."

CHAPTER VI.

THE SCHOOL UNDER DR ARNOLD.

The Rugby of Arnold's day has been so often and so ably painted, that few readers can be unacquainted with its general features. His own character and daily life—and from these the history of the school can never be separated—have found an eloquent record in the pages of his pupil, Dean Stanley; while the feelings and fortunes of a school-house boy under his rule have been graphically described by Mr Hughes. Perhaps the enthusiastic admiration felt—and justly felt—for Arnold by many of his pupils, has led them sometimes to do less than justice to previous head-masters. The great work which he did at Rugby stands in no need of exaggerated colouring. To imply, as we have it apparently implied in the pages of 'Tom Brown,' that before "Arnold's manly piety had begun to leaven the school" no boy could venture to kneel at his bedside to say his prayers without subjecting himself to outrage and insult, is to present a picture of the Rugby of former days which many living know to be untrue. No doubt such a thing required some strength of purpose at all times; and whether it could be done in peace and without fear of interruption, in a large room occupied by a dozen boys, would depend very much, under any head-master's government, on the character of the præpostor, or other head boy who slept there. If he were a bad boy, and others in the room were like him, no doubt to a little boy the thing was almost impossible. It is to be feared there were some rooms in Rugby in which it was felt practically to be so, even in the best days of Arnold. There will always be a difficulty and a discouragement to boys under such circumstances. But to assume that under former headmasters the general tone of Rugby was such as to deter of necessity a boy from such acts of private devotion, and that under Arnold it totally changed, is to do a serious injustice, and to exalt, by unfair comparison, a great man who did a great work, but who would have been the last to desire praise at the expense of others. So, again, to state that he "found the school and school-house in a state of monstrous licence and misrule" * is to bring forward a very serious charge, in somewhat unmeasured language, against Dr Arnold's immediate predecessor—a name still held by many of his old pupils in great and deserved respect; and a charge which the facts of the case would be found quite insufficient to justify. Every man of energy and ability who is appointed to the headship of a great place of public education, when his predecessor's rule has been a long one, will probably find abuses which call for remedy. A man like Arnold was sure to find much of this work to do at Rugby, and none need to be told how well he did it. But there can be no better testimony than his own, that he had not that Augean stable to cleanse which the author of 'Tom Brown' sup-

* Tom Brown's School Days, p. 141.

poses. In a letter to a friend, written soon after his entrance upon his duties, he speaks of his "generally favourable impression of it," and records that he had as yet found "surprisingly few irregularities."[*] He also expressed to one of the masters personally his satisfaction at the state in which he found the school. It is to be regretted that 'Tom Brown' did not remember, in this particular instance, that his admirable sketch of Rugby could not be regarded as wholly a work of fiction; it dealt with real names and real facts, openly and without disguise; and that if there were many of his readers to whom these circumstances made the book additionally delightful, there were also some to whom they might give pain. Many old Rugbeians, who have a hearty appreciation of the writer and his story, would be rejoiced if, in the future editions which coming generations of schoolboys are sure to call for, he could find it in his heart to modify some few of these sentences of sweeping praise or censure.

After all, the religious element which developed itself at Rugby in Arnold's days was not so exclusively of his own creation as the readers of 'Tom Brown' might be led to conclude. There was another—a kindred and yet a very different spirit—whose influence there for good, if not so patent to the world, was hardly less deep and real, and to whose share in whatever of Christian life was maintained or renewed there, none would have done more willing justice than Arnold himself. He who, even as a boy, did almost an apostle's work at Rugby, was Spencer Thornton.[†] He, too, has passed from us; but many yet

---

[*] Life and Correspondence, i. 250.

[†] Spencer Thornton, late Vicar of Wendover, entered Rugby School

living who profited by his example—many also who did not profit by it—will gladly bear testimony to his earnest profession and courageous practice. Other names might be mentioned of those who joined with him and supported him, but there was scarcely one entirely "like-minded" with him. It was round him that younger boys, whose religious feelings were earnest, gathered for counsel and encouragement. That Arnold recognised this —that he supported and encouraged Thornton by every means in his power—is to say little more than that he acted like any other Christian schoolmaster. Two more dissimilar types of religious character than presented themselves in the boy and his master it might be difficult to find. Spencer Thornton's views were ultra-evangelical; they might in these days be called narrow, if any could find it in their heart to qualify by such a grudging epithet what was so real and sincere. Arnold's creed was liberal and comprehensive: the books which the pupil loved, the phraseology which he had learned in childhood, the master would in very many cases have smiled or frowned at, according to his mood; but to both, religion and life were ideas inseparable; and each, in the case of the other, soon felt it and recognised it. It is not too much to say that there were some things in which the teacher himself would not have scorned to learn from his pupil. "I would stand to that man," he once said, in speaking of him, "hat in hand." We scarcely know to which of the two characters those words were most honourable. But

in 1829; died suddenly in the street in London, January 12, 1850. See a "Memoir" by Rev. W. R. Fremantle. It is slight, and its religious views may be thought extreme; but it is none the less the life of a hero.

Arnold never spoke of him otherwise than with regard and respect, as " a blessing to the school." " Your son has done good to the school to an extent that cannot be calculated"—were his words in a letter to the parents on Spencer Thornton's departure for Cambridge; and few who heard it will ever forget the noble tribute which he paid to him—though of course not by name—after he had left the school, in one of his sermons. The influence which a boy of strong will, self-possessed bearing, and indomitable courage obtains over his schoolfellows whether for good or evil, and especially on points of religion, is even greater than any master, however conscientious and energetic, can hope to obtain. Spencer Thornton was naturally adapted to secure this influence, and to a great extent he did. " Straightforward, manly, and upright"—as one of his most distinguished schoolfellows well describes him—he won respect even where he failed to excite imitation. "There was an open honesty in his countenance which would strike any one with the feeling that he was all that he professed to be." Many were his friends who were not his converts. In this respect, his example had something of the effect upon the little world of Rugby School which Christianity has had upon the world at large: very many were de-heathenised who were not made Christians. Boys who had little sympathy with his religious views, and still less with the peculiar phraseology in which they were sometimes set forth, had still good enough in them to honour the boldness and consistency with which they were maintained; and, often and often, an oath was checked or a ribald jest left unspoken, because he was there to hear. " Rugby School owes a great debt of gratitude to Spencer Thornton," writes one of the masters to the father of another boy; "he has done so much in putting down swearing and bad conduct." Great, no doubt, was the effect of those remarkable sermons which for so many years " seized and held three hundred boys, dragging them out of themselves, willing or unwilling, for twenty minutes on Sunday afternoons," and which stand alone to this day as appeals to a schoolboy audience; but even greater, if possible, and more effectual, was the preaching of the daily life of one among themselves.

The personal influence of Arnold over his scholars was less, perhaps, than some of his biographers would represent. Dean Stanley, in his 'Life,' admits very fairly that to many—the majority—he was but little known in his inner character, and could not therefore impress them as he did the few who were brought into more immediate connection with him. With all his great qualities, he was not always successful in winning the love of those who knew him only in his character of head-master; it was, perhaps, not in the nature of the circumstances that it should have been so. He was respected, and he was feared. No doubt, in after life, the views we take of those who once had authority over us undergo, in many cases, a wholesome change; we see much in them to love and to admire, to which our selfish wills once blinded us; but the question is now of Arnold's actual personal influence over the mass of his scholars at the time, not of their estimate of him in after life. His direct appeals to the conscience of individual boys on religious matters were few: he knew, and perhaps rather over-estimated, because he so dreaded it and hated it, the danger of producing unreality. None could be more ready than he was with words of kindly counsel or hearty sympathy if it was sought, or if peculiar circumstances gave opportunity for it; and in a large school it would often be difficult, and in some cases might not be thought advisable, to do more. But it might be gathered from some expressions of Dr Arnold's more enthusiastic eulogists that every boy in the school was of necessity brought into personal contact with him, and had the opportunity of that appeal from heart to heart which from such a man was invaluable. Whether this has ever been successfully attempted by any head-master of any public school, may well be questioned; it is certainly an injustice to assume it in the case of Dr Arnold to the implied discredit of others.

On one point of his school discipline especially there has always been a great misapprehension in the public mind. It is not uncommon to see ascribed to him the whole system—with its evil as well as its good—of governing the school by an aristocracy of its own members, the præpostors of the Sixth form.* Some unfortunate occurrences in another public school were at the time attributed openly to the importation there of "Arnold's system" by one of his pupils. The præpostorial or monitorial form of government was no more Arnold's invention than Rugby School was. He found it existing there, certainly ever since Dr James's accession, most probably long

---

* The most remarkable assertion of this kind appears so lately as in the 'Churchman's Family Magazine' for August 1867. The writer of an article on "Education," speaking of the system of "supervision" in schools, says:—"Dr Arnold tried something of the kind at Rugby by having monitors; but the result was some very sad instances of boy-tyranny, and one *fatal case*." (!) So many misstatements have seldom been comprised in so few words.

before. He strengthened and encouraged it; he inspired into his own Sixth form much of his own manly principle and love of truth; and he upheld, through evil report and good report, the institution of fagging, as the only possible protection in a large public school against "the evils of anarchy, or, in other words, the lawless tyranny of physical strength." In the same spirit, and with the same disregard of popular squeamishness, he maintained corporal punishment as a stern necessity; protesting against "that proud notion of personal independence which is neither reasonable nor Christian," which "encourages a fantastic sense of the degradation of personal correction." *

Though Dr Arnold might himself have shrunk from claiming to be, as a Quarterly Reviewer calls him, "the second and moral founder of Rugby," yet the school unquestionably took a decided colour from his honest and manly character, and its tone underwent a marked improvement under his strong government. He also raised the standard of work, and he especially encouraged the study of history and modern languages; though, on this point again, more modest than his eulogists, he thought that persons "were apt to attach undue importance to the fact" of their introduction at Rugby. Yet when he obtained one of the innocent ambitions of his heart—some "mark of royal recognition for the school"—he devoted the Queen's medal to a historical essay.

To Dr Arnold succeeded Archibald Campbell Tait, Tutor of Balliol College (now Bishop of London), for eight years; then Dr Goulburn for seven and a half,

---

* See an article by Dr Arnold in the 'Journal of Education,' vol. ix. p. 281, &c.

when he also resigned; and in 1858 the present headmaster, Dr Temple, was elected. In more than one case, in these elections, the claims of Rugbeian candidates were set aside, wisely or unwisely, by the trustees. The prosperity of the school, on the whole, under the men of their choice, has been their best justification. But these governments are too modern to be critically discussed in these pages. Even "*de mortuis*," it has been sought here to speak "*nil nisi bonum;*" and a discreet silence may well be preserved in the case of living bishops and dignitaries. Only let us not forget Rugby's *annus mirabilis* under Goulburn; when the school carried off, in 1857, nearly every open university scholarship both at Oxford and Cambridge; or that Dr Tait raised the numbers to the highest point which had been yet reached—493;* or that Dr Temple, to his great credit, has abolished the "goal-keeping" at football, which made a cold winter half-holiday a misery to many small boys who are now men. The time may come when their own pupils will speak of *their* days as the golden age of Rugby, even as the scholars of Arnold do now: all honour to the generous and scholar-like spirit which will see no failing in the old master or the old school!

* Dr Arnold wished to *limit* the school as nearly as possible to 300: the numbers of late have been slightly over 500.

CHAPTER VII.

PRESENT CONSTITUTION.

The present constitutional government of Rugby consists of the head-master and twenty-one assistant-masters, who are university graduates. Of these, thirteen are specially classical; five are for mathematics and natural science—a study which has been introduced of late years; and three for modern languages,—one an Oxford M.A., who has resided some years in France, and the other a foreign graduate of Berlin. Seven of these masters are on the foundation; *i.e.*, they receive certain allowances from the Sheriff estates; the others are paid chiefly by capitation-fees. But nine of the classical masters have an important additional source of income from their private pupils, averaging about forty each, who pay £10, 10s. annually for such assistance; three others have a distinct salary for assisting the head-master; and one as the master of the Lower School. The privilege of keeping a boarding-house is also now confined exclusively to masters (the "dames"* hav-

* The following note may help to preserve some record of the old boarding-houses during the first quarter of the present century:—

ing been gradually extinguished by Dr Arnold), and this, of course, implies a certain amount of profit; not so considerable, however, as might be supposed: the high price of provisions, the better style of living, and the increased accommodation provided for the boys, diminish the gains very materially from their proportion in the good old times. Not to mention that the responsibility is of a kind which many masters would rather be without; and Dr Arnold, it is well known, found a difficulty in persuading some of his best men to undertake it. There are now seven of these boarding-houses (exclusive of the school-house), accommodating each from forty to

"Mrs Bucknill's house was that now inhabited by Mr Cropper, not far from the school gates. Mrs Wratislaw's house is now Messrs Butlin's bank. Dr Bloxam's is now divided into three, the centre one being inhabited by Dr Bucknill. Mr Gascoigne's is Mr Loverock's shop. Stanley's has been converted into additional schools. Townsend's is at present the residence of Mr Bromwich, the builder. Several of Lawrence Sheriff's almshouses are built on the site of Mr Birch's boarding-house. Mr Moor's is still a boarding-house—Mr Wilson's. Before this house was built, Mr Moor resided at the rectory, where he had his boarders, but at this period the favourite houses with parents were always those belonging to the surgeons of Rugby—Bucknill, Fosbrooke, Williams, and Powel. Mr Williams's house adjoined Mr Gascoigne's on the south side. The latter gentleman was bookseller to the Lower School; as the dinners at his house were considered better than those at Williams's, some of the boys at Williams's would occasionally climb over the wall between the yards at one o'clock, and dine at Gascoigne's, who was too near-sighted to distinguish his uninvited guests from his own boarders. His son was a Lieutenant of Marines, and once published a book called 'Natural Reflections,' in which he described his pleasure at seeing his father on one of his returns to England, 'for,' said the author, 'Benevolence beamed in his countenance, as Temperance was his constant companion.' John Macaulay, afterwards head-master of Repton School, used to quote this passage with much unction, at dinner-time, when senior praepostor in Gascoigne's house, to the old gentleman's great annoyance."—T. L. B.

fifty boys. Several important improvements have been introduced of late years into the domestic regulations. Dr Arnold took the first step in that direction, by the abolition of the "spending-houses"—pastry-cooks' shops, very pointedly so called—where the boys had to go night and morning in order to get their breakfast and tea in any comfort; the custom having been, from time immemorial, to give out from the buttery merely a certain dole of bread and milk (cold), which had to be converted into a civilised meal by the said pastry-cooks—tea, coffee, and butter being extras provided at the boys' private charge. The comfortable spread which may now be seen in the school-hall was one of his earliest introductions. But the most desirable innovation of later times, and one of which the value will be apparent from many points of view, is, that in some of the present houses the master and the ladies of his family dine in hall *with* the boys, instead of his merely presiding there officially to say grace, and taking his own dinner at a later hour, as was formerly the custom. More than this, in some of the houses he spends a certain part of the evening in the boys' hall, at his own work, thus effectually preventing those undesirable congregations of bigger and idler boys round the fires (which, as old Rugbeians may remember, the most zealous præpostor, far off in the quiet of his study, could not always prevent), and being at hand to give any reasonable help or advice in preparing for the next morning's work. Nor does his presence seem to interfere in the least with the cooking of the sausages or other delicacies which were Tom Brown's delight at Rugby, and at which Miss Martineau assured us "the dissenters generally are amazed and shocked," as "a disclosure of the sensual cast of mind of the boys in a great public school."* These iniquities are still perpetrated, both at breakfast and tea, under the very nose (without any metaphor) of a clergyman of the Church of England, and with at least his tacit connivance. The old bread-and-cheese-and-beer supper at eight o'clock has been slightly modified by the substitution of butter, or the old-fashioned hot bread-and-milk, according to fancy; to obtain which latter delicacy, in "dame's" houses of an earlier generation, required strong personal influence with the matron. The comforts of the sick were always perfectly well attended to in earlier times, and indeed the sick-room, in bad weather or literary difficulties, was supposed to possess rather too much attraction; but the new Sanatorium, built a few years ago, has great advantages in cases of serious illness or infection, as well as in those which require quiet and seclusion. It is a pleasant house, standing apart in its own grounds, but within easy reach of the boarding-houses, and commanding a view of the new "Bigside" ground, so that the invalids can watch the games from its windows. It is under the management of an excellent resident nurse.

Rugby begins to stir about 6.30 in summer; that is to say, prayers begin at 7 to a second; and half an hour is not too much to dress and get into school.† In

---

* Health, Husbandry, and Handicraft, p. 20.

† There is indeed a terrible bell which begins ten minutes only before morning school, and to this last moment a sleepy lower-boy (who is not an elaborate dresser) too often defers his getting up. The horrors of such a practice, especially on cow-fair mornings, are so

winter, first lesson is at eight; and for a month before and a month after the Chrismas holidays, breakfast is taken before going into school, *i.e.*, at 7.30. This has been found not only an effectual remedy for the old excuse of "staying out" (going on the sick-list) on a cold wet morning, but a really useful sanitary precaution. Fortified with hot tea and rolls (and possibly sausages), a boy is found to brave snow and sleet, and even the chance of a "floorer" at lesson, with comparative indifference. So, at least, say Rugby doctors, medical and scholastic; but some of the boys contend that it involves a hurried and unsatisfactory breakfast; that they scald their throats, upset their digestions, and are, in consequence, unable to construe when called up. Second lesson is from 9.15 to 11.15; another from 12.30 to

vividly set forth in the following parody, that it may be well to quote it as a warning:—

THE SONG OF THE BELL.

With hair dishevelled and waste,
  With eyelids heavy and red,
A fellow rises at early morn
  From his warm and cosy bed.
    Splash! splash! splash!
Through dirt and cows and mud,
  And still he hears the dismal crash,
    The bell's far-distant thud.

    Dress! Dress! Dress!
While I listen to the chime.
    Dress! Dress! Dress!
Four minutes to the time.
    Vest and collar and coat,
    Coat and collar and vest,
The stomach is faint, the hand is numbed,
  But we cannot stay to rest.
    New Rugbeian (School Magazine), vol. i. p. 85.

1.30; then comes dinner; then third lesson and fourth (with no real interval) from 2.30 to 6. This is the work for whole-school days—Monday, Wednesday, and Friday; the three alternate days are nominally half-holidays, when there is no lesson after 11.15. But the only real half-holiday is the Saturday; for the Tuesdays and Thursdays are cut up by the finishing and correcting the composition for the Middle and Lower Schools—occupying from half an hour to two and a half, according to proficiency; and upon both Tuesdays and Thursdays there is a composition lesson from 12 to 1.30. These hours, however, are not all spent in school, and must be taken as indicating generally the time assumed to be employed in preparing the lessons as well as saying them. Besides these public lessons, every boy has to find three hours a-week out of his play-time for his private tutor. Every third Monday is also a half-holiday; called "Middle Week"—modern Rugbeians say, "because it never was the middle of anything." Altogether, the school-work claims about five or six hours *per diem*, on an average, from a boy below " the Twenty;" in the higher forms, of course, the amount varies according to individual industry.

At Rugby no charity is shown to the dunces, and a boy may look in vain for any kind of promotion on the ground of mere seniority. The evil of his being " utterly and hopelessly thrown out in the fair competitions of the school" is met there by a very different remedy. "Boys, on failure to reach the Middle School at 16, or the Sixth Form at 18, are required to leave, unless the headmaster, after inquiry made, deems it right to suspend the rule on special grounds." The limits of indulgence appear to be fixed with a charitable allowance for incapacity, and the rule is not strictly enforced, except when idleness or other faults are combined with slowness.

Another feature peculiar to Rugby amongst the schools to which the late Commission extended, but adopted also at Cheltenham and Marlborough, is that of "parallel" forms, first introduced at Rugby by the present Bishop of London when head-master, and now revived by Dr Temple. In a very large school, where the subdivision into anything like manageable classes or forms makes these very numerous, it is apt to involve what cannot be described more clearly than in Dr Temple's words :—

"I found, when we had so many forms, one under another, two bad effects—the clever boys went up through the forms with a system of promotion so rapidly, that no one master saw a boy of that sort for more than a quarter of a year; he never got hold of him at all, and the result was to encourage a great deal of very superficial working. On the other hand, slower boys got disheartened by the sight of the terrific ladder which they had to climb—they had a sort of feeling that they would never get to the top."*

Five of the larger forms are now subdivided, not into an upper and lower, but into two parallels, both doing the same work, both holding the same rank in the school, but each having its separate master. For all purposes of promotion they are still one large form, an equal number from each parallel being moved up at each remove into the form next above. There are some difficulties in the

* Public Schools Evid., Rugby, 592.

working, owing to the two parallel masters being not always supposed to be exactly parallel in efficiency; but, on the whole, the system seems well adapted for a very large school.*

* The arrangement will be best understood by a tabular view :—

<pre>
                    Sixth Form.
                    The Twenty.
       (Parallels.)   Fifth.   (Parallels.)
       Lower Fifth   =   Lower Fifth.
       1st Upper Middle   =   1st Upper Middle.
       2d Upper Middle   =   2d Upper Middle.
       1st Lower Middle   =   1st Lower Middle.
       2d Lower Middle   =   2d Lower Middle.
                        Remove.
                        Fourth.
                        Third.
                        Second.
</pre>

CHAPTER VIII.

THE GAMES.

Notwithstanding a large amount of honest work, young Rugby finds plenty of time for play. Cricket, though it has been a Rugby game from the earliest records, was late in assuming there its present scientific character. The Schools which claimed, justly or unjustly, the exclusive right to the title of "Public" would only play matches with each other; and while they were distinguishing themselves at Lord's, Rugby was content with occasional victories over the "the Town," or a Warwickshire club. Dr Wooll brought with him some boys from Kent and Sussex, and they seem to have been the first to raise the game to something of a science. True, we hear from Nimrod that in his day "cricket was in high repute;" and Rugbeians may cherish, if they will, the glorious names of Joseph Port, Harry Wise, and Ned Tomkinson, whom he hands down to fame, but it is only as "hard hitters." William Ayling, afterwards one of the best gentleman-players in England, astonished, and at first disgusted, his new schoolfellows by his new-fangled notions of batting; he made clever "draws," and obtained runs faster than the established school champions, whose only use of the bat was to "swipe." Loud were the protests against such "sneaking," as it was called; but in course of time science, as usual, carried the day, and Ayling was voted what would now be called "Captain of the Eleven." But it is only in very modern times that such names as Wynch and Sandford have made a cricket reputation for Rugby.

The Rugby game *par excellence* is the old English sport of football, popular in this country for immemorial centuries, threatening to rival even archery in the days of Edward III., and still holding its place more or less in villages from which other sports have died out, but having its special temple and most imposing mysteries at Rugby. Less scientific and more energetically active than cricket, it is specially adapted to English schoolboy taste. King James, indeed, debarred it from his court as "meeter for lameing than making able the users thereof;" but he was neither an Englishman nor an athlete. It has certainly served both purposes in a high degree at Rugby. The only complaint now heard is, that it is scarcely played so "viciously" as in the generation just gone by; that it is assuming a somewhat more delicate and *dilettante* character. But it is a noble game still, and has more of the fierce and thrilling excitement of battle than any other national sport. For two months, or thereabouts, it continues to be the one absorbing subject of outdoor interest in the school. It is played, or rather fought, under somewhat different laws from those of other public schools, and the rival principles have formed of late important subjects of discussion. It would be utterly hopeless to explain its points to any one who does not know the game, and quite unnecessary for those who do. To drive a ball in one direction against all the efforts of the opposite party who are driving it in the other, is the players' object; and to effect this, pretty nearly every species of bodily force is in turn called into requisition. Kicking is the main principle—whether your adversary's shins, or the ball in preference, depends entirely upon circumstances. "Mauling"—which is also allowable in certain defined cases—is so expressive a word as to explain itself; but for the consolation of any tender-hearted reader who may consider football a *very* dangerous game (especially for horrified mammas, who see the death's head and cross-bones on the schoolhouse jerseys), it is pleasing to be able to quote the following provisos from the last amended Rugby rules:—"1st. Though it is lawful to hold any player in a *maul*, this holding does not include attempts to *throttle* or *strangle*, which are totally *opposed to all the principles* of the game. 2d. No one wearing *projecting nails* or *iron plates* on the soles or heels of his boots or shoes shall be allowed to play."

There are few more lively sights than the school-close on the day of one of the great matches—the "Sixth" against the rest of the school, or the "Old" against the "Present Rugbeians." Each side plays in jerseys and flannels, with velvet caps of distinctive colours, which old Rugbeians are disposed to regard as modern vanities, but which certainly add very much to the picturesque of the game, and no doubt increase its interest in the eyes of the ladies, who, since the late Queen Dowager set the example, crowd the ground on bright winter afternoons whenever a match of any special interest is to be played;

sometimes, in their enthusiasm, venturing outside those mysterious posts which mark out the "line of touch," and thus occasionally getting mixed up with the combatants, to their own detriment and the general confusion. The scene has been already so well described by more than one enthusiastic writer—by Tom Brown, by William Arnold, in his 'Sixth-Form Match,' and by George Melly, in his 'Experiences of a Fag,'—that it would be mere repetition to do more than refer to those truthful pages any curious readers who may not prefer to halt a few hours at Rugby, some winter Saturday afternoon, and see a match played with their own eyes. For scientific play, for magnificent "drops" and gallant "runs in," one might recommend the Old Rugbeian match, usually played about 1st October, where the heroes of two or three generations of players meet in the field, and "maul" and "hack" each other for very love—vowing, like Arthur's knights, that "it doth them good to feel each other's might;" but for "vicious" play, perhaps the contest between the Sixth—forty-five only in number, but a host in size and pluck—against the remaining 450 of the school, or the match in which the two champion houses are pitted against all the rest, had better be selected. Yet probably no struggle now is so fierce as that which used to take place when, in earlier times, the Upper Bench (the first twelve) of the Sixth used to challenge the whole school, and beat them. That match had to be stopped by royal proclamation of King Wooll, so little like "play" was it. Those were the days of the giants, when William Adey drove all foes before him like an Ajax; terrible in his strength and size, though not so great at "drops," it may be, as the more modern "White of Ansteys." But all this is "caviare to the general."

"Hare and Hounds" has also had its sacred bard,[*] and needs not any weaker celebration. Only that in these brief notes, dealing as they have done more largely with the past than with the present, the modern heroes of the run may be reminded that there was a time when it was very differently conducted; when fags were hounds and præpostors huntsmen, who carried hunting-whips, as the hounds could testify; nay, that some enterprising spirits hired horses for the run, and the game was stopped for that reason during many years at the close of Dr Wooll's mastership, and in the early part of Dr Arnold's. At present it has become a mere foot steeplechase, a good test of wind and pluck; and the great object in life for an enthusiastic "hound" is to do the "great Crick run" (thirteen miles) in something less than eighty-four minutes; that, we believe, being the shortest time at present on record. Enthusiastic Rugbeians might perhaps remind the reader that in the earliest class-list ever issued at Oxford, when there were but two Firsts, one was a Rugby man; that a Rugbeian first ascended Monte Rosa, and first stood on Mont Blanc without a guide; and that their rifle marksmen beat Eton and Harrow at the first meeting for the Wimbledon Shield. It might be added, that in the three centuries which have passed since the school's foundation, only one Rugbeian has been committed for highway robbery, and he was a baronet,[†] and it was a very gentlemanly

---

[*] *Vide* Experiences of a Fag.

[†] Sir Charles Burton, committed for highway robbery near St Alban's.—Luttrell's Diary, 1706.

offence in his time; only one, so far as the records go, was ever hung, and that was for high treason,* which is always, to say the least, respectable; that of the many exhibitioners sent to both universities, one only was transported, and he but for seven years; and that no head-master has ever yet come upon the parish, though at one time such a result was very much feared. So, *Floreat—et valeat—Rugbeia!*

* Rev. William Paul, chaplain to the rebels at Preston in 1715, "hung, drawn, and quartered" at Tyburn. He went to the place of execution in full canonicals.—Rugby Register.

INDEX.

I.—WINCHESTER COLLEGE AND COMMONERS.

ALWYNE, Thomas, head-master, 21.
Arthur's round table, 4.
Athelwold, St, 6.

BADGER-BATING, 57.
Baker, John, warden, 18.
Barter, R. S., warden, 65.
"Bethesda" (sick-house), 53.
Bible-clerk, 18.
"Bibling," 18, 37.
Bilson, Thomas (Bp.), head-master, 33.
"Bloody hand," legend of, 69.
"Bluchers," 55.
"Books," 24, 36.
Bowles, W. L., 45.
Bull-baits, 24.
Burton, Dr, head-master, 28, 39.

CHAPEL, 52.
Charles V., emperor, visits the college, 12.
Cheyney, Thomas, head-master, 39.
Chichele, Archbishop, scholar, 32.
"Child," Winchester term, 53, 64.
Choristers, 9, 60.
Civil wars, 35.
"Cloister-time," 24.
Commoners, early, 24, 26, &c.; numbers of, 28.
"Commoners," Old (the building), 28.
Coryatt, George, 17.
Cricket-matches, 64.
Crimean memorial, 52.
Cromwell at Winchester, 35.

"DISPARS," 22.
Domum tree, 68.
Drake, Sir F., verses on, 34.
"Dulce Domum," 68.

"EDOM," 45.
Edward VI., his Statute of Exceptions, 13; Injunctions, *ib.*; visit of, 16.
Election, 31, 61, &c.; festivities at, 68.
Elizabeth, Queen, her visit, 17.
Erle, Sir W., 52.
Erlysman, Thomas, head-master, 11.
Evered, William, head-master, 21 note.
Expenses of college, 47.

FAGGING, 48.
Fiennes, Colonel Nathanael, 35.
Football, 66.
Ford, William, "*hostiarius*," 13.
Founder's kin, 32.
Fromond, John, 53; his chantry, 60.

GABELL, Dr, head-master, 47.
Games, early, 24; modern, 64, &c.
Gauntlett, Dr, warden of New College, 62.
Goddard, W. S., second-master during rebellion, 40; head-master, 46; his munificence, 46.
——— scholarship, the, 47.
Gown, 29.
Grammar, study of, enjoined by Wykeham, 8.

HALL, the, 50.
Harpsfield, John, 15.
Harmar, warden, 37.
Harris, John, head-master, 39; warden, 35, 53.
Henry VI., patron of college, 11.
Henry VII. visits the college, 12.

INDEX. 407

Henry VIII. visits the college, 12; his statute for dissolution, ib.
Herton, Richard de, master, 10.
"Hills," 24, 56.
Horeman, William, head-master, 11.
Huntingford, warden, 40.
Hutton, scholar, his bill, 34.
Hyde, Thomas, head-master, 15.

Informator, 9.

JAMES I., his interference, 33.
Johnson, Christopher, head-master, 20; his descriptive poem, 21.

KEN, Bishop, 38, 53.
Kitchen, 51.

LIBRARY, 53.
Love, Nicholas, 35.

MARY, Queen, her visit, 16.
"Meads," 30, 57.
Meals, 22, 57, 59.
Melanchthon, 8.
Middleton, Thomas, 26.
Milton, John, *informator*, 10.
"Moab," 45.
Moberly, Dr, head-master, 49.
More, Edward, head-master, 21 note.
Morris, John, warden, 10.

"NAIL," punishment of, 37.
Newbury, election held at, 62.
New Forest, hunting in, 34.
Nicholas, John, warden, 36.
"*Non-licet*" gate, 35.
Numbers at Winchester, 49.

"OLIVER's Battery," 39.
Ostiarius, 9.
Otterbourne Mead, 7.

PHILIP, King of Spain, his visit, 16.
Philpot, John, martyr, 15.
Plays performed, 19.
"Posers," 61.
Potenger, John, head-master, 35.
Prefect of tub, 22, 23.
Prefects, 24, 25, 54.

RAINOLDS, William, 17.
Rebellion (College), of 1793, 40, &c., 70 (App.); the second, 47.
Reformation, the, at Winchester, 13.
"Remedies" and half-remedies, 55, 56.
Richard II., charter of, 11.
Ring used on "remedies," 56.
Rod, the Winchester, 18.

ST ELIZABETH's College, 27.
St Giles's Hill, 7.
"Scheme," 58 note.
Scholarship, Winchester, 63.
Schoolroom, present, built, 36.
"Scobs," 37.
Scrutiny, 62.
"Seventh Chamber," 23, 36.
Smith, Sydney, 44.
———, Courtenay, 44.
Smyth, Clement, head-master, 11, 21 note.
Statutes, 7.
"Stuckling," 64.

THEATRICAL performances, 19.
Thurburn, warden, 53.
"Tower of the Two Wardens," 66.
"Toy-time," 58.
Trelawny, Sir J. (Bishop), 54.
Trevilian, E. B., cricketer, 65.
"Trusty servant," the, 51.
Turner, Francis (Bishop), 38.

WARD, William, cricketer, 64 note.
Warden's lodgings, 24.
Warham, Archbishop, scholar, 32.
Warton, Dr Joseph, head-master, 39; collision with Dr Johnson, ib.; his scholarship, 40; resigns, 44.
———, Tom, 19, 58.
Wayneflete, William, head-master, 11.
White, John, warden, 13; his "black" sermon, 14.
Whitehead, William, the poet, 19, 56.
Williams, Dr, head-master, 48; warden of New College, 66.
Windebank, Secretary, 33.
Wykeham, William of, builds Windsor Castle, 5; founds New College, 7; St Mary's, Winchester, 9.

II.—WESTMINSTER SCHOOL.

ADAMS, John, head-master, 83.
Allen, J. H., 132.
Andrewes, Lancelot, Dean, 86.

Aston, Lord, 132.
Atterbury, Francis (Bishop), 110, 180 note.

INDEX.

BAGSHAWE, Edward, second-master, 98, &c.
Barber, John, 120.
Barry, David, 90.
Beale, Robert, 106.
"Beaver," 92.
Bedford, Grosvenor, 133.
Beds, 166.
Bentley, Dr, 123.
"Bingham's Leap," 139.
"Bishop's boys," 87.
Blanket-tossing, 121 note.
Bluecoat-boys, fight with, 122.
Boarding-houses, 169.
Boat-races with Eton, 172, &c.
Booth, Barton, the actor, 144, 147.
Bourne, Vincent, 128.
Boyle, Hamilton (Earl of Cork), excellent actor, 146.
Breakfast, 167.
Buckland, Dean, 162.
Burdett, Sir Francis, 130.
Busby, Richard, head-master, 97, &c.; his feud with Bagshawe, 98.

CAMDEN, Wm., head-master, 89.
"Cap," the, 157.
"Captain of Election," 161, 184.
Carey, Dr Wm., head-master, 131, 135, 136, 185 note.
Carow, scholar, 88.
Carrick, John, 104.
Cartwright, Wm., 101, 104.
"Challenge," old form of, 82 note; present form of, 182.
Chiswick, college-house at, 86, 112.
Churchill, Charles, 146 note, 148.
'Cleomenes,' Dryden's, acted, 143.
"College John," 155.
Colman, George, the younger, 130, 134.
———, ———, the elder, 146.
Coronation, ceremony at, 188.
Cowley, Abraham, 106; his juvenile plays, 149.
Cranstoun, George, 134.
Crighton, Robert (Bishop), 106.
Croft, James, 104.
Cumberland, William Duke of, 143, 145.
Cumberland, Richard, 127, 138.
urll, Edmund, his punishment, 120.

DEBATES in Parliament attended by scholars, 188.
Declamations, 95.
Dictamina, 92.
Dinners, 168; annual Westminster, 118, 122.
Dodd, James, usher, 152.
Dolben, John, canon of Christ-Church, 104; Archbishop, 113.
———, William, 177.

Dormitory, the, 165, 179.
Dryden, Charles, 116.
———, John (the poet), 178.

ECKERSALL, John, good actor, 146.
Election, "The Golden," 123 note; of scholars, 84, 180, 182; to Universities, 85, 88, 114, 123, 185; suspended, 103.
Elizabeth, Queen, restores school, 83; at the Play, 144.
Epigrams, 119, 160, 166, 168, 171.
Epilogues, 153.
Eton, boat-races with, 172, &c.; cricket-matches with, 174.
Evelyn, John, visits school, 114.
Exhibitions to Trinity Cambridge, 185.
Expenses under Busby, 111, 114; present, 181.

FAGGING, 161.
Fell, Dean of Christ-Church, 104.
Field-Marshals, Westminster, 136.
Finch, Hon. Wm., Henry, and Daniel, 111.
Fire of London, 113.
'Flagellant,' the, school magazine, 133.
Football, 175.
Forms, how numbered, 187.
Forster, J. H., stroke of boat, 173.
Franklin, Thomas, 123.
Freind, Robert, head-master, 117.
Frodsham, Bridge, actor, 149.

GALE, Richard, 105.
George IV., his visit as Prince of Wales, 166.
Glynne, Sir John, 108.
Goodenough, Dr, head-master, 137.
Goodman, Gabriel, Dean, 85.
Graham, Sir James, 139, 188.
Grant, Edward, head-master, 89.

HALL, 178.
Harley, Earl of Oxford, 131.
Hastings, Warren, 183.
Henry VIII.'s charter, 83.
Henry, Philip, 107.
Heydegger, "Count," 119.
Hinchliffe, John (Bishop), head-master, 129.
Hobart, George, 146.
Hodges, Nathaniel, 106.
Home, Sir Everard, 186.
Hook, James, 131, 133.
Hoop-races, 175.
Hussey, Edward, cricketer, 174.

'IGNORAMUS' acted, 145.
"*Ignoramus* Lewis," 145.

INDEX.

Impey, Sir Elijah, 125.
Ingulph, Abbot, his school-days, 82.

Jackson, Cyril, 135, 180, 183.
James, Mr, under-master, 99.
Jonson, Ben, 149.
'Julius Cæsar' acted, 144.
Juniors, duties of, 162; their hardships, 112, 163.

Kingston, Duchess of, her trial, 134.
Knipe, Thomas, head-master, 117.

Lansdowne, Marquess of, 186.
Latin formulæ, 170; spoken in school, 94, 95, 116, 171.
Laud, Archbishop, 91.
Liddell, Dr, head-master, 137.
Litlyngton, Abbot, 178.
Littleton, Adam, second-master, 102.
Llewellyn, Matthew, 104.
Lloyd, Pierson, usher, 127.
———, Robert, usher, 146.
'Lusus Alteri Westmonasterienses,' 153.
Lynn, Francis, his diary, 114.

Maidstone, Lord, 111.
Mansfield, Lady, 169.
Markham, William (Archbishop), head-master, 129.
March, Lord, 139.
Mary, Queen, abolishes school, 83.
Mattaire, M., second-master, 121.
Mead, Dr Robert, 104.
Monitor Monitorum, 94, 185.
Monitors, 91, 94, 185.
"Monos," 183, 186.
Montagu, Charles, Earl of Halifax, 110, 113.
'Mourning Bride' performed, 144.
Mure, James, his 'Account of Westminster School,' 178.
Murray, William (Lord Mansfield), 125, 183.

Neale, Edmund, 124.
Newton, Bishop, 123.
Nicoll, John, head-master, 126.
Nobility, Westminster list of, 1726, 118.
Nonsense Club, 146 note.
Nowell, Alexr., head-master, 83, 143.
Numbers under Busby, 111; under Knipe and Freind, 117; under Carey, Goodenough, and Williamson, 137.

Oliphant, Robert, 132.
Oppidani, 83.
Osbaldiston, Lambert, head-master, 95.

Page, Dr William, head-master, 137.
Paget, Arthur, 166.
Pancake-tossing, 171.
Park, Mother, 175.
Pearce, Zachary (Bishop), 124.
"*Pensionarii*," 83.
"*Peregrini*," 83.
Petre, Father, and Busby, 109.
Phillimore, Sir R., his evidence as to the Play, 159.
'Phormio,' the, of 1855, 154, &c.
Plautus, 'Trinummus,' 144; 'Amphitryon,' *ib.*; 'Aulularia,' *ib.*; 'Rudens,' 151.
Play, the, 142, &c.; attempts to suppress it, 158; advantages of, 159; stopped on account of deaths in Royal Family, *ib.*; royal visitors at, 160.
Plays, English, performed, 143, 144.
"Plays," "early" and "late," 186.
Plump-walkers, 94.
"Posers," 84.
"Presbyter," "Jack," burnt in effigy, 115.
Price, Owen, master of Magdalen College School, 101.
Prior, Robert, 124.
"Private study," under Carey, 136.
Prologues to the Play, 152.
Pump, the college, 141; discipline of, inflicted, 140.
Puritans attack the Abbey, 103.

Quin, James, 105.

Rats in the dormitory, 167.
Ravis, Thomas, scholar, 88.
Reforms at Westminster, 164 note.
Richmond, Duke of, steady patron of the school, 138.
Roberts, Jack, the waterman, 134.
Ross, David, actor, 148.

Salter, John, wicket-keeper, 175.
Saunders, Charles, 150.
Scenes and dresses, 151.
Scholars, social position and expenses, 181.
Schoolroom, 176.
Scott, Dr, head-master, 138.
"Seventh" form, 187.
"Shadow" and "substance," 187.
Shrove-Tuesday custom, 171.
Silver pence as rewards, 188.
"Ski," derivation of, 129 note; fights with, 140.
Smalridge, Bishop, 123.
Smith, Dr Samuel, head-master, 130, 146.
Somerton, Lord, 173.
Songs, Latin, 151.

410 INDEX.

South, Robert, 104, 111, 120.
Southey, Robert, 133, 148 note.
Speed, Samuel, 105.
Stevens, Robert (Dean), excellent actor, 147.
Studentships at Christ-Church, Oxford, 185.
Study, course of, *circa* A.D. 1600, 91, &c.
Supper, 163.

TASWELL, William, his autobiography, 112.
Taunton, Sir William, 132.
Terence's comedies, 143, 144, 159.
Tothill Fields, 138.
'Trifler' magazine, 132.
Twisleton, Hon. Thomas James, 132, 149.

UDALL, Nicholas, head-master, 88.

VINCENT, Thomas, 107; (another), 108.
———, Dr William, head-master, 103, &c., 171.

WAISTCOAT, college, contents of, 164.
Wake, Colonel William, 109.
Wall, canon of Christ-Church, 104.
Waring, Robert, 104.
" Watch," 163.
Whitehall, Robert, 105.
Whitford, David, 104.
Wigs worn by boys, 125.
Williams, Dean (Archbishop), his scholars, 87.
Williamson, Dr, head-master, 137.
Wilson, John, head-master, 95.
Wingfield, Dr, head-master, 135.
Wynn, Sir Watkin, 186.
———, Rt. Hon. Charles, 148 note.

YORK, Duke of, 135.

III.—SHREWSBURY SCHOOL.

Alieni, 197.
Archery enjoined, 203.
'Arundines Cami,' 253.
Ashton, John, head-master, 196, 200; his "ordinances," 202; his death, 204.
Atcherley, Thomas, head-master, 236.
Atkys, Richard, third-master, 196, 206.

BAKER, John, second-master, 206, 210.
"Beef Row," the, 247.
Birch Hall, 223.
Black Hole, 241.
Blakeway's MSS., 209.
Boarders, 212, 246.
Boarding-houses, defective arrangements of, 246.
Boats, 248.
Books enjoined by Ashton, 204.
Bradshawe, President, 227 note.
Bromfield's hall, 240.
Brooke, James, second-master, 213.
Bury St Edmund's school, 238.
Butler, Dr Samuel, head-master, 327; his character, 238; anecdotes of, 239, 242, 248, 252; resigns, 243.
"Butler" exhibition, 243.

CHALONER, Thomas, head-master, 217; ejected, 222; at Birch Hall, 223; at Hawarden, 224; at Ruthin, 226; restored, 228.

Chapel, "the scholars'," 210; present chapel built, 211; services, 245.
Charles I. at Shrewsbury, 221.
Cheltenham College, boat-races with, 248.
Choir, the school, 245.
Civil wars, 221.
Corporation, their rights, 194, 202, 217, 232, 237.
Cotton, Mr, second-master, 227, 230.
Cricket, 248.

DAY-BOYS, 251.
Devereux, Robert, Earl of Essex, 201, 208.
Dinah, Dr Butler's housekeeper, 239.
"Douls," 250.

EARNLY, Sir Richard, 220, 222.
Edward VI., 193; his charter, 195.
Edwards, Hugh, 194.
"Election," ceremonies of, 243.
Elizabeth, Queen, 197, 200.
Eton Montem, 206.
Evans, David, third-master, 213, 219, 222.
Eyton, John, master, 195.

FAGGING, 250.
Fees, scale of, 203.
Football, 248.
"Fourth-form School," 241, 252.
"Free" school, meaning of, 194.

GITTENS, Mr, second-master, 212; ejected, 213.
Greville, Fulke (Lord Brooke), 198.
Grinshill, sick-house at, 205.

"HALL-CRIERS," 249.
Harding, John, 217.
Hare and hounds, 248.
Harrington, James, 199.
Hawarden, Chaloner's school at, 224.
Hildyard, James, 253 note.
Honours, list of, 252.
Hotchkis, Leonard, head-master, 233.
Hyson Club, 235.

I———, Mr, second-master, 240.

JAMES II. at Shrewsbury, 231.
John "Bandy," 239.

KENNEDY, Dr, head-master, 243, 253 note.
Kent, Roger, accidence master, 206, 211.
"Kitty Pry," 242.

LAURANCE, Thomas, head-master, 205; letter of resignation, 209.
Lee, Sir Richard, 220, 228.
"*Libera schola*," its meaning, 194.
Library, 215, 245.
Lloyd, Richard, head-master, 231.
"Lord High Constable," 249.

MEIGHEN, John, head-master, 210; his disputes with corporation, 212; care of library, 215; resigns, 216.
Morys, "Sir," master, 195.
Moss, H. W., head-master, 253.

NEWLING, Charles, head-master, 235.
Numbers under Ashton, 197; Laurance, 207; Meighen, 215; Chaloner, 218; Lloyd, 232; Butler, 237; Kennedy, 244.

OATLEY, Sir Francis, 220, 221.
Oppidani, 197.
"Ordinances," Ashton's, 202.
Owen, Hugh, head-master, 232.

PARR, Dr, 215, 236, 241.
Parry, Mr, second-master, 234.
Phillips, Dr Robert, head-master, 232.
Pierce, David, 225.
Pigot, Richard, head-master, 219, 222, 227, 229.
Plague at Shrewsbury, 205, 227; at Hawarden, 225.
Plays, early, 200; modern, 242.
Porson prize, 252.
Præpostors, 250.
Prichard, Archd. Thomas, 215.
Public Schools Report, 244, 246, 252.
Puleston, Sir John, 225.

"QUARRY," the, 200, 203.

"R. S. S. H.," the, 248.
Regatta, 248.
Ruthin School, 226.

'SABRINÆ COROLLA,' 253.
Sacheverell, Dr, 233.
Salaries of masters, 202.
Sandys, Archbishop, 200.
Savill, George, Marq. of Halifax, 221.
School, present, built, 213.
School-buildings, 245; insufficient, 246.
"Sextry Club," 219, 228.
Shilleto, R., 253 note.
"Show," Shrewsbury, 200 note.
Shrewsbury, the town, 193.
Sidney, Sir Henry, 198, 205.
———, Philip, 198, 205.
———, Thomas, 208.
"Skytes," 251.
Speeches, 241.
Sweating-sickness, 195.

TAYLOR, Dr Andw., head-master, 230.
———, Dr John, 235.

VAUGHAN, Sir William, 220, 228.

WARING, Edward, 235.
Welsh scholars, 215.
Wem, school at, 234.
Whitaker, Richard, 194.
Wylton, Thomas, second-master, 196.

IV.—HARROW SCHOOL.

ALLIX, C. W., 305.
Archery enjoined, 260, and note; 304.
Arrow, the silver, 305.
"Articles" of admission, 260.

BATHING, 322.
Baxter, William, 271.
Beckett, Thomas, 258.
Bennet, Bishop, 282.

INDEX.

"Bills" of the school, 275, 286, 307.
"Bloody Porch," 320.
Boarding-houses, 283, 293.
———, "small," 294.
Bolton, William, prior of St Bartholomew, 258.
Books prescribed, 263.
Brian, Thomas, head-master, 272.
Butler, Dr George, head-master, 265, 275, 287, 291; his reforms, 315.
———, Dr H. M., head-master, 293.
"Butts," the, 305.
Byron, Lord, 266, 286, 288, 309, 313.

CHAPEL built, 268.
"Charity" removes, 297.
Charles I., 257.
——— II., 257.
Choral music, 321.
Correction to be administered, 263.
Cox, James, head-master, 272.
Cricket, 309; matches with Eton, ib.; with Winchester, 310.
Cricketers, celebrated, 310, 311.
"Crimean Aisle," 268.

DARTMOUTH, Lord, 284.
Dibdin, Dr, 285.
Drury, Dr, head-master, 286, 287.
———, Mark, under-master, 287.
"Duck-Puddle," 322.

ETON, cricket-matches with, 309, &c.
Evans, Benjamin, assistant-master, 287.
Expenses, 293, 294.

FAGGING, 302; former severity of, 318.
Farmer, Mr, 321.
"Finds," 316.
Flogging, 319.
Football, 311; early mode of play, 312.
"Foreigners" to be received, 261.
Forms, names of, 262, 275.
Fourth-form Room, 266.

GAMES, 304, &c.
Glasse, Dr, his boarding-house, 283.
Goding, the barber, 305.
Grant, Sir W., his judgment, 261, 262.

"HANDING-UP," old custom, 317.
Hare and Hounds, 313.
Harrow, derivation of the name, 258.
Head-master, 259; his lodging, 264; house assigned him, 265; burnt down, ib.; his salary, 259, 260.
Heath, Dr, head-master, 265, 279, 285, 300, 306.
Hoadly, Bishop, 272.

Hockey, 312.
Horne, William, head-master, 271.
Hours of work, 297, &c.
"House-songs," 321 note.

"JACK o' Lantern," 313.
Johnson, Thomas, head-master, 271.
Jones, Sir William, 273, 278, 282.
Jonson, Ben, 271 note.

KING, Rufus, 286.

LIBRARIES, celebrated, at Harrow, 320 note.
Library, monitors', 320; the Vaughan, 312.
Longley, Dr, head-master, 291.
Lyon, John, his "Will and Intent," 259.

MARTIN, Dick, 300.
———, Jem and Jack, ib.
———, Thomas, head-master, 271.
Meals, 299.
Monitors' library, 320.
Monitors, system of, 263, 275, 301, &c.
Motto of the school, 306 note.
Music popular in the school, 321.

NORWICH, Parr's school at, 281.
Numbers, 280, 291, 293.

PALMERSTON, Lord, 266, 321.
Parr, Dr, 273, 277, 287, &c.; at Norwich, 281.
Peel, Sir Robert, 266, 289.
Perceval, Spencer, 266, 321.
"Pinching-in," old custom of, 316.
Plays acted, 308.
"Prayer-book" form, 276.
Preston, hamlet of, 259.
"Private Tuition," 296.
Prize compositions, 307.
Promotion, system of, 297.
"*Pugna Maxima*," 284.

RADNOR, Earl, 284.
Rebellion on Heath's election, 279.
Rifle corps, 306.
Roads, London, repairs of, 259, 270.
Roderick, Mr, under-master, 279.
"Rolling-in," old custom of, 316.
Roxeth Green, 311.

"SCAN and Prove" Form, 275.
Schoolhouse built, 264; enlarged, 265.
Schoolrooms, new, 267.
Sheridan, R. B., 283.
"Speeches," 266, 290, 307.
St Albans school, 260 note.

INDEX. 413

Stanmore, Parr's school at, 280.
"Squash" at football, 312.
Sumner, Dr, head-master, 273, 277, 278, 284.

THACKERAY, Thomas, head-master, 272, 296.
Tutors, private, 296.

USHER, 259; his lodging, 264; his salary, 269.

VAUGHAN, Dr, head-master, 268, 292, &c., 321.

"Vaughan" Library, 321.
Vigne, Godfrey, cricketer, 310.

WARBURTON (Lytton), Richard, 283.
Wellesley, Marquess, 280.
Wilkinson, Sir Gardner, 321.
————, Tate, 308.
Williams, Sir Fenwick, 268.
Wordsworth, Charles, 310.
————, Dr, head-master, 265, 268, 291, 310.

V.—RUGBY SCHOOL.

ABERCROMBY, Sir Ralph, 346.
Adey, William, 403.
Allen, John, head-master, 338.
Apperley, Charles ("Nimrod"), 357, 359, 366, 368, 400.
Arnold, Dr, head-master, 374, 383, &c.; his personal influence, 388; system of discipline, 389.
————, William, "Sixth-form Match," 403.
"Ash-planting," punishment of, 349 note.
Ashbridge, Robert, head-master, 338.
Ayling, William, cricketer, 400.

"BARN School," the, 356.
Bath built, 366.
Birch, William, assistant-master, 358.
Bloxam, R. R., assistant-master, 358.
Boarding-houses, early, 358, 392 note; modern, 393.
Boughton, Edward, 336.
Bryant, Jacob, 356.
Burrough, Stanley, head-master, 350, 354.
Burton, Sir C., 404 note.
Butler, Samuel, 360, 373.

CHAPEL built, 374.
Chariot races, 371.
Chartres, James, second-master, 354.
Churchyard, the original playground, 341.
Clerke, Edward, 327.
"Clodding," old custom of, 381.
"Conduit Close," the, 330, 333, 338.
Costume of boys in 1778, 351.
Cotton, Sir Willoughby, 370.

Craven, Lords, 340.
Crewe, Sir George, 377.
"Crick Run," the, 404.
Cricket, its introduction, 400.
Cricketers, celebrated, 400.
Crimean window, 374.
Cromwell, Oliver, quartered in the town, 329.
Crossfield, Thomas, head-master, 344; his epitaph, 345.

DOUGLAS cause, the great, 351.

ETON, discipline adopted from, 355.
Examiners, 372.
Exhibitions established, 353; examiners for, 372.
Expenses, school, 365, 367.

FAGGING, early, 359, 381.
Farrer, Robert, 331.
Field, Barnard, 333, 336.
Flogging of the Lower Fourth, 380.
Football, 401; modern laws of, 402.
Forms, arrangement of, 399 note.

GASCOIGNE, Mr, his boarding-house, 393.
George III., his remark, 356.
Goulburn (Dean), head-master, 390.
Greene, Willigent, head-master, 337.
Greenhill, Nicholas, head-master, 336; his epitaph, 337.

HARE and Hounds, 404.
Harrison, George, 333.
————, Knightley, head-master, 338.
Head-master, salary of, 353, 353.

INDEX.

Heyrick, William, 351, 365.
Hodgkinson, Joseph, assistant-master, 344.
Hodson, of "Hodson's Horse," 375.
Holyoake, Henry, head-master, 339, 342, &c.; his will, 342.
Homer, Philip, assistant-master, 357.
Hours of work, 395.

INGLES, Dr, head-master, 367.
Innes, George, under-master, 357.
"Island," the, 365, 370.

JAMES, Dr, head-master, 354, 361, 362.
Jeacocks, Leonard, head-master, 339.

KNAIL, William, head-master, 346.

LANDOR, Walter Savage, 361.
Lower Fourth flogging, 380.
Lyttleton, Lord, 362; his "Farewell," 363 note.

MACAULAY, John, 377, 393 note.
Macready, C. W., 377.
Manor-house purchased for school, 348.
Mansel, General John, 346.
Marbles played, 356.
"Mauling" at football, 402.
Meals, 394, 395.
Melly, George, 'Experiences of a Fag,' 403.
Modern languages, study of, 392.

"NIMROD," his 'Life and Times,' 357.
Numbers of the school, 345, 355, 372, 382, 393 and note.

"OVER School," room so called, 349.

"PARADISE," room so called, 349.
"Parallel" Forms, 398.
Parr, Dr, 377.
Paul, William, hung, 405.
Pearce, Raphael, head-master, 337.
Peterborough, Earls of, 340.
Pinley, Mr, assistant-master, 343.
Playground, originally the church-yard, 341.
Plomer, John, head-master, 344.
Post-chaises, 352.
Præpostors, 389.
Private tutors, 359.
Promotion, system of, 396.

REBELLION of 1745, 346.
——— (School) of 1797, 368, &c.; a second attempted, 379.
Register, the Rugby, begun, 338.
Richmond, Joseph, head-master, 347, 350.
Richmond, Margaret Countess of, 329.
Robinson, Hastings, 378.
Rolfe, Augustine, head-master, 337.
"Rugby Register," begun, 338.
Rushes, school strewn with, 364.

SANATORIUM, 394.
School rebuilt, 347; again, 373.
School-close, original, 341.
Schoolroom, original, 339, 364; of 1755, 348; new ones added, 355.
Science, Natural, study of, 392.
Seele, Richard, master, 335, 336.
Sheriff, Laurence, 328, 331; his will and intent, 332; codicil, 333; death of, 334.
Sleath, John, assistant-master, 358.
———, W. B., assistant-master, 357 note, 359.
"Song of the Bell," 395 note.
Speeches, 364, 366.
"Studies," 355.

TAIT, A. C. (Bishop), head-master, 390.
Temple, Dr, head-master, 391; abolishes "goal-keeping," ib.
Theatricals, 377.
Thornton, Spencer, his influence on the school, 386, &c.
"Thos." Woolridge, 376.
"Tom Brown," his account of the school, 383.
Tripe an article of consumption, 343.
Trustees of the school, 335, 353.

"USHERS" provided, 353.

VOLUNTEERS, early, 371.

WATERLOO, Rugbeians at, 372.
Whitehead, Peter, head-master, 338.
William III. passes through, 329.
Wimbledon Shield won, 404.
Wooll, Dr, head-master, 373; enters Rugby in a tandem, 376; resigns, 382.
———, Mrs, 376.
Writing-master appointed, 353.

By the Same Author.

ETONIANA, ANCIENT AND MODERN:

BEING NOTES OF THE

HISTORY AND TRADITIONS OF ETON COLLEGE.

In fcap. 8vo, price 5s.

"The volume before us is just the kind of book to make outsiders acquainted with the living spirit of a great English school as it used to be, and, in fact, as it must always continue to be. It is not a disquisition on Eton education, nor is it a reproduction of the Report of the late Public Schools Commission. It is a collection of illustrations of the history, and what we may call the life, of the school, as distinct from its formal teaching by means of books and lessons."—*Pall Mall Gazette.*

"We must refer our readers to the pages of 'Etoniana' for a most amusing account of all the customs of Montem and its past glories, as well as for equally amusing accounts of other Eton traditionary ceremonies. Even to non-Etonians, thanks to the author's rare good feeling in personal matters and rare good taste in everything he touches, there is a fascination about the book which must call forth a regret that he does not at once commence a task he could accomplish so well—the full history of our greatest public school. As for Etonians, they will be ready enough to appreciate this—we hope we may say instalment—without a word from others."—*Spectator.*

"A most learned and withal readable account of the early records of the school, a full history of the Montem, and a host of anecdotes of bygone Etonians, besides a very reliable notice of its present condition."—*John Bull.*

"These scholarlike pages will be welcome to every Etonian; indeed, we may add, to the reading public generally."—*Morning Advertiser.*

"A most valuable account of the foundation and growth of one of our most famous public schools. . . . The book deserves cordial commendation."—*Morning Star.*

WILLIAM BLACKWOOD & SONS, Edinburgh and London.

Just published, the Nineteenth Edition of
LAYS OF THE SCOTTISH CAVALIERS, and OTHER POEMS.
By W. EDMONDSTOUNE AYTOUN, D.C.L. Foolscap octavo, price 7s. 6d.

ILLUSTRATED EDITION OF
AYTOUN'S LAYS OF THE SCOTTISH CAVALIERS.
By Sir J. NOEL PATON and W. H. PATON. In Small Quarto, printed on Toned Paper, bound in gilt cloth, 21s.

TRANSLATIONS BY THEODORE MARTIN.
GOETHE'S FAUST. Second Edition. 6s. cloth.
THE ODES OF HORACE, with Life and Notes. 9s.
CATULLUS, with Life and Notes. 6s. 6d.
THE VITA NUOVA OF DANTE, with Introduction and Notes. 7s. 6d.
ALADDIN. By OEHLENSCHLAEGER. 5s.
CORREGGIO. By the Same. 5s.
KING RENE'S DAUGHTER. By HENRIK HERTZ. 2s. 6d. cloth.

Ninth Edition.
THE BOOK OF BALLADS.
Edited by BON GAULTIER. With numerous Illustrations by DOYLE, LEECH, and CROWQUILL. Gilt edges, post 8vo. 8s. 6d.

Second Edition.
POEMS AND BALLADS OF GOETHE.
Translated by W. E. AYTOUN and THEODORE MARTIN. 6s. cloth.

Third Edition.
BOTHWELL: A POEM.
By WILLIAM EDMONDSTOUNE AYTOUN, D.C.L. Foolscap octavo, 7s. 6d.

FIRMILIAN; OR, THE STUDENT OF BADAJOZ.
A Spasmodic Tragedy. Foolscap octavo, 5s.

Third Edition.
THE BALLADS OF SCOTLAND.
Edited by PROFESSOR AYTOUN. 2 vols., Foolscap octavo, 12s.

WILLIAM BLACKWOOD & SONS, Edinburgh and London.

www.ingramcontent.com/pod-product-compliance
Lightning Source LLC
Chambersburg PA
CBHW030549300426
44111CB00009B/918